DAISY
DE MELKER

DAISY
DE MELKER

Hiding among
killers in the
City of Gold

TED BOTHA

Jonathan Ball Publishers
Johannesburg · Cape Town

© Text: Ted Botha (2023)
© Images: Museum Africa and Johannesburg City Library
© Published edition: Jonathan Ball Publishers (2023)

First published in South Africa in 2023 by
JONATHAN BALL PUBLISHERS
A division of Media24 (Pty) Ltd
PO Box 33977
Jeppestown
2043

ISBN 978-1-77619-277-9
ebook ISBN 978-1-77619-278-6

jonathanball.co.za
twitter.com/JonathanBallPub
facebook.com/JonathanBallPublishers

Cover by Sean Robertson
Cover images from *Souvenir of Johannesburg Suburbs and Mines on the Rand*,
Braune & Levy Printers & Engravers,
Johannesburg, Circa 1904-1908, and Museum Africa
Design and typesetting by Catherine Coetzer
Maps by Roland Metcalfe
Set in Abril Text

She was one of the world's great poisoners, a classic who, because her stage was remote, has not had fair recognition in the annals of crime.

Sarah Gertrude Millin

Could this be the tin town of mud and filth I knew in 1897, the pestilential settlement I was warned against, the waterless region in which there was nothing but dust, fleas, objectionable characters and an early grave?

Louis Cohen

Contents

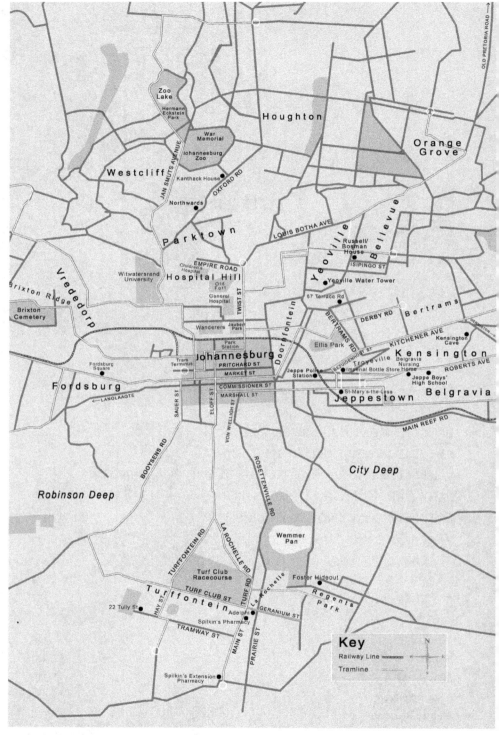

Map of Johannesburg

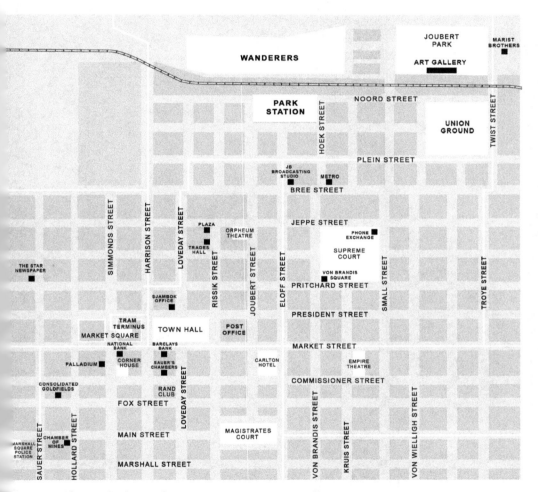

reet map of central Johannesburg

Introduction

From 1914 to 1932, a woman of extremely modest means, who might have been described as innocuous and even uninteresting, lived in Johannesburg. She was a wife and a mother, and had more than a passing knowledge of medicine.

It was one of the most turbulent and opulent times in a city that had become famous the world over for the impossible riches that lay in the gold-bearing reef under the 60-mile stretch of mining towns. Two bloody rebellions, one of which almost toppled the government, and innumerable strikes led to widespread destruction and hundreds of deaths. At the same time, a number of high-profile murders and subsequent trials kept the public both horrified and spellbound by the crime in their midst.

Into this scene of gold dust and bombs, strikes and limousines, shacks and gargantuan mansions wandered a schoolteacher, a rodeo man, an escaped prisoner, a peddler, a young female student, a motor-bike enthusiast, a prudish novelist, a witch doctor, a farmer's widow, a gun-runner, an extremely talented lawyer and a son who wanted too much from his mother. In a way that made the mushrooming city feel more like a small town, the players sometimes crossed paths, an unintended concert of killers and victims. Each murder had its own motive and weapon – gun, knife, rope, witchcraft, dynamite, poison.

The murders, besides their connection to Johannesburg, were mostly resolved fairly quickly – all except hers. In the shadow of the ever-growing mine dumps, she went about her business, quietly and unnoticed, the most unlikely of all the killers. Even though people close to her kept dying, for 20 years no one suspected a thing. When someone finally spoke up, it led to the most sensational trial the country would ever see.

PART 1

THE SET-UP
1913–1915

CHAPTER 1

Their aliases

The Union Limited made a rhythmic sound over the tracks, as sparks shot off to the sides of the blackened wheels. The sunset, red and indigo sliced by striations of white cirrus clouds, gave way to a pitch-black sky studded with more stars than the man with the bad arm could remember.

As he sat in the cheapest section of the train steaming from Johannesburg to Cape Town in early March 1913, it was perhaps inevitable that John Maxim would meet and quickly fall under the sway of William Foster. The men had two very important things in common – a weakness for aliases and crime.

Maxim, a moustachioed, black-haired American in his late thirties, had a good story to tell. At the turn of the century, he had arrived in South Africa and quickly became a trick rider and shooter with the Wild West Show & Circus. It was owned by a fellow American, Texas Jack, who had taken the name of his adopted father, a famous cowboy and actor with one of the very first Wild West shows in America. The son started his own version of his father's act, and eventually landed up in South Africa, taking it to towns and cities, promising 'Marvelous Feats of Horsemanship, Shooting, Lasso Throwing!'

Young men like Maxim, drifters most of them, joined the Wild West Show & Circus for a while and then left – one of them, a teenager who would one day become a famous Hollywood star, was named Will Rogers – but Maxim stayed on. One arm was badly crushed during a performance, as were both his pinkie fingers, which remained crooked. When Texas Jack died, in 1905, Maxim didn't have much money and his talents weren't in high demand. He took to selling liquor to Africans, which was illegal, and ended up in jail several times. To evade the law, he sometimes used the names Maxwell or Milton.

Sitting opposite him on the Union Limited, as the train crossed the Great Karoo, sat William Foster, who also called himself Bailey, Ward Jackson and 'Captain White'. Ten years younger, just shy of five foot ten, full of face with a high forehead, light hair, grey eyes and a long nose, Foster already had a powerful presence and a temper that was known to explode quickly.

Born of 'a perfectly normal and responsible middle-class family in Griqualand East', Foster's father was Irish and his mother came from Grahamstown. After the Anglo-Boer War (1899–1902), when he was 16, his family – three boys and three girls – moved to Bertrams, east of the Johannesburg city centre. Foster went to a good school, Marist Brothers' College, but 'he hated discipline and baulked at authority', which was where the trouble started.

He tried his hand at surveying on a gold mine, and then at photography, before his first brush with the law, in 1908. First, it was a drunken brawl, then being caught without a ticket on a train, small things that would have carried little penalty, but he fought back and ran away. In German South West Africa, he 'borrowed' some donkeys, and despite not meaning 'very serious harm [for a] not very heinous crime', he fell victim to a harsh stock-theft law: 'This started him on a career of crime and he carried his vendetta against society and its laws to a point which approached madness.'

More ominously, some detectives at Marshall Square, the headquarters of the police's criminal division in Johannesburg, believed that Foster had killed one of his sisters, although they couldn't prove it. Her death had been declared a suicide, and as events unfolded over the next year, the detectives were more convinced than ever that they had been right.

After the Union Limited reached Cape Town, Foster and Maxim took rooms at Ebenezer House on Hope Street, not far from the

Company's Garden. By the time they came up with a plan to rob the American Swiss Watch Company, on the lower end of Longmarket Street, Foster had already established himself as their leader. They stole a car for their getaway and called in the help of Foster's younger brother Jimmy, who came down from Johannesburg with Fred Adamson, the son of a butcher who knew the Fosters from Bertrams.

At 7 pm on Wednesday 19 March, Maxim waited in the car on Longmarket Street while the three others, masked and sporting fake moustaches and beards – disguises that would soon become their trademark – entered the store. The owners, two men named Hirschsohn and Grusd, were busy closing up, removing the window displays. The robbers put pistols to their heads, then bound and gagged them, putting hoods over their heads and cords around their necks. From the displays and safe they got jewels, watches, necklaces, foreign coins and cigarette cases worth £5 000. (If true, this figure is staggering. A sum of £100 in 1913 would now have the purchasing power of £13 000, meaning the gang had in its possession a haul of £650 000!)

'One of us will watch the place for a quarter of an hour,' Foster told the bound men. 'He'll shoot if you try to raise the alarm.'

The robbers went their separate ways, with Foster taking the loot, which he planned to hide away and then distribute when the heat died down. On 20 March, he took a taxi from Hope Street, placing four items in the back of the car, including a leather trunk and a very heavy 'cabin trunk'. The taxi drove to the Cape Town railway station, where Foster intended to leave the bags in the baggage storage, right under the nose of the authorities.

But Foster made two mistakes. The cabin trunk was so heavy that it could barely be carried, which a baggage handler at the station later remembered. When Foster didn't have the right amount to pay for the storage, he made a fuss about getting the exact change back. When the police did a check of the station two days later, the handler recalled Foster and the heavy trunk, and the police found the loot. They told the handler to alert them as soon as Foster returned. Within a few day Foster was caught in Cape Town, and his brother and Adamson Johannesburg. The only one they didn't catch was the American ro man, Maxim.

The three men – Foster, his brother and Adamson – were arrai for trial a few days later. Sitting in court was a young woman who paid particular interest to the main accused, who was calling himself Ward Jackson. Pretty with dark hair, Peggy Lyons, formerly Peggy Korenico, was a showgirl at the Empire Palace of Varieties on Commissioner Street in Johannesburg. She was also Foster's girlfriend.

The men were taken to the Roeland Street jail in Cape Town to await their trial in May, two months later. Several days before their appearance, special dispensation was given, for the very first time in the Cape Province, for a prisoner to get married. Foster wed Peggy, who was also pregnant with their first child.

On 22 May, the three men were brought to the Supreme Court on Keerom Street. When Foster entered the courtroom, he was dressed in oversized clothing that he had borrowed from other prisoners, and his hat was pulled low over his eyes. He smiled at Peggy, who was in the public gallery. During evidence, the confusion of names was finally cleared up, when the heavily coated man admitted that he wasn't Jackson but William Foster, while the man they thought was William Foster was his brother Jimmy.

All the shenanigans didn't impress the judge, John Kotze, who was nearing the end of a long career and had a reputation for being smart and fair. He quickly summed up the insouciant, disrespectful Foster, and so did the jury. Within 25 minutes, they returned a verdict of guilty for all three men, and Kotze threw the book at them. Each man was sentenced to 12 years of hard labour at the country's main jail, Pretoria Central.

Peggy fainted, while Foster stood in the dock, frozen. The punishment was outrageous, he cried out, especially for his brother Jimmy, who was younger than him and had his whole life ahead of him. As he was led out of court by a side entrance to be driven away in the large motor van – 'a sinister dark conveyance' called a Black Maria – swore that he would get his revenge.

orter covering the case described Foster as 'dark and saturnine and his face wore an air of suppressed fury', little knowing how rds were, an omen for the bloody murder spree that was

ilding behind the stone walls looked not entirely st glance: solid, red brick, two storeys, lying solitary between the koppies on the outskirts of Pretoria. On closer inspection, though, one noticed the armed men in uniform standing in its shadows, the barred windows, the castle-like turrets on each side of the main gate. Behind the walls, the corridors were long, the stairs cold metal, the cells small and dark. Pretoria Central was also known as just 'Central', and sometimes as 'the Citadel'.

Criminals of every stripe were kept inside its walls – political renegades, thieves, rapists, fraudsters, con artists, murderers – although it was perhaps most famous for being the main place of execution in the country. Since its opening eight years earlier, in 1905, only men had swung from the gallows, and another seven years would pass before the first woman would take that last walk.

Prisoners fell into three categories. First offenders, which included even murderers, were meant to be kept apart and only allowed to mix with others for weekend exercise, but they all had to come together during work hours anyway. Second offenders could include men who hadn't been in a prison before – say, if they had paid a fine instead – and for them it was technically their first time too. The last group, the so-called Blue Coats, were 'incorrigible' repeat offenders who had been given indeterminate sentences, which could be up to 15 years.

Each prisoner was given a small ticket that they had to keep on them at all times. If a prisoner had a 'clear ticket' – that is, no marks for bad behaviour against their name – they could get a remission of at least a quarter of their sentence. But should they be convicted again, their unserved time was added to the new sentence.

By the beginning of 1914, William Foster, Jimmy Foster and Fred Adamson had served six months of their 12-year sentences. Their routine was 'deadly monotony [and] very depressing ... searches, parades, roll calls, exercise, etc'. All Foster could think about was how to escape, and slowly he concocted a plan. He watched the guards and the routes the prisoners followed when going on work detail to break stones at the quarry, and he made contact with any prisoner who might give him information or even help him to get out.

In a nearby cell was another repeat offender plotting to get out of Pretoria Central before his time was up, but his method for doing so was very different to Foster's. Andrew Gibson was hoping to charm his way out – and if anyone could do that, he could.

Gibson was legendary, his exploits talked about as far away as the United States and Australia. Depending on which story you believed – and Gibson told many of them – he had been born in New South Wales, Australia, or in Canterbury or Manchester, England, in 1867. Orphaned from an early age, he 'very early in life took to crime'. One of his first crimes – 'always distinguished by amazing audacity' – was to sell two chemist's shops in Manchester that he was meant to be looking after, and then to open another one nearby.

From then on, Gibson had conned his way around the world, apparently little deterred by the lengthy periods that he spent in jail, from Yass in Australia to San Quentin, near San Francisco. The crimes he most favoured were fraud and forgery, although in San Quentin he had picked up another pastime – medicine – by helping out the prison doctor on his rounds. Before long he was masquerading as a doctor in Burraga, near Sydney, and in Halifax, Canada, where he also impersonated a priest, taking over his parish for a month while the clergyman was on holiday.

It was hard to imagine the small man as a world-famous criminal. Gibson was five foot seven inches tall and slight, with blue eyes, dark hair turning grey, hollow cheeks and high cheekbones. He had a perpendicular scar on his forehead and a tattoo of clasped hands and the number 11 on his upper left arm. But he had fooled many people with a list of aliases so colourful, they could have been plucked straight from the pages of adventure novels.

There was Henry Westwood Cooper, Charles Ernest Chadwick, Dr Milton Abrahams, Norman Ebenezer McKay, Harry Cecil Rutherford Darling, and his own favourite, 'Surgeon, Sir Swinton-Hume, VC, DSO, 5th Dragoon Guards'. As Sir Swinton-Hume, he told people, he had been knighted by the Queen of England. Along with the aliases and phony professions, Gibson had accrued a string of girlfriends and wives, and with them he had even 'mixed in good society in London'.

Johannesburg, the City of Gold, was a particular favourite of Gibson's, a place to which he kept returning. Then, as the law started catching up with him, he disappeared. The last time he'd done that was in 1912; on the run once again, he caught a ship from Durban or Lourenço Marques – the two main ports for steamships heading east –

to Australia, where he was caught and sent back to stand trial. In 1913, he received an 18-month sentence for falsity, forgery and theft, and was sent to Pretoria Central.

Next to William Foster, who was really only just starting to learn about aliases and had used just a moustache during the American Swiss robbery – a disguise so amateurish that the jeweller Hirschsohn had no trouble picking him out in a police line-up – Gibson was a master.

As repeat offenders, it would have been impossible for the two men not to have met, in the dining hall, the exercise area or the infirmary – where Gibson, once again, was helping the doctor. In the 'brother hood of convicts', as Gibson called his fellow inmates, his notoriety must have been a topic of conversation. Plus, he was eminently likeable, sometimes being mistaken for a harried accountant rather than a criminal. What with all his stories, he 'must have been good company', especially in the monotony of prison life.

But Foster, suspicious and angry at the world, probably stayed away from the wily old-timer, which was wise. For Gibson was not beyond betraying the 'brother hood' if it could help him. His idea of getting out of prison was to have his sentence reduced or wiped out completely, either with a 'clear ticket' or by convincing the authorities that he reformed. Information about Foster's plan to escape would have helped him do just that.

But Foster shared his secret only with those who could actually help him break his chains and scale the walls.

It was a beautiful Friday morning in late summer 1914 when that happened. The weather was clear and crisp, the umbrella-shaped acacia trees outside Pretoria Central still green, even though the last wild-flowers were gone from the veld covering the nearby koppies.

After the prisoners ate breakfast, one of the work gangs was led out to a quarry behind the main fortress-like building. Among them was William Foster, his escape plan already set in motion. What happened over the next hour or two would be crucial.

Not long after they reached the quarry, a fight broke out between two prisoners, and quickly more men joined in. By the time the guards had restrained them, Foster was gone. A search of the prison grounds turned up only his overalls, discarded near one of the perimeter walls.

The police immediately put a tail on Peggy Lyons, his wife, who had recently given birth to a baby girl. Surveillance was kept on the ports of Cape Town and Lourenço Marques, in Portuguese East Africa, for there was a strong suspicion that Foster might try to flee the country. Tip-offs kept coming in, even one that the fugitive had been seen dressed up as a woman at the Empire Palace of Varieties, where Peggy sometimes worked. If it was William Foster, the police got there too late.

He had vanished.

CHAPTER 2

A cold month for death

June was always the cruellest month in the City of Gold, and June 1914 was going to be no different.

If the cold wasn't bad enough, piercing one's bones like microscopic daggers, the wind swept powdery dust off the mine dumps, such as Robinson Deep and City Deep. The dust swirled down the dirt roads, and seeped into every nook and dark corner. From Vrededorp to Marshalltown to Jeppe, every shop had a sign ready to put in the front window: 'Closed on account of the dust.'

At the home of Daisy and Alfred Cowle on Tully Street, number 22, in the shadows of Robinson Deep, June was also important for another reason. It was the month when the Cowle children had been born. The twins had come four years earlier, in 1910, another son a year later, and then a fourth in 1913.

It was also in the winter months that the children died. The twins lasted less than a year before they took ill, their two small bodies almost rising off the bed in repeated spasms in their final hours, as if controlled by a devil of torture, before expiring.

The doctor, not entirely sure of the cause, concluded that it was probably 'convulsions', a vague, catch-all diagnosis that took in any number of possibilities. The boys might have had lead poisoning, a result perhaps of chewing the paint from their cots or toys. Or perhaps their symptoms were the result of a zymotic disease, such as whooping cough, typhoid fever, measles, smallpox – there were plenty of maladies to go around. The diagnosis of convulsions in itself wasn't uncommon, especially among infants, but two deaths from the same symptoms at the same time in the same house? That was very bad luck indeed.

A few months later, Daisy fell pregnant again, and the news gave the Cowles something to look forward to. They chose the name Lester Eric, for they were sure that it would once again be a boy. And they were right. In June 1913, at the age of 26, Daisy gave birth to her fourth child.

Now, one year later, in June 1914 – at the same time that William Foster was about to break out of Pretoria Central – the Cowles were celebrating the birthday of not only Lester Eric but also their other son, who was turning three.

The older boy had been blessed from the moment he was christened. In a sign that they expected great things from him, he was given a name that set him apart. But it was also a name that cursed him, especially in a city where poorly paid miners were constantly at odds with the men they worked for. They even referred to one of the main mining company headquarters in the city centre, Corner House, as 'the sentinel to the gates of hell'.

In spite of this, the Cowles named their eldest son after the most famous mining magnate of all, one of the richest men in the world, Cecil John Rhodes. The boy would be Rhodes Cecil Cowle.

The neighbours on Tully Street could have set their clocks by Alfred Cowle's movements. Employed as a plumber in the water department of the Johannesburg municipality, he left home at almost the exact same early hour every weekday morning, and sometimes even on weekends.

A solid man of medium height with a moustache and slightly protruding ears, Alfie was reliable and never known to call in sick. Daisy ran the house and looked after her two boys without any help. The Cowles could afford a maid, but Daisy didn't like having a stranger in the house.

When she had any errands to run, she probably left her boys in the care of a friend or a neighbour, such as Mary Jane Meaker, who also lived on Tully Street. There was also her cousin Mia Melville whom she could ask.

The suburbs in the south of the city lay in the shape of a crescent, taking in Turffontein, Kenilworth, Rosettenville and La Rochelle, with the eastern tip ending at Regents Park, a loose collection of modest houses and shops that was a far cry from its opulent namesake in central London. Between them, Turffontein Road and Main Street ran north to the city, cutting through some of the largest mine dumps, before coming together for the final stretch into Marshalltown. To the east of Regents Park was Wemmer Pan, which had started life as a repository for the wet tailings and sludge from the mines, but now, in a city that had no rivers or waterfront, doubled as a lake where locals came to relax on weekends.

All of the houses on Tully Street, which ran parallel to Tramway Street, were of a kind: modest, single-storey, verandah on the front, some with a bay window, sometimes an alley down the side of the house, but always near enough for neighbours to overhear each other. In such close proximity, it was hard to imagine that any dark secrets could be kept.

The main shopping area was more than a mile away, and even though there was a tram that ran down Hay Street to Turf Club Road, the walk wasn't unpleasant. One can imagine Daisy walking down Turf Club, shaded by a long row of eucalyptus trees, skirting the southern edge of the city's popular racetrack. The air was charged with the sound of people cheering from the stands, and Daisy would have seen women in their pastel day outfits, with sashes, lace parasols and day hats, which they had probably bought on Pritchard Street, where all the fanciest dress shops were located. She envied them.

The gun went off at the racetrack for the next heat – it could have been the Broker's Handicap or the Licensed Victualler's Plate – and as the roar of the crowd grew louder, Daisy carried on walking. She headed for La Rochelle, where Meyer Klevansky had his butchery on Pan Road, right near Miller's grocery. At the corner of 7th Street was a store run by a Chinese family. The tailor belonged to Lemmer, the butchery to Sacks and the small hotel to a Herr Wies.

Near the corner of Prairie and Geranium streets, where La Rochelle became Kenilworth, stood two cinemas, also known as bioscopes, the Adelphi and the Grand. Daisy knew them well. She loved the movies. In the darkness, she could escape the city outside, blot out the thoughts of bad luck that seemed to dog her. She could forget for an hour or two the children who had died before they turned one, and, before them, the young man she had loved.

Or maybe she didn't think about them. Perhaps, like countless other women, she imagined herself up there on the screen instead of Mary Pickford and Mabel Normand and Clara Kimball Young. But when the lights went up, there was no beautiful movie star sitting on her own, just a woman who was plain, blowsy and, some people would say, ugly.

Before heading home, Daisy made her way up to the corner of Turf and Main streets, to buy some medicine. There was always someone in the Cowle house who was sick and needed a powder or a tonic. Lester Eric, now one year old, was down with something, and Rhodes Cecil was just getting over the smallpox. Her husband, Alfie, had kidney problems, which was especially troubling. A recent story in the *Rand Daily Mail* had said that kidney trouble could lead to Bright's disease, which could be fatal.

As she reached the intersection, Daisy turned in at a store that she knew well: Spilkin's Pharmacy.

CHAPTER 3

Motor bandits

The sound of an explosion in itself was not unusual, especially when there was a reef of gold running for almost 60 miles underneath the city just waiting to be dynamited open. But the blast that took place in the middle of 1914 was different; it was quick, uncushioned by a layer of earth, and it happened in the dead of night.

In Roodepoort, 15 miles west of the city centre, robbers blew open a safe at the post office and got away with British postal orders and a set of keys belonging to a branch of the National Bank. Even though no one got a good look at the robbers, they saw that at least one of them fled on a motorcycle.

A few weeks later, in Vrededorp, a poor neighbourhood just west of central Johannesburg, exactly the same event was repeated – late night, post office, safe dynamited and the robbers had at least one motorbike. They got away with money and several hundred pounds in revenue stamps.

A third robbery, targeting a small branch of the National Bank, this time east of the city, in Boksburg, didn't go as smoothly. As one of the robbers stood guard outside, his two accomplices went around the back of the building, broke into an adjacent business and then blew a hole through the wall of the bank. A bank employee who arrived at the scene unexpectedly shouted for help, which drew the attention of a barman at a nearby hotel, Alexander Charlson. When he tried to intercept the robbers, they shot him; as he lay on the ground wounded, one of the robbers, who was so young he looked more like a schoolboy, put a final and fatal bullet into Charlson. Another onlooker who tried to intervene was shot in the leg before the men hopped on their motorbikes and sped off.

This time people were able to describe the three men, finally giving the police proof that their earlier suspicions were correct: it was William Foster and his gang. This time the gang included the American John Maxim and Carl Mezar, a short 21-year-old whose neck and face were covered in freckles and small moles. Because of his size and adolescent looks, Mezar was known as 'Boy'.

The police linked the men to the two earlier heists, and also suspected them of a spate of other robberies of groceries, motorcycles and a car, and a reward of £500 was offered for any information leading to their capture. Flyers went up across the city that not only pictured the men but described them and provided their aliases. Members of the public were warned that they were armed and dangerous, and the robbers quickly became known as the Motor Bandits or the Foster Gang.

But then, on 28 July 1914, something happened thousands of miles away that gave Foster and his men an incredible break. Great Britain declared war on Germany, and the Union of South Africa descended into an acrimonious debate about whether or not to join the war on the side of the British. Even though a dozen years had passed since the Anglo-Boer War, many Afrikaners still hated the English and preferred to side with Kaiser Wilhelm. Rumours of a rebellion quickly spread, and the police and army suddenly had a new threat to worry about.

The Foster Gang used the time to disappear.

*

In the final weeks of winter, a menacingly cold wind raced down the slopes of City Deep and across the icy waters of Wemmer Pan, slicing into the small block-shaped homes in whimsically named Regents Park.

A house standing at a distance from any other, and which had been empty for some time, was newly occupied, with a motorbike and an

SOUTH AFRICAN POLICE. CRIMINAL INVESTIGATION DEPARTMENT.

SPECIAL CIRCULAR No. 7.   JOHANNESBURG, FRIDAY, JULY 24, 1914.

£500 REWARD.

MURDER and ATTEMPTED BANK ROBBERY at Boksburg North, Transvaal, on the night of Friday, July 17th, 1914. A Reward as above is offered to any person giving information leading to the arrest and conviction of the men concerned in this crime. Warrants issued for the arrest of the following three men on the above charge :

1. ROBERT WARD JACKSON, alias FOSTER, alias Bailey, alias 'Capt. White'.

DESCRIPTION : English or Colonial; has given his place of birth as Birmingham, England, and Pretoria; on different occasions, age 24, 5ft 7½, dark brown hair, grey eyes, long straight nose, small firm mouth, round chin, medium protruding ears, high narrow forehead, sallow complexion; was clean shaven; may grow beard and moustache; four false teeth upper front two gold; scar under right jaw; fine scar back of neck. Is married. Occupation, clerk or surveying. Rides a motor cycle. Finger-print classification: 19 M 8

Photograph taken at Johannesburg.   Photograph taken at Capetown.
Robert Ward Jackson, al. Foster, alias Bailey, alias Capt. White.

2. JOHN MAXIM, alias MAXWELL, alias MILTON MAXIM.

DESCRIPTION : American, age 28 or 30, 5ft. 7½, black hair, blue-grey eyes, dark complexion, dark brown moustache, right arm deformed elbow has been crushed, mole left of neck, birthmark right of neck, first joint of both little fingers crooked, body and legs hairy. Was in possession of a motor cycle, which he will probably try to sell. Finger-print classification: 28 MI 16 IO

John Maxim, alias Maxwell, alias Milton Maxim.   Carl Mezar, alias George Smit.

3. CARL MEZAR, alias GEORGE SMIT.

Photo taken in 1908. DESCRIPTION : Dutch, gives his age as 22 but looks younger, 5ft. 5 in 1908, face and neck freckled and covered with small moles, raised mole back left neck, three moles left shoulder-blade, both marks on buttocks. Finger-print classification: 9 I 17 or 16 O

These persons will probably make for the Coast, and endeavour to leave the country either as passengers or ships' hands.

K. VACHELL, Deputy-Commissioner, C.I.D. Johannesburg.

10. The Foster Gang. Police offer of £500 reward as result of the Boksburg North murder. This document has not been published since 1914.

There was a bounty.

Overland sedan covered in a tarpaulin parked outside. Anyone watching, like some of the neighbours across the open ground in between, would have noticed the new residents, who made sure to keep to themselves: three men, a woman and a baby.

Behind the darkened windows, the Foster Gang were plotting their next robbery, which would have to be their last in Johannesburg, given that they were wanted for the murder of the hotel barman, Alexander Charlson. Their faces were now plastered across the city and there was a bounty on their heads. After this final robbery, they planned to flee across the border, into Portuguese East Africa, and they were even drying out some stolen meat on a washing line in case they had to hide out for a long period of time.

The men discussed possible targets. Post offices and banks were now being carefully watched by the police, so it was decided to hit a liquor store. John Maxim knew from his illicit liquor-selling days that the biggest sales were done on weekends, and that any money made would be kept on the premises until the banks opened on Monday. So the gang needed to rob a liquor store on a Sunday.

Next, the location. They settled on a large outlet on Kimberley Road just east of the city centre, in Doornfontein, where the weekend takings would be good. The only risk was a big one: the store was barely a mile from the well-manned Jeppe police station. A few nights before the robbery, the gang drove past the store and smashed a streetlamp on a nearby corner, so they could carry out the robbery in relative darkness.

Late on the night of Sunday 13 September, the three men took off from their hideout in Regents Park on a single motorbike, with the scrawny Boy Mezar riding pillion. For four miles they stayed on back roads as much as possible, avoiding Market and Commissioner streets, and especially the area around the Jeppe police station.

After that they turned off Bertrams Road into Kimberley Road. Foster approached the store on foot holding a small crowbar, or jemmy, while the other two stood near the broken streetlamp keeping watch. At 1.30 am, an African guard sleeping in the liquor store heard the 'whirr of an electric bell', triggered by someone trying to get in. Seeing a white man standing outside, he rapped on the windowpane to try to scare him off. Then he saw the two other men standing nearby.

At that moment a police constable named James Landberg came around the corner, and the guard rapped on the pane more vigorously to get his attention. Foster rushed at the policeman and knocked him out with his jemmy. Before the three robbers took off, Foster struck another blow to the constable lying on the ground. The quick-thinking store guard immediately raised the alarm, and 'the intelligence was flashed from station to station that desperadoes were abroad'.

The Foster Gang, desperate to find a liquor store to rob, knew about the Imperial Bottle Store, which was about a mile away, on the corner of Eleanor Street and Op de Bergen, and almost the same distance away from the police station. This time it was Foster and Boy Mezar who went in, while John Maxim kept watch at a tram stop outside. It was probably the small Mezar who got through the skylight above the door and let Foster in, and then they blew the door clear off the safe.

At 4.15 am, Sergeant Neil MacLeod, who was doing a patrol of the tramline, saw Maxim sitting at the tram stop. MacLeod, a Scotsman who had worked for the Glasgow police for many years, was immediately suspicious. He went around the corner, where he met another constable, named Swanepoel, and told him to approach the stranger.

'Law-abiding citizens do not, as a rule, sit on deserted seats in the small hours.'

Both constables were unarmed and, according to police policy, had only batons to defend themselves. As Swanepoel got closer to him, Maxim immediately started whistling wildly.

'Why do you whistle?' the constable asked.

'What the **** has it got to do with you?' replied the American.

MacLeod came up and told Swanepoel to arrest him.

'We'll take no chances. Put the handcuffs on.'

A quick search of Maxim's pockets revealed a loaded revolver and housebreaking tools. They began walking Maxim down Op de Bergen towards the Jeppe police station, but as they were passing the Imperial, Maxim shouted, 'Help! Help!'

Out of the side entrance of the liquor store dashed Foster, who pointed his gun at the policemen. The constables were unarmed apart from their batons, so MacLeod told Swanepoel to use the revolver he had taken off Maxim. A volley of shots was exchanged until Swanepoel's gun was empty. That was when he saw that MacLeod had been hit – by at least six bullets, it was later discovered – and fell to the ground, dead. When Foster pulled out a second gun, Swanepoel, who had also been hit and had no more ammunition, turned and ran for cover.

The commotion had caused people in nearby houses to open their windows and watch what was happening. They saw a third man suddenly exit from the liquor store, and all three ran for a motorcycle that had been hidden in a shaded area. The men scrambled onto the bike and rode off towards Commissioner Street.

Within 20 minutes of MacLeod being shot, Major Kenneth Vachell, the head of the criminal branch of the police at Marshall Square, the CID, was on the scene. By that time, a grisly discovery had been made outside the side entrance of the liquor store – the lifeless body of another policeman, Sergeant Robert Mansfield. Going by the trail of blood, which stretched from near the exploded safe to the place on Eleanor Street where Mansfield had died, it appeared he had come across the robbery in progress. Wounded by a bullet, probably fired by Mezar, he ran out into the street, where he was shot again, at close range, and died.

There was no doubt in Vachell's mind that he was dealing with the Foster Gang. It was small comfort that the robbers had got away empty-handed, for 'the Saturday takings, usually a fairly big sum, had been taken away by the manager at closing time'. All Foster found in the safe were ledgers and papers.

*

The murder by the Foster Gang of three people, two of them policemen, 'roused the indignation of the public'.

Vachell assembled his men for what would soon be called the greatest manhunt the country had ever seen, where 'every available arm of the law has been brought into play'. Firearms were handed out to detectives and other policemen who usually went unarmed.

Roadblocks were set up across a large swathe of the city. Within hours, tip-offs started coming in from all over: three men on one motorbike had been seen in the east, the west, near City Deep, out north beyond Rosebank, in Craighall, while others claimed the gang was taking refuge in a private residence whose owners they were holding hostage. There were so many tip-offs, in fact, it was hard to follow them all up.

Something about the call from a woman in Regents Park, however, got Vachell's attention. She said she believed the Foster Gang might be in a house on the corner of Bob Street and South Road, near where she lived – in 'the most distant house in the district'.

Vachell summoned one of his most reliable officers, Detective Charles Mynott, and told him to go with two other policemen, Detective

Layde and Constable Murphy, to interview the woman. If Foster was indeed there, Mynott was instructed not to approach him under any circumstances but to call for backup first.

At 5.30 am, after speaking to the woman in Regents Park, the three policemen approached the house on Bob Street. They got close enough to see Foster and Mezar in the yard working on a car, an American Overland model they had stolen, that was partly hidden by a tarpaulin. Peggy was walking to the car with the baby and got in.

Despite Vachell's instruction to call for backup, Mynott believed that they had the element of surprise on their side. Layde tried to dissuade him, but Mynott was adamant. He posted one of the men at the fence and the other near the driveway to stop Foster from trying to make a getaway. As Mynott got closer, Foster was bent over near the front of the car, turning the crank handle to start the engine.

'Hands up!' Mynott called out. 'I want to speak to you.'

'Who are you?' Foster asked.

'I am Detective Mynott.'

'You are Mynott, are you?' he said, as he reached for a revolver on the car's chassis. 'Well, take it.'

Murphy, who saw what was happening, shouted, 'For God's sake, shoot!' But it was too late.

Foster fired, and Mynott immediately fell to the ground. Maxim, who had been under the car, came out and started to turn the crank handle. In the chaos that followed, the two other policemen, Boy Mezar and Foster began shooting at each other. Layde, his Browning quickly emptied, was confronted by Maxim.

'Sling your shooter away, you bastard, or I will shoot you.'

Layde did as he was ordered and then rushed to Mynott's body, but found him already dead. For some reason, no more shots were fired at Layde; he later said he thought it was because he was wearing a coat that covered his uniform and might have been mistaken for a civilian.

'The men then entered the car and drove away,' the *Rand Daily Mail* later reported, 'firing as they did so at the small crowd which had assembled upon hearing the noise. Fortunately no one was hit.'

The policemen and the bystanders saw the considerable firepower that the gang had with them – at least two rifles, a short-nosed carbine and several pistols. Layde was also sure that at least one of the police bullets had hit a gang member because as the car sped off, one of them was being held up by the other two.

Throughout the violent encounter, he noted afterwards, Foster 'was coolness itself, and his tone was quiet and level'. Even as he killed Mynott, he had laughed.

The main arteries out of the city were quickly flooded with constables and detectives, this time heavily armed with Mauser pistols and rifles, and the roadblocks were increased and reinforced.

The men manning them, however, were on edge. The gang had already killed three people, two of them policemen, and were heavily armed. They clearly would do anything to avoid being caught, for they faced the death penalty. Every vehicle that approached a roadblock was seen as a potential threat, 'and orders were issued that all cars were to be challenged, and fired at on failing to stop'.

Once again, tip-offs were received from all over the city, of a motor-cycle with three men on it, and a possible getaway vehicle travelling at high speed. At about 6 pm on Tuesday 15 September, a doctor named Gerald Grace, a former mayor of Springs, was driving in his Sunbeam motor car with his wife to attend to an urgent medical call in the city. Passing through Stanhope Dip near the Simmer & Jack Mine, and obviously unaware of the intention of the roadblock, he sped on. The police fired shots into the darkness toward the escaping vehicle. The doctor was hit in the neck and died instantly, and his wife was hit in the arm.

Grace's death was the fourth caused by the Foster Gang. The number was about to increase significantly, and in a very short time.

On another road, directly west of where Dr Grace was killed, another car was speeding, although for very different reasons.

The government sedan was carrying two of the most important people in the country. One of them, a handsome man immediately identifiable by his luxuriant, neatly trimmed moustache, was Brigadier General Christiaan Beyers, who until 24 hours earlier had been the chief of the Union Defence Force; the other was Koos de la Rey, the most revered Boer general, fondly known by his men as 'Oom Koos'. They were on a very secret mission, which had as its goal nothing less than the overthrow of the Union government.

The previous week, at a special sitting of parliament, South Africa had voted to support Britain in the war against Germany. One of the first things that had to be done was to send a special army contingent to take control of German South West Africa. General Beyers, who would have had to lead the invasion, was against supporting Great Britain, as were several other former Boer generals, including the older De la Rey, who was now 67. Beyers and De la Rey were on their way to meet fellow rebels in the town of Potchefstroom, where a Citizens' Defence Force 'sixteen hundred strong' was waiting on horseback, ready to storm the capital.

De la Rey's involvement was crucial, and it had been made possible because a seer, a 'simple and illiterate farmer' in Lichtenburg, had identified 15 September as a very important day. He had seen the number 15 on a dark cloud, and 'General de la Rey returning home without his hat; immediately afterwards came a carriage covered with flowers'.

The car left Pretoria at 8 pm and, after 40 miles, was on the outskirts of Johannesburg. A police sergeant and a constable who were holding a position near Orange Grove saw the car approaching and motioned for it to stop, probably not recognising who was inside. The generals, either unaware that the roadblock was for the Foster Gang and not for them, or because of a strong wind that was blowing, so 'none of the occupants heard the challenge or understood its seriousness', told the driver to keep going. From there, they 'sped along what is known as the Kloof Road by way of Killarney to the Vrededorp Subway and out towards the Western Witwatersrand'.

One of the policemen, meanwhile, ran to the nearest police station, and an alert was sent out by radio giving the number plate of the speeding car. Several miles away, near Langlaagte – the very place where gold had first been discovered on the Witwatersrand in 1886 – they were challenged at another roadblock but drove on. Using his rifle, one of the policemen fired three shots, one of which ricocheted off the road and then hit De la Rey in the spine: 'To General Beyers' intense horror the aged veteran collapsed and expired almost immediately.'

The driver stopped, and for a while Beyers and the policemen were 'at cross-purposes', for the general knew nothing of the Foster Gang and the police knew nothing of the plot to overthrow the government. Eventually, the car, with Beyers holding the general's body inside, was driven to the police station at Fordsburg.

The rebellion, at least for the moment, was still unborn.

On Wednesday 16 September 1914, the day after the shootout in Regents Park, police found the Foster Gang's Overland car abandoned, partly covered by a green tarpaulin, near Primrose Cemetery, several miles beyond Bertrams. A bullet had pierced the chassis and damaged the engine, and the blood on the front seat confirmed that at least one person had been wounded.

Assuming that Foster and the others were now on foot, it was clear that their progress would be slowed down even more by a wounded person and a woman with a baby. Police dogs were brought in and given the scent of the car – as an additional measure, one of the seats was taken out and carried with the trackers. The dogs then followed a path not east, in the original direction, but back towards the city.

The trackers reached Kensington, a neighbourhood known for its boarding-houses and tea gardens that people went to on weekends. With large expanses of veld separating the buildings, the fugitives wouldn't be able to go far during daylight without drawing attention. At one point a tracker indicated two routes, suggesting that part of the group, probably Peggy and the child, had gone a different way to the others.

Meanwhile, a second police detachment of African constables led by Sergeant Thomas Granger had started searching further up the ridge behind Kensington. When one of them shone a light into a cave and saw a man's booted foot, a shot rang out from inside, narrowly missing the constable's head. A second constable threw an assegai into the darkness. More shots were fired at them, but no one was hit. The police rolled rocks over the cave entrance to block it until reinforcements arrived. The Foster Gang had been found.

Major Sholto Douglas, the deputy chief of police, soon arrived on the scene, where he was assisted by Detective George Martin. Scores of armed policemen and sharpshooters, with bandoliers slung across their shoulders, took cover behind rocks or lay flat in the long grass. Not long afterwards, cameramen from a newly created newsreel service called 'African Mirror' arrived – followed by their counterparts from British Gaumont and Pathé News – and set up their cameras.

When the news spread that the Foster Gang was trapped in a cave, members of the public who had made sure to stay locked up at home the last few days – especially with the stream of headlines like 'Horror Upon Horror', 'Murderers Get Away' and 'Night of Tragedies' – suddenly came out and went to see the final act play out. The city had never seen anything like this. The tram terminus in Kensington was barely 200 yards away from the cave, and a crowd had soon gathered, so many people that a cordon had to be put up to keep them back. Mounted policemen patrolled the barriers.

At the cave, Major Douglas considered using firehoses to flood the gang out, but locals who knew the terrain said the cave went back 45 yards or more and water would be useless. Then they tried smoking them out by getting a marksman to shoot open two bottles of ammonia that were strung over the cave entrance. The fumes, instead of going into the hiding place, were carried by the wind towards the onlookers, sending them into a panic.

When darkness fell, the police illuminated the area with acetylene lamps hung from long poles to prevent anyone from trying to escape. As

Dozens of snipers gathered near the cave to back up the police after they found the Foster Gang's hiding place

the police hunkered down for a long vigil, a cold wind blew down the ridge, chasing away many of the remaining onlookers.

The next morning, Thursday 17 September, the sharpshooters were still in place, standing now, feeling more relaxed that no one would shoot back, and the cameramen waited as close to the cave as the police would allow.

Detective Martin suggested to Major Douglas that they try to negotiate with Foster. Several policemen went down to move the rocks out of the way, covered all the while by snipers. There was no response from inside the cave, but shortly afterwards they heard a single shot.

At midday, Foster finally broke his silence, and asked to see his family – his father, who had been there all the while, 'a sunken faced, slim old man ... obviously highly agitated at the desperate position of his son', his mother and two of his sisters. Most of all he wanted to see his wife, Peggy.

'If you let me see her, we'll all come up with our hands up.'

His voice was hoarse and weak. He gave them an address in Germiston, where he said they would find her.

'Now play the game,' he said. 'No treachery. We'll hand over our firearms. We've got four down here. But don't move the stones from the hole till I hear my wife's voice. I'll be waiting at the entrance here for her. We'll surrender to her and to no one else. You've got us here all right and we'll surrender.'

Not everyone thought it was a good idea to bring Peggy to Foster, but a policeman was dispatched in Douglas's car to fetch her. As they waited, Martin organised for cigarettes, matches and a flask of tea to be lowered to the cave.

'I'm damned sorry we had to shoot your fellows,' Foster called out, meaning Mansfield, MacLeod and Mynott. 'It was only money we were after to get out of the country.'

When Peggy arrived with the baby, the news cameramen were all lined up waiting for her. They filmed her getting out of the car and then climbing down to reach the cave. By that stage, his mother and sisters had arrived. After half an hour, Foster threw out a gun. He asked if he could also see his parents and sisters, for there were certain private matters he wished to discuss with them before he surrendered. The

The site of the cave where the Foster Gang were hiding became almost like a circus, as policemen held off hordes of spectators.

police grew more suspicious – would he try to escape dressed up as one of his family members? – but they believed they could deal with any outcome. One by one, Foster's family entered the hideout.

Inside, the first thing they saw was the lifeless body of Boy Mezar near the entrance to the cave, killed by one bullet – the single shot that had gone off earlier – either by his own hand or by one of the others as he tried to flee. Foster himself had been hit by three bullets and was very weak from loss of blood.

John Maxim, who had stood by Foster since they first met, tried to persuade him to dress up as a woman and escape as one of his sisters, but Foster said the police would see through the disguise.

As Foster played with his daughter, it became clear to the family that he had no intention of giving himself up. He told them that all the violence had been caused by the actions of one man, the old judge in Cape Town who had sentenced him and his brother to 12 years in jail for the American Swiss robbery.

'It's Judge Kotze who is to blame for this. It was his [Jimmy's] first conviction, and to think old Kotze could be so cruel towards the boy. It made me determined to exact vengeance. The price is paid. I die here.'

Peggy refused to leave Foster, saying she would rather die with him, and handed the baby to one of his sisters. Foster's mother exited the cave first, weeping, then his sisters, one of them carrying the baby. By the time his father came out, the police must have known what would happen next. Barely a few moments later, four shots went off inside the cave.

Three detectives were sent down, but they approached carefully, in case it was a trap. After climbing over Mezar's body, which was cold and stiff, they found the other three. The top of Peggy's head had been blown off by Foster, who had then put a single bullet hole in his own forehead, slumping onto her shoulder. Three feet away from them lay Maxim, who, judging by the cotton wool at his side, had shaved before pulling the trigger on himself. On his body, they found a key to the National Bank from the gang's first Johannesburg robbery, the only thing linking them to it. The bank drafts that had been stolen were still missing.

CHAPTER 4

Boom town *in excelsis*

L ife in the City of Gold got back to its own kind of curious normal. The week of violence in September 1914 probably hardened some residents' attitudes for a while, before they returned to a fairly common relationship with Johannesburg, one that swung wildly between love and hate.

The city had many nicknames, and 'deserved every one' of them. Sometimes it was the City of Gold, the Golden City, the City of Wonder, the Sunshine City, the Wonder City Built on Gold, the Incredible City, the Wonder of the World and, in those rare moments of rapture, the Miracle City.

To the Africans flooding in from across the subcontinent to work at the mines – from Portuguese East Africa, Rhodesia, Basutoland and further north – it was simply *eGoli*, the Zulu word for gold.

To white miners, it was a pit stop on the way to wealth. Mark Twain, after visiting in 1896, wrote that the salary of an engineer was 'not based on what he'd get in America, but apparently what a whole family of him would get there'. Just as often it led to perdition.

'Everyone is out for gold and you can fairly smell it in the air,' Edmund Bright, a young adventurer from Pennsylvania, wrote to his father in 1902.

When they didn't find it, they moved on.

The centre of the boom town, Market Square. Within a few years it would become a major tram terminus.

'The people here behave as if they came last month and intend to leave next month,' the American doctor Alexander Orenstein wrote in 1914, after arriving from the Panama Canal, where he had worked to help eradicate malaria. His job in the City of Gold was to try and deal with the chronic incidence of phthisis (pulmonary tuberculosis) in the mines.

And to those who hated Johannesburg – and there were many – it was Sodom, the City of Ramps, the equivalent of the British industrial heartland, Judasberg, the city of gold and sin, and the University of Crime. Almost from the moment that gold was discovered in 1886, the mining camp exploded, attracting fortune hunters from across the globe, many of them arriving after trudging across the country and then down the ridge at Baragwanath, laden with all their gear, and descending into the new Eldorado.

No other gold discovery had ever caused this kind of unrestrained excitement. In 1889, just three years later, the London *Daily News* wrote: 'There are not wanting those who prognosticate a future for Johannesburg which is positively blinding in its brilliancy. They promise a million inhabitants in five years, an output of gold which shall gild the whole world, a commercial importance threatening the established trade centres of the Old World, and a political and social position second to no city in Africa, north or south.' Cecil John Rhodes called it 'the biggest thing the world has seen'.

The flood of adventure seekers quickly generated two other phenomena: entertainment and crime. Within two years, there were 77 bars, 43 hotels, 12 billiard halls, the racetrack at Turffontein, gambling dens, circuses, boxing matches, roller-skating rinks and countless brothels.

Corruption and 'ramps', popular slang for a swindle, flourished, and by 1896 the incidents of crime that people actually bothered to report totalled at least 35 000 annually. 'The Golden City's reputation for wickedness is engraved in the South African conscience almost as deeply as the gold reef is embedded in the quartz of the Witwatersrand.' Criminals and desperadoes from around the world drifted to the mining camp, and 'it was another type of prospecting that they did'. Confidence tricksters, fraudsters and murderers hid in plain sight, their most obvious targets the people who possibly had gold or money in their pockets, probably had drunk too much and were almost asking to be preyed upon. They were often single young men – at least 80 per cent of the population – with no families or friends to ask what had happened to them if they disappeared. And disappear they often did, or their money did.

In what became known as the 'Marshall Square Murders', in 1899, several men were murdered and their bodies left right outside the police headquarters on the square, each with his pockets turned inside out. A few blocks away, another young man was shot. 'The whole town was alarmed, and the anxiety was aggravated when two or three nights later two more men were found murdered in similar circumstances.'

Even though a killer was never found, it was strongly thought to have been an Englishman, Frederick Baily Deeming, who for a time had posed as an engineer on the mines. Deeming fled to England, where he murdered his wife and four children, and then murdered another wife in Australia, where he was finally executed.

The Marshall Square Murders left a lasting impression on a young boy named Harry Morris. Just two years before the murders, when Harry was nine years old, his mother had brought him and his sister to Johannesburg to join their father, a bank manager. Until then the family had lived in Beaufort West, an 'honest little town ... where there were no brokers, bookmakers or burglars'. And then ... the University of Crime.

From the start, even before he read of the Marshall Square Murders, Morris was more suited to the cosmopolitan chaos of Johannesburg. His mother was Afrikaans, from a long line of Dutch immigrants, his father Jewish, one of the founders of the city's Hebrew congregation, and young Harry was sent to an array of Catholic and Anglican schools in Johannesburg, Durban and Cape Town. Like William Foster, he had gone to the Marist Brothers' school in Koch Street, opposite Joubert Park.

By 1898, at the age of 20, he was back in the city, just in time to witness the most sensational murder trial the country had ever seen: Baron Carl Ludwig von Veltheim had been charged with killing the mining magnate Woolf Joel in cold blood. It was the first big murder trial to be splashed across the newspapers, and it combined all the elements the city was infamous for – adventurers, charlatans, intrigue, millionaires and murder.

The accused was handsome, tanned, dashing and tall. Von Veltheim had once boasted that he 'explored the Never-Never-Land of Australia, that he went through two revolutions in South America, and was not far away when President Barros was shot dead ... that he fought in Bulgaria and joined in the search for Stanley in Darkest Africa, proceeding as far as St Paul de Loanda in West Africa, and only returning when he heard that Stanley had gone to Stanley Falls ...'

In fact, he was a German-born 'notorious arch-swindler' named Frank Kurtze, although he also called himself, among other names, Karl Broun, Captain Jackson, Captain Vincent and Louis Platten. He had been a sailor, gun-runner, spy, lumberjack, confidence trickster and 'freebooter', and had been linked to acts of kidnapping, extortion and murder around the world.

'Johannesburg, a boom town *in excelsis*, drew him as honey does a fly.'

Now, in 1898, Von Veltheim stood accused of the cold-blooded murder of Woolf Joel, a nephew of Barney Barnato and a partner in one of the city's biggest mining houses, Barnato Brothers. The prosecutor, the first ever in the city – a formidable and brilliant Afrikaner named FET (Fritz) Krause – had an open-and-shut case. Or at least it seemed that way.

Harry Morris sat in the packed court, entranced. The women were infatuated with Von Veltheim, who sat before them in the dock, smartly dressed, his moustache neatly waxed, his thick hair brushed, his eyes brooding. It was almost hard not to be in love with him. Seventeen journalists crowded into the courtroom.

Fritz Krause told the jury that the accused had, for several months before the shooting, sent a series of letters to Woolf Joel demanding money for secret information that he claimed to have about dealings on the Johannesburg Stock Exchange. Joel, accompanied by his assistant, Harold Strange, met Von Veltheim and told him there was no reason to

The con man Von Veltheim talking to one of his guards during his 1898 trial for the murder of Woolf Joel.

do business with him. A second meeting between the three was arranged to trap him. In broad daylight on 14 March 1898, 'with detectives lurking outside', Von Veltheim came to Joel's office and, even though all three men were armed, it was Joel who took a bullet and died. Von Veltheim's defence was that Woolf had fired the first shot.

Von Veltheim was clearly guilty, but after Krause's lengthy closing argument, the seven-man jury, to the surprise even of the judge, took only 20 minutes to set him free. Like most working-class men in town, they loathed mine owners like the murdered Joel, as well as the likes of Cecil John Rhodes, Sir JB Robinson and Sir George Albu. Justice was outweighed by 'the proletarian public's antipathy towards mine magnates'.

The scene following Von Veltheim's acquittal, Harry Morris recalled, 'baffled description', with people 'swarming all over the place, standing on the benches, shouting and screaming, and waving their hands. The prisoner appeared electrified.' The young Morris, swept up in the excitement of it all, was struck by two things: how thrilling a criminal trial could be, and how, under the right circumstances and with the right lawyer, you could get away with murder.

'This place showed distinct promise,' he wrote mischievously, 'and I decided to stay.'

CHAPTER 5

Dr Gibson returns

Near the end of 1914, the man described as one of the country's most famous criminals walked out of Pretoria Central, a free man after serving his 18 months.

The authorities' original plan, to deport master fraudster Andrew Gibson to the US, had, inexplicably, been 'dropped' and, with apparent ease, he went to Johannesburg, where he blended in like a chameleon and began oiling the wheels for his next scam. Of course, he already knew exactly what it would be.

In the prison infirmary, where Gibson had worked as an orderly, he had struck up a friendship with one Charles Plunkett, a 'financier' also in his early fifties, who had since been released, and whose 'cooperation paved the way for a series of bank frauds ... of a nature rarely heard of in crime'. Together with a local printer, they forged bank drafts from the Queensland government and then conned various reputable people to sign them, whereupon they were paid out.

The speed with which Gibson worked was breath-taking. He acquired a new wife, Elizabeth Stafford, whom he married at St Mary's, and even persuaded the *Rand Daily Mail* that they had just arrived from Australia. Dr Gibson, the article said, was the son of the late Justice John W Spencer-Gibson, and would be setting up a medical practice in Belgravia, east of the city centre. He even managed to fool the local medical authorities with documents identifying him as Dr A Gibson of Victoria, British Columbia. He claimed to have worked in London at an ear, nose and throat hospital in Golden Square and a maternity home in Myddelton Square, and at a refugee camp in Uitenhage during the Anglo-Boer War, before returning to London.

Plunkett by this stage was working at the Belgravia Nursing Home, in a non-medical capacity, and he asked Gibson to come and help him there, as the facility was not up to date and was losing customers to the Kensington Sanatorium. Gibson began filling in as a doctor, soon becoming the 'initiator and sole user' of the 'Twilight Sleep' system of childbirth. The procedure used scopolamine, a drug derived from plants of the nightshade family, such as belladonna, to induce labour in pregnant women. It was estimated by a man who knew him that Gibson attended as many as one hundred patients, although 'he had a couple of narrow shaves, for some of his subjects nearly went to sleep for good'.

'He also used his system – which resolved itself into a patent anaesthetic – for all sorts of operations. In one case he took the top off a man's skull, removed a tumour, and got the head in order again. I once asked him [the man told the reporter] how he came to get hold of his anaesthetic, and he said it was obtained by himself and another medical man who worked on it in Europe, and it had been used in 4 000 cases. ... He said [it] was made of three drugs, of which hyoscine [sic] was the chief, and he used to recall that this latter mixture was used in large quantities by Dr Crippen to poison Belle Elmore.'

Gibson moved to a house near the Belgravia facility, and kept fooling people that he was of the highest breeding: '[H]is skill as a surgeon was undoubted and he performed operations which gave strange relief. One, in particular, a delicate operation for a nervous complaint, resulted in a complete cure and established his reputation with all those to whom his grateful patient spoke.'

He ordered a piano from Mackay Bros, although when the manager, a Mr Landau, came to deliver it, 'there was neither the red lamp nor brass plate' that one usually found at a doctor's office. Gibson explained that he did not require these, as he 'worked privately for the profession'. When there was a chance that Gibson might have absconded, Landau returned to the property but found him there: 'His manner was exceedingly charming, so much so, in fact, that he appeared to have had a very polished education and to be able to disarm all hostility.'

But then, in early March 1915, Gibson suddenly took off. The law was on to him again, and, quite bizarrely, he was wanted not for his medical fraud – no one seemed to have complained about that – but for the Queensland government bank draft forgeries.

Plunkett saw the Gibsons off from Germiston station on 3 March, and they headed to Lourenço Marques. He followed a few days later and checked in to the Central Hotel as Dr Andrew Gibson, giving the fraudster time to escape.

'As long as I am free,' Gibson told Plunkett, no doubt as a gentle threat should the latter think of confessing to the authorities, 'you are safe.'

On the voyage to Australia, he dumped three volumes of fake Queensland treasury bonds overboard.

In late March, a detective by the name of William Hill was sent by Colonel Kenneth Vachell – who had led the Foster Gang investigation and had since been promoted – to visit the Gibson house on Main Street, Belgravia. Plunkett, who had returned from Lourenço Marques, was staying there and answered the door. He told the detective that he had first met Gibson not in the Pretoria Central infirmary but ten years earlier, in 1904, when Gibson had attended his wife and child in Bertrams.

Whatever the truth – and the two men's versions differed wildly when they finally came out – the police were on Gibson's trail. Photographs of the 'doctor', taken both during his prison days in California and during his time in Pretoria Central, were published in newspapers, saying he was wanted on various charges in various parts of the world.

The brazenness of his cons, which were becoming legendary, earned him the nickname of 'a local Koepenick ... the famous German cobbler who went to a garrison town and thoroughly spoofed the burgomaster and the military authorities'.

After the Plunkett interview, Vachell contacted the police in Australia to be on the lookout for Gibson, and by 25 August 1915 he had been arrested. Strangely enough for the master of disguises, he did not deny his identity when confronted. No mention was made in the press of 'Mrs Gibson', with whom he had disappeared.

Vachell made arrangements to send Inspector Hill to Australia to fetch Gibson, and by the end of September he was on his way. When Hill arrived and interviewed Gibson, the first thing the fraudster asked was if Plunkett had been arrested. Hill said, as far as he knew, Plunkett was still a free man. That was when Gibson made good on his promise to implicate him if he compromised his freedom. It was clear that if the police had figured out where Gibson had fled to and caught him, then it was because of Plunkett. He told Hill that he had paid Plunkett £1 500 as part of the 'robbery' of the Queensland vouchers.

And from that moment, the two partners in crime turned on each other.

CHAPTER 6

Wine of life

By April 1915 – as Andrew Gibson's name was fading from the news, while the police carried on their search for him – the war in Europe increasingly occupied people's attention. Allied forces had started what would turn out to be a long and devastating campaign against the Turks at Gallipoli, while General Louis Botha was leading an occupation force into German South West Africa.

Men across the country, especially on the gold mines, began to enlist in droves. One of those who didn't enlist – not because he didn't want to but because he would never have passed a physical exam – was Alfred Cowle, Daisy de Melker's husband.

Even though Alfie looked healthy enough, never missed a day's work and pottered around the garden when he was at home, he had already been operated on three times, for haemorrhoids and a fistula. The diagnoses for his complaints were imprecise, as most physicians at the time still relied on blood counts and urine analyses, stool tests and rigid tube proctoscopies. If they were lucky enough to have the equipment, they could take X-rays of the oesophagus, stomach, colon and gall bladder. But most of them didn't.

In the end, Alfie could have been suffering from Crohn's disease or ulcerative colitis, caused by any one of various things, all with equally confusing names: visceroptosis, a sinking of the internal organs; auto-

Dutch medicines were popular at chemists from the earliest days of the mining camp.

intoxication, a poisoning of the body through a toxin created by itself; neurasthenia, where psychological factors cause exhaustion and other symptoms; or just dyspepsia, indigestion.

For anyone seeking relief for ailments so imprecise, there was, thankfully, a world of cure-alls, promising hope for the hopeless, including Jones' Rheumaticuro, Wincarnis 'Wine of Life' and California Syrup of Figs. Doan's Backache Kidney Pills competed with Beecham's Pills, 'a valuable aperient and unequalled in regulating the stomach, bowels, liver and kidneys and restoring the powers of digestion' or the widely publicised DeWitt's Kidney and Bladder Pills, for 'rheumatism, lumbago, cystitis, stone, backache, weak back, sciatica, gravel, gout, tired feeling'. More commonly, people opted for Eno's 'Fruit Salt', Phosferine, bisurated magnesia, bismuth, pepsin, charcoal and soda, which individually or collectively promised relief from a dizzying array of maladies – biliousness, 'sick headache', constipation, errors in diet, thirst, giddiness, 'gouty poison', feverish cold, indigestion, exhaustion, lassitude, neuritis, hysteria, neuralgia, loss of appetite, dyspepsia, acidity, flatulence, rheumatism, lumbago, cystitis, stone, weak back, sciatica, gravel, gout, 'tired feeling', 'premature decay', kidney, bladder, renal dropsy, lassitude and 'brain fog'.

Traditionalists relied on Dutch medicines. They took *rooi laventel*, or red lavender, to ease faintness, indigestion, hysteria and menstrual cramps, or mixed it with goat fat, lard and drops of pimento oil to rub onto a child's wheezing chest. Or they boiled a mixture of sulphur, linseed oil and turpentine to make Paregoric Elixir, or Haarlem Oil, which was taken for bladder and liver disorders, and even for wind and gripe. For hysteria and faintness, there was tincture of asafoetida, more commonly known as *duiwelsdrek* (devil's dung).

Daisy told Alfie to have more tests done, but he continued to rely on the ever-growing array of nostrums, pills, bromides, syrups and specially made-up tonics. Some of them he got from colleagues, others from pharmacies like Spilkin's in Kenilworth. So many bottles would have filled the Tully Street house, containing so many white powders and liquids, it would have been difficult to tell them apart. And it would have been very simple – by mistake or on purpose – to mix them up.

When it was once again time for the birthdays of the two Cowle boys, in June 1915, Daisy was already five months pregnant. She had also started a job on the other side of the city, almost five miles and two tram rides away.

Leaving Rhodes and Lester in the care of a neighbour, perhaps Mary Jane Meaker or her cousin Mia Melville, she headed for the tram stop on Turffontein Road. The tram took her north, through the mine dumps and into the city, where she got off at the terminus on Market Square. From there she had the option of catching the tram up Harrison Street, past Park Station and over the railway tracks, or another that went along Market Street and then up Troye and Twist streets.

The two lines ran parallel as they approached, and then ascended, Hospital Hill, and between them at the top stood a pair of structures that had overlooked the mining camp from its earliest days: the Old Fort, which now housed a small prison, and the building where Daisy would be working, the main hospital.

After she got off and walked in the shadow of the ramparts of the Old Fort, square and foreboding, the medical buildings offered a prettier sight – five storeys, red brick and sandstone, topped by an ornate Beaux-Arts tower, and with trees and a garden spreading out in front of the growing agglomeration of wings and laboratories. These included the medical research institute, the 60-patient Barnato Block and the Queen Victoria maternity section. The new fever wing was to serve patients with infectious diseases, and would have separate wings for diphtheria, scarlet fever and measles.

The hospital, like many around the country, suddenly found itself with a shortage of staff, as more people volunteered for the war effort. Daisy got a job as a 'portress', to carry things around the wards, clean rooms and toilets, and sweep the floors, even though she could have done a lot more.

Until seven years earlier, she had been studying to become a nurse, but then tragedy struck, something that would keep happening to her – the first death of someone very close to her. Afterwards, Daisy's life took a very different turn.

*

In 1908, Daisy Louisa Hancorn Smith was about to marry Bert Fuller, an assistant native commissioner who worked at Broken Hill in Rhodesia, which was in the lead and zinc mining belt near the Congo.

Fuller was friends with Daisy's eldest brother John, who, together with their father, William Stringfellow Hancorn Smith, a descendant of the 1820 Settlers, had moved to work on a farm near Bulawayo when Daisy was a young girl. The rest of the family were left behind in Seven Fountains, a settlement not far from Grahamstown in the Cape. The middle child of 11, she was ordinary but had wild hair and was born with a slight disfiguration, a harelip. When Daisy was ten, in 1896, she was sent to live with John and William.

One of John's jobs was to set traps on the farm for animals preying on their cows. He laced meat with strychnine, a poison that, despite being deadly, could be easily bought at pharmacies in Rhodesia. To make it distinguishable from other powders, it was often coloured pink.

Bert Fuller sometimes joined John on his rounds.

Daisy was sent to a boarding school in Cape Town and then to study at the Berea Nursing Home in Durban. Each time she returned to Rhodesia, Fuller came to visit. When he asked her to marry him, she accepted but wanted to keep it a secret until she had completed her nursing studies.

In late 1907, when Daisy was 21, she and Fuller announced their engagement, even though she hadn't yet graduated, and the marriage was set for 3 March the following year. By February 1908, Fuller was gravely ill. Having suffered from malaria in the past, it was suspected he had black-water fever – so called because after parasites destroyed the red blood cells, it turned the urine so dark that it looked black.

Daisy returned from Durban and kept a vigil by his bedside, but Fuller never recovered, and he died on 3 March, the day they were meant to have married. Despite Fuller's relative youth, he had drawn up a will, leaving most of his estate, worth £95 (about £11 400 today), to Daisy.

Instead of returning to nursing school, she moved to the City of Gold, where her aunt ran a boarding-house in Bertrams. A year earlier, she had visited the city, which, as it did with everyone, had left a deep impression. It was London and New York in Africa, with bioscopes and theatres and dress shops along Pritchard Street and tasteful arcades to escape the dust storms and drink afternoon tea, all dwarfed by the 'spectacle of huge structures upon the American pattern'. There were long wide main avenues, where cabs parked outside the station on race days to take men to the track at Turffontein and ricksha boys waited at the post office in Jeppe Street. The ornate gardens in Joubert Park centred on a fountain and a bandstand, where musicians played on weekends, and women flocked to a nearby art gallery that had a sculpture by Rodin. There was a million-tree forest at Sachsenwald, right near the millionaires' mansions in Parktown, each on its acre of land. The Carlton Hotel, with heating and cooling systems, penthouses and a Turkish bath in the basement, was where the mining magnates sat in their bathrobes making deals. There were even laws about people riding bicycles faster than six miles an hour and cracking a whip too loudly.

While staying at the boarding-house, and while Fuller was still alive, Daisy had met a man of medium height, with slightly protruding ears, who worked as a plumber for the municipality. His name was William Alfred Cowle. After Bert Fuller died, they met up again, and on 3 March 1909 – the anniversary of Fuller's death – they were married at St Mary's-the-Less, the first Anglican church in the city, close to Bertrams and Jeppestown. Alfie Cowle was 35, and Daisy was 11 years younger.

Three months later, Alfie made a will, and in June 1914 a codicil was added to include an insurance policy. His executor and sole heir were the same person – his wife, Daisy.

*

In September 1915, after news had been received of Andrew Gibson's arrest in Australia, and just as Inspector Hill was setting off for the long voyage from Durban to fetch him, Daisy Cowle gave up her job on Hospital Hill. On 19 October, she gave birth to another boy, whom the Cowles named after Alfred. The eldest son, Rhodes Cecil, was now four years old and Lester Eric was two. Only one of the three boys would live beyond his fifth birthday.

PART 2

ARMS OF THE LAW

1916–1921

CHAPTER 7

Women waiting

On 16 January 1916, a large crowd of mostly women gathered at Park Station to witness the arrival of the 'notorious criminal' Andrew Gibson, who was meant to be on the train from Durban, escorted by Inspector Hill and a second detective, following their return from Australia. But he wasn't on board, and it was thought that in order to avoid any sensation, the police had sneaked him off early, at Germiston. The truth was simpler – the detectives were just late. When they arrived four days later, Gibson was taken to jail to await his trial, although that couldn't happen until documents proving all his crimes were gathered from around the world. No one knew how long that would take, so the fraudster sat behind bars, waiting to hear his fate.

CHAPTER 8

The unfortunate Jew

'It certainly seems,' wrote the young poet and journalist Sarah Gertrude Millin, herself a Jew, 'that the public eye is very semitically filled in Johannesburg. The cabmen are Jews, and the fruit vendors. The jewellers are Jews and the pawnbrokers. The variety artists and the audiences. The lawyers are Jews. The stockbrokers are Jews. The millionaires are Jews.'

The visibility of Jews in Johannesburg had been a point of fascination, but mostly of opprobrium, from the city's earliest days. The English politician James Bryce, on a visit to South Africa, thought that even though Johannesburg reminded him of the mining cities of the American West, 'a busy, eager, restless pleasure-loving town', he felt compelled to add that it was predominantly 'Anglo-Semitic'. 'On certain holidays you might imagine yourself in a Semitic town,' wrote the British journalist Richard Curle, 'and true it is that the Jews share with the English the local dominance to the virtual exclusion of the Dutch.' One traveller called it 'a printed-in-Germany pocket edition of London' with a high number of Jews.

The early magnates from England and Germany – Barney Barnato, the Joel brothers, Woolf and Solly, Alfred Beit, Lionel Phillips and Sigismund Neumann – followed up their diamond successes in Kimberley with even more minerals in Johannesburg. The first pharmacist was

Jewish, and within the first year, ten per cent of doctors were too. The first chairman of the Turffontein racetrack was Charles Marx; Emanuel Mendelssohn edited the *Standard and Transvaal Mining Chronicle*; and the president of the Johannesburg Stock Exchange on various occasions was Harry Solomon. The Transvaal president Paul Kruger had opened the city's first synagogue – apparently while joking 'I will make Christians of you yet'. The first Jewish mayor, Harry Graumann, had been elected in 1909.

The largest wave of Jewish immigrants, however, many of them fleeing persecution in parts of the Russian Empire, especially Lithuania, took more menial jobs, as tradesmen, shop assistants and peddlers, known by the Afrikaans word *smous*. By 1916, the Jewish population of South Africa numbered about 47 000, almost as many as in Algeria and more than in Egypt or Tunisia.

One person who didn't seem to fit into any group – not English, German or Eastern European – was Louis Tumpowski. Already in his early fifties, he had come from the US more than two decades earlier, although he had found no fame or fortune. After drifting from job to job, selling tobacco, working at hotels and behind shop counters, he landed up as yet another one of the hundreds of traders on the overcrowded Market Square in the heart of Johannesburg.

For the last two years, he had also started taking his business out of town. With his ox-wagon full of dry goods, knickknacks and haberdashery, he called in at settlements, small towns and distant farms. Some traders even managed to get a projector that they could prop on the back of their wagons and show poor-quality silent movies wherever they stopped.

In Lichtenburg, the 'town of weeping willows' to the west, where General De la Rey had been buried after his fatal shooting during the Foster Gang imbroglio, Tumpowski found a small Jewish community that was welcoming. David Rothschild farmed and ran a store, Louis Goldstein traded in skins and hides, and the tailor was Abe Slavin. This was perhaps a place where his luck could change.

One of his customers was a young widow in her mid-thirties by the name of Dorothea Kraft. She and her daughter, Polly, who at the age of 20 could have been her sister, lived on the outskirts of town on a farm called Treurfontein, where she tried, mostly with little success, to grow corn (maize). Kraft was pretty, with long dark hair, although slovenly and not particularly well educated, and had an unattractive habit of complaining a lot, bending the ear of anyone prepared to listen to her. Tumpowski had no issue with that, for it might lead to a sale, and Kraft, behind all the whining, was easy on the eye.

She told him that running a farm without a man was difficult, and she was sure the labourers were stealing from her. When she asked Tumpowski if he knew someone who could manage the place for her, he said he would ask around. Whether he did or not, he returned to Lichtenburg the next time with a proposition for Kraft: he would do the job.

She agreed.

Kraft's farm lived up to its name – 'fountain of sorrow' or 'misery fountain'. Treurfontein was all misery and sorrow, no fountain.

At the heart of the unimpressive piece of dry land – 'the veld being flat and stretching away monotonously' – was a dismal 'comfortless' homestead of galvanised-iron walls and poky rooms with small windows letting in little light. Incredibly, there wasn't even a verandah. Kraft's crop of corn yielded at most a meagre 300 bags a year, but Louis Tumpowski saw opportunity.

The arrangement they came to was that he would manage her land in return for lodgings and £25 a year. He also negotiated an option – one that Kraft would very soon come to regret – to buy the farm for £3 per morgen (about two acres or just less than a hectare) if her debt became too large. Despite their 20-year age difference, they also started sharing a bed, even though Kraft complained about him behind his back, calling him names, her favourite being 'the old Jew'.

Every now and then Tumpowski left the farm for several days, staying tight-lipped about what he was going to do. He had a married sister named Hetty Saltman in Johannesburg, which he might have told Kraft. But he probably never said anything about his bank account in Johannesburg, where his savings were not insubstantial. Tumpowski had good reason to keep his money a secret, especially in a city full of murderers, thieves and con men. But maybe also because he had his doubts about the widow Kraft.

CHAPTER 9

Eighty per cent chance

Along Pritchard Street, dozens of men dressed in black robes and white bibs scurried about their business. Barristers and solicitors, their destination was the grand Beaux-Arts building that stretched out along the northern side of the intersection with Kruis Street.

The long frontispiece of columns crafted from cream-coloured sandstone converged at a massive recessed entryway topped by a copper dome already covered in verdigris and which 'for the imaginative [had] the appearance of a mosque'. The building, the Supreme Court, was more popularly referred to by the name of its most famous division, the 'Criminal Sessions'.

Among the black-robed men, on 17 October 1916, was one of medium height with tousled curly hair and round spectacles. It was Harry Morris. Almost 20 years had passed since, as a law clerk, he had watched the trial of Baron Von Veltheim. After studying and being admitted to the Inner Temple in London, he had returned to Johannesburg – the city 'with distinct promise'.

For the past ten years, Harry had been building up a reputation for representing the most unwinnable cases, which usually also meant the most reprehensible acts possible – arson, rape, illicit diamond buying, fraud, theft, embezzlement, murder. And today, his client was none other than the 'most famous prisoner in the country', Andrew Gibson, who had been languishing in the Old Fort on Hospital Hill for ten months awaiting trial for forgery and fraud. His former conspirator, Charles Plunkett, was being tried separately.

Two things attracted Harry to Gibson's case. Not only was it going to be impossibly difficult – the fraudster had been jailed so many times, it was unlikely a jury would find him anything but guilty – but he also had a soft spot for the con artist, who reminded him of 'an over-worked broken-down bookkeeper', a man who 'radiated gentleness [and] spoke in a sweet dreamy voice that lulled his hearer into a coma of attention and interest'.

Maybe Harry also recognised something of himself in the criminal. They were both wily, sharp and charming, and their spirits were indomitable – the one trying to pull off the classic scam, the other an unwinnable case. Both had uncertainty and the power of suggestion to their benefit, studying their targets and wheedling into their confidences before they struck. Exploiting the shortcomings of human beings was their mutual gift.

As usual, Harry arrived at the Criminal Sessions an hour before proceedings started, which was when the detectives from Marshall Square got there. A good deal of banter always followed between the police and the prosecution – also called the Crown – that often did not appear in the preliminary-trial record. There was always the chance that Harry could pick up something that he could use to his client's benefit.

In almost all cases, Harry believed, it took 20 per cent skill and 80 per cent chance, although in Gibson's case the odds were a lot worse. The prosecution had not only solid witnesses – the detective who had chased him, Inspector Hill, as well as the man who had printed the forged Queensland bonds and the bank managers who had paid them out – but also Gibson's own affidavit that he had signed in Australia, in which he admitted to a crime.

Two people who eagerly wanted to testify in Gibson's favour, and attest to his good character, weren't allowed to because the judge said their evidence had nothing to do with the case. One was a policeman whose broken finger Gibson had fixed, the other a 'dear old lady' who said her daughter was at death's door until 'Doctor Gibson' had given her a blood transfusion.

When Harry put Gibson on the stand, the latter denied everything, told a fantastic tale of how it was all Plunkett's idea and said he'd been blackmailed to take part in the crime and that Plunkett had made his life a misery. When he'd finally learned of the crime, on 3 March 1916, he'd fled the country with his wife. Gibson even disputed his previous convictions, all except the one in 1913 that had sent him to Pretoria Central.

No one was fooled by Gibson's performance, and the jury took only 19 minutes to reach a unanimous verdict: guilty.

'Well, Gibson,' the judge said, taking into consideration all his past convictions, 'with a record like this there is only one sentence I can impose upon you, and that is the indeterminate sentence.'

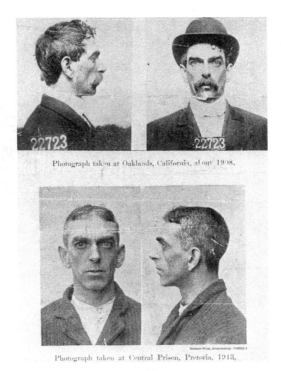

Photograph taken at Oaklands, California, about 1908.

Photograph taken at Central Prison, Pretoria, 1913.

Andrew Gibson in several photographs published while the police were searching for him.

This sentence, reserved for habitual criminals whom the court had repeatedly found guilty, meant that Gibson would be returning to Pretoria Central for up to 15 years. He would become a Blue Coat, although that wouldn't stop him from thinking about ways to escape.

CHAPTER 10

The last son

The year came to an end, as it always did, with the strange sight of Santa Claus in heavy winter clothes decorating shops while the temperatures outside were often sweltering. In Chudleigh Bros department store, there was an entire window display of 'Whyte's Famous Christmas Puddings', and at Blinmans, among the toys and games for sale there was, besides a 'Harmless Pistol', an Eskimo doll.

But at 22 Tully Street, there were no plum puddings and pretty toys. The Cowles' youngest son, Alfred Eric, now one year old, was severely ill. He began to show the same symptoms as the twins before they died, and his body was also overcome with spasms before he expired in early 1917. The doctor, not unexpectedly, gave the cause of death as convulsions.

Next came Lester Eric, who was four.

Over the low fences and bushes between the small properties on Tully Street, it was hard for the neighbours not to hear his cries. They would, in any case, have already known that something bad was going on at the Cowles because Daisy made sure to inform them of the latest news. It was as if she was preparing herself – and them – for the worst.

Lester lasted until spring. The doctor said the cause of death was an abscess of the liver, but it also could have been convulsions. Out of the five children Daisy had given birth to since 1911, only one was left – the boy named after Cecil John Rhodes.

CHAPTER 11

A potion to love her

By early 1917, the only claim that Dorothea Kraft had over Treurfontein was in her head.

Louis Tumpowski, according to the option she had signed, could at any time rip the carpet from under her. A local storekeeper had already made an offer to buy the property from him for £250, not a bad price for the fountain of sorrow, but Tumpowski had said no. Dorothea knew it was only a matter of time before she lost her farm and her home.

Tumpowski kept making secret trips to Johannesburg, leaving her behind with Polly. In May 1917 – one month after the US entered the war – Treurfontein was visited by a burly man in his thirties, well over six feet tall, who had met Polly at the railway station and taken a fancy to her. Hermanus Swarts, who drifted from farm to farm and had already had several run-ins with the law, did some small jobs around the farm. Kraft complained to him about 'the old Jew' and what he was doing to take Treurfontein away from her.

People in town sometimes saw or heard Kraft and Tumpowski quarrelling. Her complaints about him grew into wild threats, and soon she was asking neighbours how to get African *muti* to 'infect the Jew', and told a butcher who visited the farm that she would poison or murder 'the old man' and bury him in the ashpit outside the kitchen or under the kitchen floor. And yet no one ever knew whether to take her

Transport riders, or smouse, like Louis Tumpowski worked alone or with a small support team.

seriously or not – maybe hers were just the crazed rantings of a woman who talked too much and tended to exaggerate.

After other avenues failed, Kraft heard of Jim Bird, who lived on his own in a hut on the outskirts of town, and whom people called 'Whiskers' because of the unappealing wisps of hair always sprouting from his face. Bird sometimes preached but mostly performed *Slaamse toordery* – Malay witchcraft.

When Kraft went to see him, Bird threw cards for her to determine whether Tumpowski loved her, and concluded that he did. Then she asked him if he could make a potion to get the Jew not only to love her, but to love her so much that he would marry her. Bird concocted a brew of *rooi laventel*, *doepa* and *duiwelsdrek*, herbs normally used for flatulence, 'lentils [also] being one of the ingredients'. Kraft used the potion in a tea that was taken to Tumpowski by Polly, but he was ill for two weeks and a doctor had to be called. Tumpowski accused her of trying to poison him, and from then on refused to take any more food or drink that she prepared.

Next, Kraft asked Bird for something that didn't need to be

consumed, so he instructed her to bring him some of Tumpowski's hair and other small possessions. Over them he muttered an incantation and then placed them in a matchbox, which he told her to bury under the floor at the front door. When the old man stepped over it, Bird promised, he would get sick and die. Nothing happened.

Kraft started visiting Bird more often, and 'having immoral relations with him'. The arrangement might well have been prompted by an idea Kraft had, which she eventually put to him: she would pay £100 if he killed Tumpowski.

CHAPTER 12

His perfect day at trial

In Johannesburg, a man very much like Louis Tumpowski – Jewish and a resident in the country for a quarter century – was about to stand trial for an offence his lawyer, Harry Morris, considered the hardest to defend. Harder even than murder.

Unlike the American-born Tumpowski, Lazar Schmulian was Russian-born, and he owned the United Printing and Publishing Company. In August 1917, he and his wife were arrested and accused of being in possession of £1 700 worth of stolen postal orders, which they had started using in March of that year. Because the bonds were from 1914, more than three years old, the dates on them had to be falsified. It wasn't clear how the Schmulians had come upon the postal orders, or if they even knew about their link to a famous robbery. The drafts had been part of the Foster Gang's very first robbery, when they had blown open a bank safe in the middle of the night in Roodepoort.

The charge against the Schmulians was theft, which might have seemed comparatively modest next to murder, rape, arson, manslaughter and fraud, but for Harry Morris, it was the hardest crime to try and disprove. The very moment that thievery was mentioned in a courtroom, whether or not your client was guilty, the odds grew substantially. The hint of something being stolen 'has a smell of its own and makes your case stink'.

The trial was scheduled to take place at the Criminal Sessions in the middle of October.

The Schmulians had chosen to have a jury – rather than be tried only by a judge – and that was what Harry preferred. A jury, which had to be nine men, he could manipulate and influence, and so he carefully went over the list checking the names, professions and other details about the jurors. Johannesburg was still small enough that he might even know things about some of them that he could use to his advantage.

Witnesses called by the prosecution were a bigger challenge, but they all had one thing in common – they were all extremely fallible. Harry knew that some of them would lie blatantly, and these he quickly unmasked, but the vast majority would come to court intending to tell the truth but then not do so.

'I speak of the man who says he heard, saw and remembered accurately what he is telling you,' Morris wrote. 'What he is telling you is generally a little of what [he] saw and heard, something of what others said, and a good deal of what [he] imagined.' And this mix of fact and fiction could often land an innocent person behind bars.

Of all the witnesses, none appealed to Harry's vanity more than the technical expert, whose wisdom it was his job to undermine, a job he repeatedly proved he could do shockingly well: '[W]ith a smattering of knowledge, you can confound the medical man, the ballistic expert, the toxicologist and the handwriting expert.'

Even the people in the public gallery, which was usually packed if Harry was in court, helped his performance. To gain attention or create 'a moment', he sometimes fidgeted with his robe, gripping a shoulder or pulling it down on either side of his chest, his elbows back. When examining evidence or addressing a witness, he folded his arms behind him, underneath the gown, and then slowly rolled up the material with his hands, sometimes leaning forward to emphasise a point. His glasses he would take off, clean or readjust – slowly.

For any witness, even if they hadn't heard of Harry's reputation, those must have been very anxious moments. He quickly put them at their ease, to get them on his side, only to turn their evidence against them moments later, especially if they appeared to be lying: 'For the witness who strayed from the truth, [he had] a trenchant vocabulary and a tongue like a whiplash.'

Harry Morris.

Harry's style mimicked, perhaps intentionally, that of a well-known barrister of the Inner Temple in London, Edward Marshall Hall, whose cases often made headlines, for his theatrics, his ability to defy the odds in impossible cases and his expert command of difficult subjects.

In 1907, Marshall Hall had defended an artist named Robert Wood, who was accused of killing a prostitute – the case became popularly known as the 'Camden Town Murder' – and despite all the evidence pointing to Wood as the killer, he was acquitted. Five years later, Hall's clients were Frederick Seddon and his wife, accused of poisoning a woman with arsenic, with Hall 'masterfully grasping the subject of poisons'. And in 1915, in the famous case of the 'Brides in the Bath', his client George Joseph Smith was charged with drowning his new wife, which, it transpired, he had done to several other wives.

Elements of each of the three Marshall Hall cases would soon crop up in Harry's own work; with the Schmulians it was the Seddon trial. Against Marshall Hall's advice, Frederick Seddon had insisted on taking the stand. He came across as cold and insensitive, which destroyed any chances he had with the jury. He was found guilty, and hanged. His wife, who said nothing in court, was set free.

Morris told the Schmulians that he wanted them to stay out of the witness stand, but Lazar Schmulian had other ideas.

When the Schmulians were brought into the courtroom, they sat quietly, their chances of being acquitted most unlikely. But then, each time Harry Morris began questioning a witness, there was a perceptible shift, in the jury and even the judge, and you could see why he liked to call cross-examination 'a good horse to back'.

He used simple English words and terms that everyone could understand – both jury and witnesses – his voice always audible. He went chronologically, so no one lost the thread of the argument. He was brief, never asked more questions than were necessary, and did it calmly, for to cross-examine crossly, he maintained, was 'bad for your client and your blood pressure'. If anyone's interest flagged or someone was restless, he cracked a joke. His mistakes and omissions were always intentional, calculated.

As usual, he started courteously with a witness, but if someone was cocksure, know-it-all, pompous, rude and offensive, or prejudiced and partisan, he quickly went on the attack. He would 'destroy an untruthful witness and make an honest witness wonder whether he had not really been dreaming'.

One hostile witness kept referring to his diary, saying that he carried it about with him wherever he went, making copious notes. But he made the mistake of pronouncing the word 'dairy'. After he had answered one of the defence's questions, Harry quipped, 'I suppose you took the *dairy* with you.' The audible chuckling from the gallery didn't help the prosecution.

Morris's movements across the courtroom, all the while, were nothing less than theatrical, punctuated by the adjusting of his glasses – taking them off, wiping them and then putting them on again – placing his hands behind him as he adjusted his robe in various ways, shuffling papers on the lawyers' table.

And then – no one could ever tell exactly when it happened in Harry Morris's trials, or whether it was the way he framed questions, the favourable replies he got or the wave of sympathy emanating from the jury – the case took a turn in the Schmulians' favour and 'a case that was airtight suddenly was full of holes'. So much so that Lazar Schmulian felt confident enough to want to give his own version of events, even though Morris had warned him against it.

It was the wrong move. Schmulian, just like Frederick Seddon, turned the jury against him. It took only five minutes for them to find him guilty and, despite the defence's arguments for leniency, he was sentenced to 18 months of hard labour. Schmulian's wife, who had obeyed Harry and hadn't taken the witness stand, was acquitted. She jumped up, cried and hugged Harry, almost shocked at the fact that she was free.

Harry was pleased. Outbursts of emotion like this, handshakes and embraces, clapping in the gallery, were the signs that he had done his job well. He had got his client, guilty or not, acquitted. 'There are few thrills like the thrill of a successful cross-examination,' he wrote. 'There are few triumphs like that of an acquittal following what you believe to be an inspiring address to the jury.'

For Harry, this was the perfect day.

CHAPTER 13

Tumpowski's last breath

The weather on the first Thursday in February 1918 was just what the plotters on the miserable farm needed. It was dark and thunderous. Rain and hail pelted down on the metal roof of the ugly farmhouse and against the walls, in a deafening concert.

Assembled with Dorothea Kraft in the cramped kitchen were five men: the drifter Hermanus Swarts, the witch doctor Jim Bird, and three African labourers from the farm. They made their way through the dimly lit house to Louis Tumpowski's bedroom, Bird first, holding a knobkierie, and Swarts behind him with a large pocketknife.

Swarts opened the door to the bedroom but then pushed Bird in front of him. Before Tumpowski had time to defend himself, Bird struck him across the ear and Tumpowski dropped to the floor, dazed. Bird kept hitting him, while Swarts placed a leather thong around his neck. Tumpowski 'kicked and struggled', and then Kraft and the African helpers held him down by the chest and feet. Swarts cut his throat and blood shot out onto the floor around them. Kraft fetched a blanket to soak it up, and then wrapped the material around his neck to stop the flow of blood. As they were picking up Tumpowski's body, Bird panicked and ran out of the house. He went to a nearby reservoir, where he cleaned the blood off his weapon and hands, and then hurried back to his hut.

The other five took Tumpowski's body outside and dug a hole near the ashpit, not far from the kitchen door – the very place where Kraft, in her wild rantings, had threatened to bury him. In their haste, they failed to notice that he was wearing a signet ring, and they didn't hear, through the deafening storm, that someone was knocking at the front door.

The disappearance of Tumpowski went almost unnoticed.

When anyone asked about him, Kraft said he had gone to Johannesburg. Since he used to travel so often, they thought nothing more of it. Soon the questions dried up, and people began to worry once again about the more immediate problems – the state of their crops, the shift in the war since the US had joined the Allies, and then, from April 1918, a new and deadly influenza virus that was spreading across North America and Europe. The old man who had gone missing was forgotten.

Kraft, who had apparently also started sleeping with Swarts around this time, sold Tumpowski's oxen and the leftover corn, and then made arrangements to leave the farm. Before she did, Jim Bird turned up and demanded the £100 he had been promised for killing Tumpowski, but Kraft angrily accused him of being a coward and fleeing the murder scene. If she paid him anything, she said, it would only be after she had sold her fountain of sorrow. She asked a neighbour to keep an eye on the farm, and then she packed her meagre belongings and headed for the City of Gold.

CHAPTER 14

Bertrams

At the same time that Dorothea Kraft was moving, so were Daisy and Alfie Cowle.

Number 22 Tully Street, a house that had seen four deaths in five years, was filled with too many bad memories, and the Cowles were ready for a fresh start. They decided to make a clean break from the area, and looked on the east side of the city, in Bertrams, the same place where Daisy's aunt had the boarding-house where they had first met. A friend of Alfie's, a supervisor at the municipality named Leonard Bradshaw, and his wife, Frances, lived on Terrace Road, and opposite them there was a house for sale.

It was an ideal place for the Cowles. They left behind the mine dumps, the grinding headgear and the incessant thump-thump-thump of the rock-crushing machines. Bertrams had none of that. The lack of gold deposits in the area had led to the establishment of suburbs – Bertrams, Lorentzville, Jeppestown – named after some of the early settlers. A tramline ran close by, but went east–west and not north–south. Instead of the dust and noise of the mines, they now backed on to the green ridge of Yeoville, topped by an onion-shaped water tower.

Like their house on Tully Street, 67 Terrace Road was also simple – one storey, tin roof and red granolithic verandah out front – but the setting made all the difference. The trees were bigger, jacarandas and cypresses mostly, the lanes quieter, and if you strolled over to Saratoga Avenue, there was a view of Eastington House, the grand hillside home of the mayor. Unlike Tully Street, it was a world of possibility.

The neighbourhood was also linked, every few years, to some of the city's most famous criminals. Within a one-mile radius could be found the house where William Foster had grown up, the liquor stores where his gang had murdered two policemen, and the cave where they had hidden out, as well as the house where Andrew Gibson had first met Charles Plunkett in 1903 and, in the small enclave of Belgravia, the nursing home where he had worked, practising his method of 'twilight sleep'.

Since then, Bertrams had been out of the news. But that wouldn't last for long.

A rare, undated photograph of Daisy and Rhodes, probably taken outside 67 Terrace Road.

In Daisy's usual fashion, she made friends quickly, including Frances Bradshaw across the street and Ethel Balderow next door. Nearby was her cousin Mia Melville. Margaret Walker lived a few houses down, and Emily Stricker on Berea Road. And it's easy to imagine that they took an instant liking to Daisy.

She overcame her appearance with a personality that was 'bright and chatty', always sociable, and she clearly liked women. It was clear that she liked to do things just so, held her teacup the English way, didn't tolerate bad language. The poor thing, they knew, had endured the death of four young children, which was perhaps why she doted on her son Rhodes.

Alfie spent time in the garden and began building a big stone wall down one side of the small property – the plan was to make it 50 feet long and 10 feet high. Sometimes he was visited by Leonard Bradshaw, or by another friend named William Johnson. Occasionally, he brought with him a 'work mate' who also worked as a plumber. Robert Sproat was friendly, not unhandsome, younger than Cowle and a bachelor.

A street running through Belgravia, bordering on Bertrams, where Daisy and Andrew Gibson, among others, spent time.

CHAPTER 15

In fearful squalor

When Dorothea Kraft arrived in Johannesburg, she was going by the name of Sweeney. The City of Gold, as 1918 drew to a close, looked hardly better than Treurfontein, at least the part where she settled. Martindale, a tiny enclave just west of the city centre, was so undesirable that it drew only those people who, no matter what race they were, could afford nothing better.

In this 'fearful squalor' there had recently been an outbreak of smallpox, and then, from September 1918, the Spanish flu. The virus that had been killing hundreds of thousands in the northern hemisphere was brought into the country by returning soldiers and spread quickly. Ten thousand miners were unable to report for work, schools and courts were closed and tram and rail services severely affected. Even though Johannesburg was less badly hit than the rest of the country, because of a specially constituted Influenza Epidemic Committee, poor people in areas like Martindale were 'heavy sufferers'. If there was any respite, it was on 11 November, when the Armistice ended the war: '[T]housands of people danced in the streets and celebrated until the early hours of the following morning. Bonfires blazed on mine dumps along the Rand and nearly all the churches held thanksgiving services.'

Even in this turmoil, Kraft was able to move quickly. She was soon married again, to a transport driver named Van der Merwe who was in his early twenties – 14 years her junior – and people were calling her not Dorothea but Dina. She had also found a potential buyer for Treurfontein. But on learning of Louis Tumpowski, and that he had rights over the property, the man wanted to meet him. Kraft insisted that he had left the farm long ago, and then fabricated a story about his owing her money. But the man instructed his lawyer to make every effort to find Tumpowski, which was when things started to go wrong for Kraft.

The lawyer tracked down Hetty Saltman, Tumpowski's sister, and sent her a letter asking if she knew his whereabouts. Unaware that her brother had left the farm, or was missing, she and her husband, whose name was also Louis, started asking questions. At her brother's bank, they learned that his accounts were all in order but hadn't been touched for several months. At the same time, Hetty Saltman had a dream that her brother had been killed.

They went to the police headquarters at Marshall Square, and enough suspicion was aroused for a detective to be dispatched to Treurfontein. Kraft was not there, having already left for the city and taken on a new name, and attempts to get in touch with her and Polly took time.

When she was finally found in Martindale, now calling herself Dina van der Merwe, she didn't answer the door and a constable eventually had to break it down. At first, she denied knowing Tumpowski, but then admitted that she had loaned £100 to 'a Jew' who had left her his oxen and a wagon as security. Later, she confessed to knowing him but repeated the story that she had told others: Tumpowski had left her farm in January 1918 and she had never seen him again.

The detective didn't believe her, but without a body there was nothing more the police could do. As a last resort, a reward of £100 was offered for any information that might lead to the discovery of Tumpowski or his body, and the conviction of any guilty parties. Despite that, no one from Lichtenburg came forward with any information.

The case went cold, and Tumpowski's name was mentioned less and less. The farm remained unsold, while Kraft and her new husband moved further west, to Roodepoort. Almost 14 months would pass before there was a strange turn of events that would reignite people's interest in the old Jew, and it took place in the infirmary of Pretoria Central, where Andrew Gibson, still serving his indeterminate sentence, was helping out the prison doctor.

CHAPTER 16

'If a man's throat was cut'

On 24 April 1919, Andrew Gibson and the prison doctor were doing rounds in Pretoria Central, with the con man now respected enough to be called a 'senior medical orderly'. Assisting them was another prisoner, a murderer who had been reprieved.

Lying in a bed in the infirmary was a burly Afrikaans man in his thirties who had been jailed more than a year earlier for various crimes, including desertion. He overheard Gibson and the doctor talking about the assistant's crime, and asked a question that immediately raised Gibson's curiosity.

'Doctor, supposing a man was killed and was buried, how long afterwards could they tell from what he died?'

Gibson replied that it would all depend on how he was buried and what he had died from.

'Supposing he was put in a hole.'

Again, Gibson said it would depend on the cause of death.

'Suppose his throat was cut.'

Gibson said they might be able to tell years afterwards, so long as the skeleton existed. The patient asked if a blow on the head would leave any mark, and Gibson said it probably would.

'Why are you asking all these questions?' he asked.

The patient said there had been an argument in the cell, and he had contended that one could not tell what a man had died from 16 months after he was buried.

'How long would it take after a man died,' he asked, 'before one could not tell what the cause of death was?'

'It all depends on what he died of,' replied Gibson.

'Suppose he was killed,' the patient carried on.

'Even then it would depend on how he was killed,' Gibson continued. 'If he was poisoned, for example, the decomposition sets in. You would not, in the case of some poisons, be able to tell [who the person was] in quite a short time after death and burial.'

The patient thought a moment before speaking again.

'And if a man's throat was cut? Could they tell then [who he was], after a time?'

'Well, that would depend on how long he had been buried,' Gibson said. 'If he was buried in a coffin, doctors might be able to tell a long time afterwards what the man died of.'

Gibson, forever on the lookout for an opportunity to have his sentence reduced, realised that the burly man might be a murderer whom he could turn in to the prison authorities.

'But why are you asking me all these questions?' Gibson asked. 'Have you been reading detective stories?'

'Oh, it's nothing important,' the patient said, realising he might have said too much already. 'I had an argument with another fellow over it. He said doctors could tell a long time afterwards what a man died of. I said they wouldn't be able to after 16 or 17 months.'

Over the next few weeks, Gibson spent more time with the patient, giving him tobacco and doing him small favours, hoping to gain his confidence. With 'cruel avidity', Gibson set down every word the man said, hoping he could use it to barter for his freedom.

When Gibson finally reported what he had learned to the chief warder, the police followed up by looking for a case that bore some resemblance to what had been described, but they found nothing. They decided that the man's questions must have been prompted by an argument or idle curiosity, and the matter was dropped.

The patient was serving three years for fraud and desertion from the army. His name was Hermanus Swarts, and 14 months earlier he had cut the throat of Louis Tumpowski.

Hetty Saltman and her husband didn't give up as easily as Andrew Gibson did.

They kept calling in at Marshall Square. There had been no progress on the case, and no one had been drawn by the reward of £100. But now, two years after Tumpowski had disappeared, there was a new officer in charge, Colonel Alfred Trigger, and for some reason he took a special interest in the case.

'In my opinion,' Trigger concluded, '[Tumpowski's] option [to purchase the farm] is at the root of the trouble. But we will have to find the body first, if there is one. Until then we can do little.'

He dispatched one of his detectives, Sergeant Frederick Williams Daniell, to Treurfontein. In Lichtenburg, Daniell spoke to a woman who brought up an incident that she had previously thought of little importance. Calling in at the farm one stormy night early in February 1918 – the very night that Tumpowski had been killed – she had heard an unusual noise, something like a spade hitting the earth, maybe someone digging. She knocked at the front door but no one answered, so she left.

Then Daniell learned of Jim Bird. The witch doctor quickly broke down and confessed, but because he had run away before Tumpowski's body was disposed of, he had no idea where it was. Once he had arrested Bird, Daniell took him to the farm with eight convicts to help dig. They began on 9 July and continued for 49 days.

They began at the ashpit outside the kitchen, but found nothing. Then they began draining wells, knocking through walls, pulling up floorboards and uprooting the tall grass around a nearby cemetery.

In frustration, Daniell returned to the ashpit, which, he discovered, was larger than first suspected. And then they found the body. It was badly decomposed, but there were still wisps of grey hair on the skull, and on one finger of the left hand was a signet ring that neighbours identified as the one that Tumpowski used to wear. A local cobbler also recognised the boots on the skeleton as a pair he had mended for the missing trader.

The district surgeon in Lichtenburg did a post-mortem and concluded that the victim had been about 60 and had died from blows to his skull and a laceration of the brain. It was impossible to see if his throat had been cut, but material was found in the neck that might have been used to stop the flow of blood.

Three days later, a series of arrests began. Dorothea Kraft, aka Dina van der Merwe, was the first. Hermanus Swarts was still in Pretoria Central. Finally, the police also arrested the three African helpers, who were identified only by their first names: Hermanus, Andries and Piccanini. Jim Bird turned king's evidence, and would testify against the others, in exchange for a more lenient sentence.

At the preliminary trial, in November 1920, it was agreed to try them all separately – Kraft first, and then the others. If found guilty of murder, she would be the first white woman in the country to be executed.

The circuit court hearing began on Monday 13 June 1921, in Potchefstroom, the closest large town to Treurfontein. The murder of Louis Tumpowski was being called 'one of the most astonishing stories heard in a South African criminal court in recent years'. A 'large proportion of interested women' filled the crowded courtroom.

In his opening address, prosecutor William Hoal told the jury that it was unnecessary for the Crown to prove that Kraft had struck the blows or inflicted the injuries that killed Tumpowski. If it could be shown that she had instigated others to commit the crime, she would be just as guilty of murder as those who actually killed him. The witch doctor Jim Bird turned king's witness to give evidence against the others.

Kraft sat in the dock wearing a shabby sealskin coat, her hands deep in her pockets, her head hanging down and looking either at the ground most of the time or straight ahead of her. Alongside her at all times sat a wardress from the prisons department. At first, Kraft seemed almost disinterested in what was going on. Even the most damaging evidence, and Bird's description of the murder scene, which made people in the gallery gasp, failed to elicit a reaction from her.

Bird re-enacted the murder scene in a 'pantomime', with a court orderly playing Tumpowski, and he showed how the old man had been held down by the feet, chest and head. Swarts first tried to strangle him and then pulled out a knife and slit his throat.

The judge, Daniël de Waal, warned the jury to be cautious when considering anything Bird said, for he had already admitted to being 'a liar, adulterer, witch doctor and murderer'. At one point he himself even said to Bird, 'You are such a liar that one must always question your every statement.'

As if that wasn't enough to weaken the Crown's case, Swarts had suddenly come up with a very credible alibi, which put him hundreds of miles away from the scene of the crime. In October 1917, he had joined the 10th South African Horse but had deserted that same month and been arrested. Discharge papers from the army showed that he had been released from service only on 6 February 1918, four days *after* the murder took place.

In a strange twist, Colonel Alfred Trigger was the person who could prove that this wasn't true. At the time of Swarts's discharge, Trigger had been a major in the Union Defence Force and the Acting Provost Marshal; he was able to get the military records to show what had actually happened. Swarts, after serving 20 days for desertion, had been released in January 1918 to return to his unit. Instead of doing so, he had deserted again, giving him more than enough time to get to Treurfontein by the time of the murder.

Kraft's case took only a few days, and after 100 minutes of deliberation, the jury returned a verdict of guilty. Judge De Waal asked Kraft if she had anything to say before he passed sentence.

'I have not been able to say anything while everyone else has said what they liked about me,' she declared. 'I know before God and man that I am innocent. I did not commit a crime. Only lies have been told about me.'

The judge then read out the sentence.

'You shall be taken from where you now stand to a place of lawful execution and there be hanged by the neck till you are dead. I can hold out no hope to you that the sentence of the court will not be carried out.'

Only once she was outside the Potchefstroom court did Kraft break down and cry.

The trial of Hermanus Swarts, her accomplice, took place two days later, and spectators packed the court 'to the utmost'. The drifter appeared before the same judge and prosecutor, De Waal and Hoal. He was unshaven and looked unkempt, even though dressed in a grey suit and tie, with violets in his buttonhole.

'Sensation was provided' when one of the first witnesses to be called was the 'forger and thief' Andrew Gibson, although the judge warned the court, as he had with Jim Bird, that Gibson had been repeatedly jailed and they should be wary of his testimony. In his calm, gentle voice, Gibson told his version of events in the Pretoria Central infirmary, when Swarts had asked about how long it took for the body of someone with a slit throat to decompose. Gibson's testimony was corroborated by the reprieved murderer who had been on rounds with Gibson and the doctor that day.

The judge asked Gibson if he was giving evidence because he thought it might get him released from jail. Had he not perhaps learned things about Swarts by reading news of the preliminary trial? Gibson denied this, saying there was a severe penalty in prison for reading newspapers. 'I have a belief that I have a duty to perform to all men. I am not so utterly lost, and I have the assurance that if there is any real danger to myself, I shall be removed from Pretoria Prison.'

Another prisoner, a convicted murderer who had been in the bed next to Swarts, said he had overheard the throat-slitting part of the conversation with Gibson.

Swarts was in the witness box for three hours on the last day of his trial, and denied he had ever met Gibson, and had no idea why Gibson would tell that story about him. He denied a lot of the evidence against him, and said he'd been at his father's farm at the time of the murder.

Hoal said he didn't know what Swarts's motive might have been for killing Tumpowski – perhaps he had been hardened by war or was convinced the old man had been terrible to Kraft – but it was not essential to prove motive in a murder trial. It took the jury only 16 minutes to return a verdict of guilty. Asked if he had anything to say, the condemned man continued to claim his innocence.

'My lord,' he said, 'the people who are guilty of this murder are the three [Africans]. I want them sentenced to death. One day you will all know I am innocent. You can do what you like with me, but there will come a time when you will repent of it. I know I am innocent and that my heart is pure.'

In the trial of the three African accomplices – Hermanus, Andries and Piccanini – the charge against one of them was withdrawn for lack of evidence, while the judge ruled that the other two men had clearly been influenced by Swarts. They were both acquitted.

*

Two months later, on 16 August 1921, Dorothea Kraft became the first woman to be led from the women's section of Pretoria Central down the corridor between the men's cells to the gallows, which lay at the end of one wing. Andrew Gibson was there to see her pass, as well as, the following day, Hermanus Swarts, the man he had implicated. Kraft's body was given to Johannesburg's medical school to be dissected.

A full decade would pass before another white woman was sent to the gallows – and it would also be over the death of a man. Several men.

CHAPTER 17

Sarah's destruction

Trials, especially the criminal ones, were entertainment. Each one drew more attention than the one before, and Dorothea Kraft's had been no exception, where 'all day long people waited at the entrance in the hope of being permitted to fill any seats that might fall vacant'.

Spectators carefully guarded their places, never moved till the hearing was adjourned, bent forward to get a closer look at the accused, and to hear declarations of murder and infidelity, gasp at the revelations, laugh at the lawyers' asides and be reprimanded by the judge, waiting for his gavel to slam down or his threat to clear the court if they should misbehave again.

The best trials, Harry Morris believed, were pure theatre, better than any play or movie because they were real. 'The tears shed by [the accused man's] wife come from her heart. Her shriek is the shriek of anguish and despair. The night watchman departs feeling that he has earned a good night's rest.'

At the Criminal Sessions, there was often one spectator who returned frequently, although she sat not in the crush of the public gallery but in the jury box, on her own, a place usually reserved strictly for men. She had dark hair and wore suits that, although well tailored, accentuated her plainness, while she rarely removed her round, thick-lensed tortoiseshell glasses, except perhaps for photographs to be used in the newspapers or on the jackets of her books. Behind the glasses were the eyes of someone who struggled to sleep at night and had a very unyielding view of things – marriage, politics, the rights of women and her own talent.

Sarah Gertrude Millin had just turned 32, although she looked older. Her first novel, *The Dark River*, had come out a year earlier, in 1920, published by Thomas Seltzer, who had also just brought out an author who couldn't have been more different from the prim and proper Sarah Gertrude – namely, DH Lawrence, and the book was *Women in Love*. The overseas reviews for *Dark River* were almost unanimously good, and one of the longest came from the pen of a young New Zealand writer, Katherine Mansfield.

At her home in the leafy suburb of Parktown, where she was finishing her third novel, Millin had taken to reading the law books in her husband Philip's library. He was a barrister, and sometimes she came to court to listen to him argue cases, or to listen to his colleagues, such as Harry Morris or her friend Jenny Greenberg's husband, Leopold, who was on track to become the youngest judge on the Supreme Court. Because of her association with the legal profession, she was permitted to sit in the jury box – that is, if it wasn't occupied by nine men.

The court hearings, like major events in the news, gave Millin ideas for her writing. In one of Philip Millin's most recent cases, a salacious murder, he had defended a small, slight man named George Leech, 'a phthisis victim' who worked as a banksman monitoring a shaft entrance at the Modderfontein B mine, near Benoni.

On Christmas Eve, some of the family had been staying over at Leech's mother's house near Modder B. After a lot of drinking and 'jollification', it came out that Leech's brother and Leech's wife were having an affair. Usually the brothers got on well, but suddenly George Leech became a 'madman'.

'I have caught him red-handed,' he called out. 'She has encouraged him. She is the cause of it all.' At one point his brother, who was much bigger than him, caught Leech by the throat and said, 'I'll murder you, you —.'

After the two fought that night, with the smaller Leech getting the worst of it, the two men and Leech's wife had all gone their separate ways. But early the next morning they all arrived at their sister's house at about the same time. Leech came in with a gun threatening to kill both his brother and his wife, although he later said he never meant to actually pull the trigger. A fight broke out, during which Leech was hit across the eye. He drew the gun, which went off and killed his brother.

The case, like that of Dorothea Kraft, had an element that particularly fascinated Sarah Gertrude Millin. At the centre of each murder was a woman and wanton sex, all leading to some kind of destruction. The widow Kraft had slept with Tumpowski, Jim Bird and Hermanus Swarts to get what she wanted, resulting in murder. The banksman's wife – who, during the trial, was suddenly the picture of dutiful mourning, sitting in the front bench of the crowded gallery alongside her mother- and sisters-in-law, 'dressed in black and heavily veiled' – had enticed her brother-in-law and had an affair with him, leading to his violent death.

Millin was the exact opposite of these two women. She believed, almost sanctimoniously, in the bonds of marriage, duty and faithfulness, even though she knew it was the unexciting choice. She believed most spouses 'cling together through age and ugliness and failure and disillusionments till death does them part. They slip their wedding rings over their bodies as if they were life vests, and leave the rest to heaven.'

Yet she was fascinated by the other side – sex and destruction, 'how easily murderers mated' – and it would only be a matter of time before Millin wrote a novel about a woman who fit that mould.

*

In Bertrams, that woman was about to set a plan in motion that would eventually bring her and Millin face to face – in a courtroom of the Criminal Sessions.

PART 3

THE QUIET EXECUTION OF HER PLAN

1922–1926

CHAPTER 18

Blood on the streets

Colonel Alfred Trigger almost didn't notice the new year had started. His work at Marshall Square intensified almost from the moment that he returned from testifying at the trial of Dorothea Kraft; besides the normal caseload of murders and shootings and rapes in the University of Crime, there were rumblings of a new strike.

Johannesburg was not unused to labour action, by both white and black men – the miners, workers on the railways and trams, engineers, garment workers, teachers, sanitation workers and night-soil gatherers – but this one was very different and it kept gathering momentum. It was going to be the biggest ever.

As 1921 was ending, the price of gold fell by ten shillings, and there was talk of the mines laying off 10 000 white miners, almost half their total, and 'many thousands' of Africans. Even though the white miners had a backlog of grievances – accidental deaths on shift, long hours, the scourge of phthisis – they kept coming back to the fear of Africans taking over their jobs. On 23 December, Sir Lionel Phillips added fuel to the fire when he was quoted in *The Star* saying that the colour bar, a law protecting white jobs, was 'both immoral and irrational'.

The African miners, who outnumbered whites by almost nine to one, were on their own path of dissent, not only over wages but also over identity documents, single-men taxes and rules segregating blacks on trains and trams. It was all a ticking time bomb, and by Christmas 1921 some of the families who could afford it were talking of sending the women and children out of town.

The new year began with a coal miners' strike in Witbank, the main grievance being, once again, the use of lower-paid African labour. Railwaymen who transported the coal went on strike in support. Then, in their own strike action, it was men in the city's building trades, followed by tailors, who drew so many people that they crowded out a meeting at the Trades Hall in Rissik Street.

Not a day seemed to go by without the newspapers carrying stories of strike action, strike ballots, strike committee meetings and strike notices, either in the city or close by. The African Mirror newsreel put together a segment that bestowed yet another nickname on Johannesburg, 'City of Unrest'.

On the night of 9 January 1922, after the last shifts were over, the white miners on the gold mines downed tools, leaving the African miners without bosses and bringing operations to a standstill. Deliberations between government, the mine owners and labour dragged on until the end of the month. The success of the workers' revolution in Russia gave renewed strength to the strike action, and the protest quickly became known as the 'Red Revolt'.

'There was a calculated design to repeat on the Rand the unnatural outbreak of crime in Russia that horrified the entire world,' wrote one journalist. A Reuters correspondent said there was proof that the strikers were financed by Moscow.

Trigger's men went undercover to infiltrate the ranks of the miners to try and pre-empt acts of sabotage. He quickly grew convinced there was a conspiracy among white strikers to kill Africans. Rumours spread of a 'native uprising' and a 'black peril', of African miners rising to kill white people, especially poor ones. The newly founded Communist Party of South Africa, after initially being conciliatory towards Africans, eventually took as their motto 'Workers of the world, unite and fight for a white South Africa!'

By the middle of February, Trigger regarded the strike not as peaceful, as was being claimed by the unions, but as 'definitely revolutionary'. His men started deciphering a secret code used by the strikers, in which the word 'vegetables' meant explosives, and 'cabbage and potatoes' dynamite and detonators. By late that month, the first violent clash between police and strikers had taken place, leaving three dead.

Intimidation was rife, with firebombs used on the homes of 'scabs' who kept working on the surface to protect the mine properties from attack, and people were stopped in the street as they headed to work and told that if they went any further they would be shot. Trade was paralysed, and rows of sandbags were placed around Marshall Square and other police stations and public buildings.

The strikers quickly formed themselves into a daunting force. Many of the men had fought in the First World War and, with that experience, instilled the same type of military discipline in their ranks. Those who didn't have rifles armed themselves with sticks and knives, and made firebombs out of condensed milk cans filled with paraffin. Gunfire could be heard in the city centre and at railway stations, while random explosions went off daily. Electricity pylons were dynamited and railway tracks bombed. At the height of the strike, in March, clashes between whites and Africans broke out in various places, with each side blaming the other for provocation.

By early March 1922, after more than six weeks of unrest, a state of anarchy reigned. On the first Monday of the month, a strike was finally announced, and within hours mobs were roaming the streets, thousands massing in Rissik Street, outside the Trades Hall and the post office. Passengers were pulled from their cars, which were set on fire. Railway property and police posts came under renewed attack, and a long-distance passenger train coming into the city was derailed. Sympathetic workers at power plants walked off the job, cutting off the electricity supply to most of the city. Streetlights stopped burning, and coal reserves were nearly exhausted. Towns along the Rand fell to the strikers. In the miners' stronghold of Fordsburg, just two miles west of Market Square, trenches were dug around the main square, and armed men patrolled the streets in neighbouring Brixton, Vrededorp and Mayfair.

'One no longer spoke of strikers, but of Reds, or Rebels, or Revolutionaries,' wrote Sarah Gertrude Millin, who had a bird's-eye view from her home in Parktown of the battle playing out on the Brixton ridge, next to Fordsburg. 'They had the appurtenances of warfare.

Thousands of strikers massed outside the Rissik Street post office (at left) on 7 March 1922.

They had also – and did not take their advantage – Johannesburg itself. Excepting the railway stations, the law-courts, and a few central streets, they had complete control of the city.'

By the end of the week, Black Friday, Prime Minister Jan Smuts had declared martial law. The government had amassed a force of army, police and reservists numbering 20 000 men. The main thoroughfares of Oxford Road and Jan Smuts Avenue were crowded with military trucks and staff cars, and reconnaissance aircraft 'wobbled like kites in the sky'.

On 10 March, as the battle was at its height, Alwyn Petrus Marais, a shopkeeper in Fordsburg and a father of five, was accused of being a police informant, taken to Mayfair and put against a wall behind Union Furnishers and shot, allegedly by one of the strike leaders, Taffy Long. Long was well known to Colonel Trigger as the head of the 'Irish Brigade', also known as 'the bombing section'. From their windows in the city centre, people watched a tank rolling down an otherwise empty Commissioner Street. By Sunday 12 March, the tide had begun to turn as the government arrested more than 2 000 strikers. The next day the towns of Brakpan and Benoni were relieved. On 15 March, five biplanes began to drop bombs on Brixton and Fordsburg from early in the morning.

Two strike leaders, Percy Fisher and Henry Spendiff, committed suicide rather than be caught. The three most important leaders, Taffy Long, Herbert Hull and David Lewis, were arrested and sent to Pretoria Central to await trial.

No one doubted how it would all turn out – the trio were doomed.

At a Special Criminal Court in October, Long was sentenced to death for shooting the shopkeeper Marais, and Hull and Lewis received the same sentence for killing a military intelligence officer, Lieutenant Rupert Taylor.

One month later, the three were taken from their cells in the Pretoria jail, and walked down the same hall that Dorothea Kraft had walked before them. On the way they sang the Irish revolutionary song 'The Red Flag' – *Then raise the scarlet standard high / Within its shade we'll live or die / Tho cowards flinch and traitors sneer / We'll keep the Red Flag flying here* – and in what was described as 'the biggest funeral ever witnessed', 10 000 people marched to the English section of Brixton Cemetery to see them buried.

Barely two months later, at a plot not far from where they were buried, a much smaller funeral would take place. Another member of the Cowle family would soon be dead.

CHAPTER 19

The green bottle of salts

The Red Revolt had come dangerously close to the Cowles. On 11 March, at the height of the fighting, the sound of gunfire and bombs ricocheted off the Yeoville ridge behind the small house on Terrace Road. Barely one mile away, at Ellis Park, 600 strikers had attacked an army depot, leaving eight soldiers and an unknown number of strikers dead.

But across the city, the sandbags were soon removed from the fronts of public buildings, shops took off the barricades to stop looting, railway tracks were repaired, trams started running again and residents fell back into their love-hate relationship with the city.

Alfie Cowle returned to work at the municipality as soon as he could, and Daisy to cleaning the house and cooking meals for the family. Rhodes had just turned 11, and would soon be starting senior school. He wasn't living up to the promise of his name, and was less interested in his studies than in playing football. Maybe if he went to a better school, a private boarding school like Michaelhouse or Hilton College, he would do better. But that was an expense the Cowles couldn't afford.

In early September, six months after the Red Revolt, Daisy left home one weekday morning after Alfie had gone to work and Rhodes was at school. She caught a bus east to the mining town of Germiston, even though there was a branch of the African Life Assurance Society in the city centre, closer to Terrace Road.

She took out a 15-year endowment policy of £100 on the life of Rhodes that would mature in 1933, when he would get £500. The only beneficiary of the policy was Rhodes, unless he died before it matured.

As the Christmas holiday season approached, some of the neighbours noticed it for the first time – Alfie Cowle was not looking well. Ethel Balderow, who lived at number 69 Terrace Road, later recalled him as being unhealthy and deadly pale. Even though Alfie kept working in the garden, building the wall along the side of the property, things went downhill quickly at the end of 1922.

He had been having restless nights, or at least that's what Daisy told people, although that didn't keep him away from work the next day. She said she watched him in bed at night as he twitched terribly and breathed laboriously. She wrote to her sister in Kimberley, Fanny McLachlan, that Alfie was 'not doing well'.

On Christmas Day 1922, he felt especially poorly, but the Cowles went ahead with their plans anyway. They took the tram from Bertrams to Market Square and then south to City Deep, near their old house on Tully Street, to the home of Selina Poplawski, who had known Daisy from before her marriage.

Alfie only pecked at his food, and on the way home he nearly fainted while they were getting off the tram. By the time they reached Terrace Road, he had severe pains in his neck and his back. He thought it was from some medication a friend had given him a few days earlier.

Daisy told Ethel Balderow that Alfie was suffering from some 'bad spells', and warned her that if things got particularly bad, she might come calling for help during the night.

On the morning of 11 January 1923, heavy summer rain came down in sheets against the ridge behind Terrace Road, and for the first time in six months Alfie didn't go to work. Each time the lightning flashed across the dark sky, it lit up the onion-domed water tower on the ridge like an alien creature out of HG Wells's *The War of the Worlds*.

Ethel Balderow heard Rhodes calling over the wall for her to come quickly, and she arrived to find Alfie Cowle in bed, covered in perspiration, his face pressed into a pillow. Other people were there already, as

Daisy had raised the alarm in several quarters, telling neighbours, 'Come at once, my husband is dying!'

Each person in the room, when they were asked about it later on, had noticed something different. Leonard Bradshaw, who lived across the road and worked with Alfie, arrived first and found him collapsed in a chair, still fully dressed except for a jacket. Asked what was the matter with him, Alfie put his hands to his stomach and said, 'God have mercy on my soul.'

Bradshaw's wife, Frances, arrived next, and saw Cowle foaming at the mouth. After her came Margaret Walker, also from Terrace Road, who saw Alfie with his knees pulled up to his chest and groaning. Balderow, for her part, was struck by the fact that he was clenching his fists, and he seemed to be turning purple in the face. Last to arrive were Emily Stricker, from one road away, and a Miss Williams.

After a fit of rigidness, lasting only a few moments, Alfie's body suddenly went limp and then relaxed. Then, quite unexpectedly, it happened again. Daisy tried to give him something to drink, but he refused to take it. If anyone touched him, it increased his pain, and he screamed. He was fearful of anyone even approaching him.

Daisy told some of the visitors that Alfie had been lacing up his boots earlier when she came into the room and saw him fling himself backwards uncontrollably. He had taken some Epsom salts that morning, and she had brought him some tea afterwards because he was thirsty. He believed the Epsom salts had made him feel ill. After that, his condition quickly worsened.

The doctor for the city's Municipal Provident and Pension Fund, Albert Ernest Hardman Pakes, who had attended to Alfie and Daisy in the past, had been called at eight that morning but was held up. Rhodes then went with a friend to fetch a Dr Leighton, who lived nearby. After Leighton arrived, Alfie had three more convulsions. When Leighton asked Daisy if her husband had experienced convulsions before, she said he hadn't but that they were not unlike the convulsions she had witnessed in her four children who had died.

Leighton suspected it was some kind of hysterical seizure, but it also reminded him of the shell shock he had seen in returning soldiers. He gave Daisy a prescription for a bromide mixture, which Rhodes took to a nearby pharmacy on Derby Road, while Leighton left to fetch something at home. While he was gone, the municipal doctor, Pakes, arrived.

Pakes found Alfie on the bed in a back room, conscious and lucid, able to speak but afraid to and not letting anyone touch him. A few moments later, he had a violent fit, went stiff, flung his head back and arched his back. After about five seconds he collapsed, limp and exhausted.

Alfie started telling Pakes that he had taken Epsom salts from a green glass bottle that morning when he was struck by another convulsion, accompanied by a similar arching of the back and throwing back of his head. Pakes thought it might be opisthotonos, a paroxysm of the muscles that causes horrific and unbearably painful backward arching of the head, neck and spine. If he was right, that hardly narrowed down the causes, which could have been cerebral palsy, a traumatic brain injury, hydrocephalus (water pressure on the brain), tetanus, lithium intoxication or, in the final instance, poisoning from strychnine.

Pakes rushed home to fetch some medical instruments. It wasn't far, but while he was gone Alfred Cowle had another convulsion and died. Someone in the room held a mirror to his mouth to make sure he was not breathing. It was 9.30 am.

When Pakes returned and examined the body, he looked for lockjaw and cerebral haemorrhage, both of them signs of tetanus, but found neither. He asked Daisy about the green bottle of Epsom salts, which she brought to him. Before leaving, he told her that he would not be able to issue a death certificate until she had given the bottle to the police for analysis.

When James Basnett, from the Jeppe police station, arrived at Terrace Road to take Cowle's body away, no green glass bottle of Epsom salts was mentioned. The body was taken to the government mortuary, where it was received by Dr Basil William Henry Fergus, the acting district surgeon.

Without any suggestion that there was something unusual about the death, Fergus began a post-mortem. He found the meninges were adhering to the brain, below which there had been some haemorrhaging, while the membrane of the stomach was slightly congested. His conclusion was that Cowle had died of a cerebral haemorrhage or

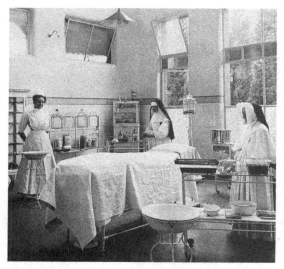

Among Daisy's duties at the Children's Memorial
Hospital was assisting in the operating theatre.

chronic nephritis, or Bright's disease – an inflammation of the kidneys that, as was commonly stated in newspapers, could be fatal.

Dr Pakes, upon hearing the results of the post-mortem, assumed that Daisy had followed his instructions to hand in the Epsom salts for analysis, and he accepted Fergus's findings.

On 12 January 1923, William Alfred Cowle was buried in Brixton Cemetery, not far from the leaders of the Red Revolt. Under the terms of his will, Daisy inherited the house at 67 Terrace Road – the house on Tully Street already belonged to her – and she was paid out £1 245, as well as a further £553 from the Municipal Provident and Pension Fund.

At the age of 37, she was suddenly a woman of means, with only one surviving family member, the 12-year-old Rhodes.

Daisy lost no time arranging her new life.

She enrolled Rhodes at the best and most expensive school in the country. Hilton College, hundreds of miles away in Pietermaritzburg, was fashioned after traditional English public schools such as Rugby and Eton. The boys educated there came from the wealthiest, most privileged families on the subcontinent, and afterwards were almost guaranteed a place in the highest circles of business or politics, sometimes even in England.

She rented out 67 Terrace Road, left her neighbours behind – all the people who had watched Alfie Cowle die – and returned to Tully Street. It is unclear if she moved back into number 22, although it is unlikely. At some stage she became a lodger with one of her old neighbours, Mary Jane Meaker.

She started working again on Hospital Hill, at the new Children's Memorial Hospital, which had just opened. Her duties were more considerable this time, not just the work of a portress but a 'theatre portress', assisting in the operating theatre, which included the cleaning of surgical instruments. Without anyone to care for at home, she would be able to keep the job longer this time, a full three years. By then, there would also be a new man in her life.

CHAPTER 20

At sea

R obert Sproat walked up the gangplank of the mail ship in Cape Town harbour, followed by his brother William, younger by seven years. They were two bachelors at the start of a very long holiday, so it was hard not to be excited and a bit giddy at the thought of this temporary freedom from the daily challenges of the City of Gold.

The elder Sproat was not the kind of man to boast, but he could have. Travelling abroad was not common, least of all for someone like him, a municipal employee who earned seven pounds a week. But he was careful with his money, regularly contributed to his savings account, and had municipal stocks and shares in a gold mine. He was probably also helping pay his brother's passage, for William also worked for the municipality, but in Pretoria.

For a trip like this, they needed a financial cushion, for it meant taking at least three months off work. The trip alone took two months: after taking the overnight Union Limited to Cape Town and spending a few nights at a hotel before embarkation – the wealthier people stayed at the Mount Nelson Hotel – the sea voyage took almost one month in each direction. That left them with a month in England.

In Cornwall, they would visit their mother, Jane, whom both brothers had last seen more than a decade earlier. Robert had left for South Africa in 1903, at the age of 23, and had gone back to visit her in

1912. When he returned, William joined him. A third brother stayed behind in England.

Even though there were at least six British shipping lines, as well as Dutch and German, offering regular sailings – some even to the US – for most people the undisputed choice was Union-Castle. By now the ships commandeered by the Royal Navy during the war and painted in camouflage colours had been returned to the company's distinctive livery: a lavender-shaded hull and elliptical red funnels tapered with a thick black stripe. The dozens of Union-Castle vessels took their names from castles across Great Britain, such as Kinfauns, Edinburgh and Pendennis.

Since the brothers had last travelled, in 1912, things on board had changed substantially, especially since the end of the war. Now there was the *Arundel Castle*, launched in 1921 – 'a floating palace', 'nothing like her had been seen in South African waters' – which offered private bathrooms in first class, ventilation in the inner cabins and an 'ample supply' of single-berth cabins, as well as a swimming pool, a gymnasium and an elevator. First and second class had been merged, with a greater choice of berths and prices, making accommodation 'more democratic'.

For women, liberties had also increased since the end of the war, so that they no longer had to be in their cabins by 10.30 pm, and by the mid-1920s they 'could no longer be barred from [the] one-time sanctuary of the males' – the smoking room. One of those women on the voyage back from England drew the attention of William Sproat. She was on her way to Australia, but she and William got on so well that they decided to start a correspondence.

Perhaps it was the fact that William was keen on someone that made Robert think about his own future. He was 43, not bad-looking although on the short side, only five foot six inches tall, and had a good complexion and was healthy. He had never been married, although he had enough money to support a wife and family. His mind wandered to a woman he had met a few times in Johannesburg whose husband had recently died. He decided that when he got back to Johannesburg, he would call on the widow – Daisy Cowle.

Later that year, after the Sproat brothers had returned, Sarah Gertrude Millin and her husband boarded the smaller, older *Windsor Castle*. It

Sarah Gertrude Millin.

was a momentous trip for the childless couple, their first trip abroad.

Unlike the Sproat brothers, the Millins were well known enough that their journey was mentioned in the weekly announcements in the newspapers of people who would be travelling to or from England. Those mentions were usually reserved for people like Solly Joel, Sir Henry Rider Haggard and General Jan Smuts, but Sarah Gertrude was important enough to mention too.

International acclaim had been slowly building up for the author. Her fourth novel had just been published – she had based *The Jordans* on the Red Revolt, part of which she had seen unfold from her own house – and she had just completed another novel, titled *God's Stepchildren*.

The trip was meant to be Sarah's introduction to literary England, although things went badly from the start. She and Philip found London, the city they had heard so much about, cold. Katherine Mansfield, the one person she had wanted to meet, had tragically died of tuberculosis in January. Mansfield's husband, the author John

Middleton Murry, became their friend, though she thought him 'kind and simple', and organised a meeting with DH Lawrence. While Lawrence and Millin shared an American publisher – who had brought out *Dark River* and *Women in Love* at the same time – they couldn't have been more different, the one writing about sex in a way that regularly saw his work banned and the other a prude in the extreme.

Their first meeting, at Lawrence's home in Hampstead, did not go well, and she found him and his friends 'very kind, but very childish and queer'. The following night, Millin invited the author and his wife, Frieda, 'a stout and untidy' woman, for dinner at their hotel. Everything seemed to go wrong – the room was cold and the conversation did not come easily.

'She felt grateful to Lawrence for the effort he had made to enliven the party, but could not get over her distaste for him and his obsession with sex. The writer in her greatly admired his work, but the puritan rebelled against much of it.'

The Millins returned to Johannesburg shortly afterwards, in January 1924.

CHAPTER 21

1924

In the new life Daisy had made for herself, she was suddenly single again. But that wasn't to last for long. Two men started to play a bigger role in her life, the one by intention and the other because she had no choice – Robert Sproat and Rhodes Cecil.

Now in her second year of working at the Children's Memorial Hospital, Daisy turned 38 in 1924. Her annual salary had increased, from £90 to just over £100, and so had her duties at the hospital. She showed in visitors, took children to the operating theatre and cleaned surgical instruments. One of the biggest changes was that, for the first time in her work, she came into contact with doctors.

Despite her penetrating blue eyes, which were too icy for some, she had 'a cheery and forceful personality'. Her harelip was barely noticeable, betrayed only by a slight lisp, and her prematurely grey hair, usually unruly, was kept in place by a nurse's cap. Sometimes Rhodes used to visit her at the hospital. The receiving nurse, Adelaide Warby, found him a 'cheerful nice boy'.

Rhodes had returned to Johannesburg at the end of 1923, unhappy about being far away at Hilton. It was also clear by now that he wasn't a good student, and wasn't going to live up to his name. Daisy gave in, as she usually did, and let him stay at home. She enrolled him in Marist Brothers, the private Catholic school in Koch Street, where the lawyer

Harry Morris and the murderer William Foster had been educated.

Robert Sproat started calling on Daisy, whom he had met when he and Billy Johnson had visited Alfie Cowle in Terrace Road. He told her about his trip to England with his brother, and Daisy started thinking about the day she could afford a similar journey. She told Rhodes that one day they would also travel abroad.

In any woman's eyes, especially at Daisy's age, Sproat was a good catch – stable, unmarried, with no dependants to look after, a Freemason. People who had known Cowle also noticed something uncanny: he bore a striking resemblance to Daisy's dead husband. He was short and stocky but proportionately built and in much better health. In addition, he was a plumber.

CHAPTER 22

Gibson at large

G iven all the media exposure Andrew Gibson had received over the past 12 years, it was astonishing that no one took notice of the fact that the 'notorious criminal' with countless names and bogus professions was released in the middle of 1924. After serving six years of his 'indeterminate sentence' at Pretoria Central, he was allowed to leave.

He had spent his time behind bars productively, as usual, and 'it was said he used his medical knowledge considerably', making friends with the people whom he could make use of later on. One of them was a warder by the name of Wallis. And then, much as he always did, Gibson disappeared.

One year later, in August 1925, he was arrested in Bournemouth, on the coast of Dorset in England, on a charge of forgery. When he appeared in court in Winchester, in December, it turned out that he had left South Africa with the help of Wallis, who had retired before Gibson got out and had moved to Bournemouth.

Gibson convinced Wallis to send him money for the passage to England, where he immediately got to work. In the seaside town, he set himself up in his two favourite positions, as a medical practitioner and as the 'deputy agent-general for emigration to the South Australian Government'.

Once again, it was the forgery and not the medicine that got him into trouble. The court in Winchester soon found him guilty of forging the signature of the Australian government's treasurer on one of its bonds, and he was sentenced to seven years of penal servitude.

CHAPTER 23

The Sproat marriage

Robert Sproat proposed to Daisy in the first month of 1926, and the wedding was set for July.

Shortly before that, she stopped working at the Children's Memorial Hospital, where she had been for almost three years. At the same time, Rhodes left Marist Brothers, at the suggestion of one of the teachers, who told Daisy something she had probably known for some time already – he was 'not a very clever boy'.

Rhodes, who had grown into a handsome if sullen young man, had no drive. He was passionate about football and, more recently, motorbikes. About to turn 16, he had already started pestering Daisy to buy him one so he could join the other young men racing out along the Heidelberg Road to Zuikerbosch River Drift or in Stanhope Dip.

After leaving Marist Brothers, he was sent to a technical school to learn a trade, to become a plumber like his father, Alfie Cowle, and his new stepfather, Robert Sproat. He and Sproat seemed to get on well, and the three of them moved back to 67 Terrace Road. Daisy settled back in at the old address, with many of the same neighbours, and once again became a housewife, maintaining the home and cooking meals on her own.

It's unclear when Daisy learned how much 'Bob', as she called him, was actually worth, which, with his savings and stocks and shares, was at least £4 000 (about £290 000 today). He was also a member of the Municipal Provident and Pension Fund, the same society that had paid her more than £500 on the death of Alfie Cowle.

Daisy also discovered that Sproat had already made out a will, in which he was leaving everything to his mother in England. She needed to change that.

CHAPTER 24

'To get the feel of death'

Across the city, into the small hours of the night, the sense of excitement was palpable. Choirs, marching bands, Boy Scouts and African dancers from the mines practised their movements; floats and Chinese dragons as long as a city block were pieced together; horse races and boxing matches were organised. Even a song was being specially composed by John Connell, a Scotsman who conducted the Johannesburg Philharmonic and Choral Society. The City of Gold, the University of Crime, the Wonder of the World, was turning 40.

The inescapable sense of anticipation grew even more intense in July 1926, when the schools emptied for the winter holidays. Children played in the streets, rode their bicycles, went to the Palladium and the Empire cinemas to see Buster Keaton in *The General* or Rudolph Valentino in *The Son of the Sheikh*. Rhodes Cowle joined his friends racing their motorbikes out at Stanhope Dip.

Another motorbike enthusiast, the 23-year-old David Russell, lived not far from the Sproats, just over the Yeoville ridge. Russell's father, William, an engineer, had married a widow named Elisa Bosman in the middle of 1925. David lived with them and one of his two grown-up sisters, Peggy, at 19 Isipingo Road, Bellevue. Through the marriage there were also two stepbrothers, Pierre, a customs official, and Herman Charles. There were immediately tensions between them all:

'They were on a different level to us,' Peggy later said. Her father was 'in good circumstances financially and well connected', whereas Elisa was not.

'The emotional climate between Elisa and William Russell was scarcely an improvement on that of her first marriage, and the second generation found themselves flung together in uncomfortable proximity rife with resentments.'

Herman, at the age of 21, had just started teaching at a school in the Marico district, not far from where Dorothea Kraft had lived. When the schools closed for the mid-year holidays, he came to visit. With him he brought, among other things, a .303 rifle that he used for hunting guinea fowl. It was shortly before his departure back to school, and the weapon was 'cleaned, oiled and loaded, ready to use'. At his stepfather's house, Bosman shared a room with David Russell, while Pierre slept on a couch in the living room.

Shortly after midnight on Sunday 17 July 1926, Russell returned home. Not long afterwards, his father, who was already in bed after going to the bioscope, heard a scuffle break out in his son's room, followed by a gunshot. By the time he got there, he saw that David had fallen off the bed onto the floor, a bullet having pierced his lungs and heart. Herman Bosman was holding the rifle. The Bosman brothers rushed to the kitchen, where another shot went off, and William Russell came in to find Herman and Pierre struggling with the weapon.

'Shoot me, Mr Russell,' Herman implored. 'I want to be dead too.'

Peggy had rushed into the bedroom, and the neighbours heard wild screaming and someone shouting, 'Oh God! Oh God!'

The police arrived and Herman was arrested and charged with Russell's murder, and sent to jail to await trial. Rumours quickly began to circulate about what might have happened that night. Was it really an accident? Had there been a fight between Pierre and David? Was it over a girl they both liked? Had David's sister Peggy called Herman Bosman a murderer? Did Herman just make up a story about an intruder in the room? The questions multiplied and the two families were torn apart.

Some of Bosman's friends, such as Benny Sachs and Eddie Roux, who had known him since high school, suspected that Bosman might have shot Russell to understand the act of killing, 'just to see what it was like, to get the feel of death, as it were'. It wasn't the first time that such strange and macabre things had been said about Bosman.

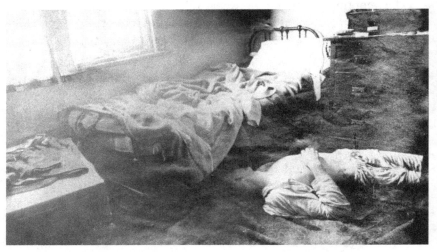

David Russell died instantly after being shot by Herman Bosman.

When Bosman's mother moved him and his brother to Johannesburg as teenagers, they lived in a modest area just east of the city centre, on the southern side of Bertrams. His father, who had got a job as a waste-picker, wasn't around much before he died in a mining accident.

What Bosman lacked in material things, he made up for in intelligence, and people noticed. At Jeppe High School, 'an establishment that might have been transplanted whole – structure, staff and tradition – from England of the public schools', he struck his friends as a smart, voracious reader making his way through the works of Shakespeare, Melville and George Bernard Shaw, and penning his own stories with titles like 'The Mystery of the ex-MP' and 'The Mystery of Lenin Trotsky'.

But there was another side to him. Bosman was a bit of 'a mad genius', 'an outsider', 'a misfit, and essentially an unhappy youth', wrote Sachs, '[but] his humour, like his literary fits, was inimitable ... It is the same nihilistic mental thrust that he shared with the Marx Brothers.' Bosman 'came into life with a very high voltage ... Call it a touch of madness, if you like.'

His behaviour regularly inflamed a situation. Outside the Town Hall he heckled speakers, and in bioscopes he did things to antagonise the other patrons, talking loudly or upsetting live performances. Once, on unmasking a 'bogus mass-hypnotism act', he was chased into the street by the performers. At the Johannesburg, Normal College, while studying to become a teacher, he could have entered his own poem for a competition but instead used one written by Percy Bysshe Shelley – and won third place.

On 26 July, ten days after the shooting, as the city suffered its coldest winter ever, causing water pipes to freeze, the preliminary hearing took place. Under the headline 'Bellevue Shooting Tragedy', quite uncharacteristically for the *Rand Daily Mail*, which rarely used photographs, especially of trials, was a large picture of Herman Bosman entering the court.

'University students, women dressed in black and a mixed throng of interested spectators crowded' into the gallery, watching Herman, who cut a handsome figure on the stand. He was tall, with a strong nose and dark eyes, wore a dark suit and held his wide-brimmed fedora in front of him. There was, however, a certain nonchalance about his bearing, and he even winked at his friend. '[L]eaning carelessly on the side of the dock, and occasionally smiling to himself, Bosman appeared entirely unconcerned.' He nodded at his friends and waved to the students in the gallery.

Bosman's brother, Pierre – who said Herman and David Russell rarely spoke to each other – caused a stir in court when he said that Herman liked to write murder stories for the newspapers – 'Tragedy, told in the Russian style', was how one person described them. Pierre told the court that after the shooting, he took the rifle from Herman and asked him why he had fired. He replied, 'To see if the gun was loaded.' Bosman had then tried to cut his throat with a breadknife.

After entering a plea of not guilty, he was taken back to the jail at Marshall Square in a Black Maria.

In the third week of September 1926, while Bosman sat awaiting trial, more than 100 000 people flocked to the city centre to celebrate Johannesburg's 40th birthday. It was the greatest pageant the City of

Throngs of people in Pritchard Street, outside the Supreme Court, for a boxing match to celebrate Johannesburg's 40th anniversary.

Gold had ever seen, and the news teams from African Mirror and Pathé News perched their cameras on rooftops and balconies at various points along the route of the parade.

People hung from windows and balconies, and for more than two miles it was impossible to move. Overhead a squadron of low-flying planes made loops to thrill the crowd and dropped thousands of leaflets. Triumphal arches lined the way for the long, elaborate procession that made its way through the crowds, with dozens of floats of early pioneers, miners of different ethnicities, long Chinese dragons, ox-wagons, papier-mâché giants, African dancers from the mines, and even a group of *abakwetha*, young Xhosa men painted in white and dressed in blankets traditionally worn during a circumcision ceremony. As the day wore on and more people arrived, space was made between the throngs for a donkey race and a boxing match.

*

Herman Bosman's choice, like anyone facing a criminal trial, was whether to have a jury or not. He chose to be tried only by a judge.

In the second week of November, his trial began at the Criminal Sessions. Judge Gey van Pittius, using his prerogative, chose to be assisted by two magistrates, whose job was to give him advice, and even to ask questions of witnesses if they wished. Bosman was represented by the barrister JG van Soelen, while the prosecutor was a smart young Rhodes scholar who had studied at Oxford, Cyril Jarvis.

Van Soelen maintained that the shooting of David Russell had been an accident. Bosman told the court that he had arrived home after midnight. He was leaving for his school job in the Marico district early the next morning, and was putting together his things, including his rifle – he didn't know whether or not it was loaded. On hearing a noise down the hall, he went to Russell's bedroom. He tried to turn on the light, but it didn't work, and then suddenly the gun went off. Pierre told him he had shot David.

Recalling the night, Pierre said that he had gone to fetch a book in David's room, which was dark, and a scuffle had broken out between them. In the darkness, a shot rang out. Bosman's mother recounted how her distraught son had tried to cut his own throat with a breadknife before Pierre took it away from him.

Few people appeared to accept Bosman's version of events. Jarvis even brought in an astronomer from the Johannesburg Observatory to attest that the position of the moon that night would have meant there was more than enough light for Bosman to have seen his victim. To make matters worse, the prosecutor presented the court with several short stories about murder that Bosman had written, including one in which the body was dismembered.

On 15 November, after a five-day trial, Judge Van Pittius found Bosman guilty of murder and sentenced him to death by hanging. Describing the case as 'a sad and pathetic one' that had torn the Russell family apart, he clearly sympathised with Bosman but couldn't see his way to reducing the charge to manslaughter. He strongly recommended that the sentence be commuted, but that would be up to the minister of justice.

'Many women produced handkerchiefs and the general atmosphere was pregnant with tragedy,' the *Rand Daily Mail* wrote. 'The ticking of the clock could be heard as Bosman bent forward towards the bench.'

Unlike others found guilty of murder who pleaded their innocence until the end – including Dorothea Kraft and Hermanus Swarts – Bosman didn't. His words after sentencing were poignant and strangely poetic but, given his taste for the macabre, maybe just something to play to the gallery.

'My lord,' he said, 'in this strange world of laughter and sighs I am in a strange predicament strengthened by the knowledge that there are those who I love and who love me and who still have faith in me.

'In that tragic minute, the happenings of which are still not clear to me, I was driven by some wild and chaotic impulse in which there was no suggestion of malice or premeditation.

'Throughout these dark months, my lord, I would like to say that I have been upheld by the sublimity of a mother's love.'

Almost from the moment they left the court, Bosman's friends and family began to seek a reprieve. His uncle was a lawyer. Benny Sachs and another friend, Fred Zwarenstein, gathered signatures from their fellow students for a petition urging leniency. Letters were written to the minister of justice.

Bosman, in the meantime, was sent to Pretoria Central to await execution. Locked in a dark cell, he began to reflect on the terrible isolation of a man sentenced to death: 'In prison, the murderer, unlike the blue-coat, does not wear a distinctive garb. He is not dressed by the authorities in a way to single him out from the others – bank robbers, forgers, illicit gold buyers, rapists and the rest. There is no need for men to put any distinguishing marks on the murderer's clothes. Cain's mark is there for all to read. Murder is a doomed sign to wear on your brow.

'Even the imagination was caged. Self-expression was strangled. Sleep was mostly a nightmare in which I was a hunted animal fighting for freedom. Occasionally a poor brute raised his voice in a desire to break the stillness of the night.'

Two days later, Bosman's sentence was commuted to ten years in jail with hard labour. As he began to serve out the rest of his sentence, two passions had taken hold – writing and the issue of capital punishment. They would eventually bring him to the doorstep of Daisy Sproat, although both of them would have different names by then.

CHAPTER 25

A secret request

For their first summer holiday as a married couple, at the end of 1926, Daisy and Robert Sproat travelled to Durban, where she had studied at the Berea Nursing Home.

The reason for the trip was to accompany Robert's brother William, who was going to fetch his future wife. Amy, the same woman he had met when the brothers returned from England in 1923, was arriving from Australia. The day after she disembarked, Robert and Daisy attended their small wedding.

Afterwards, the two couples joined other holidaymakers crowding the promenade that ran along Ocean Beach, past the best hotels, such as the new Hotel Edward, where people sat on the verandahs drinking tea and milkshakes. Whether or not Daisy overheard her husband, he told William that he had drawn up a will leaving his entire estate to their mother, and that it could be found in his Masonic bag.

Daisy, even though she barely knew her sister-in-law, brought up the subject of Robert's will, in which he was leaving everything to his mother in England instead of to her. She raised the subject several times over the next few days. When Robert went off to fetch the car, she asked Amy about it.

'I wish you would speak to him about it,' she told her.

Amy never did, and when the two couples returned home, they

rarely saw each other, even though they only lived 40 miles apart. The next time William saw Robert, his brother would be much changed.

CHAPTER 26

Lock, stock and barrel

It was unusually cool and damp for a spring weekend in early October on Terrace Road.

The Walkers, Margaret and Archibald, who lived near number 67, were walking to church when they passed Robert Sproat working in the garden. He had been to the dentist the previous day, where he'd had two teeth extracted, but that didn't stop him from pottering around. Before they walked on, he told them that he and Daisy hoped to go out in the afternoon.

That evening, Sproat was on the verandah reading the *Sunday Times* and drinking a beer. He went inside and asked Daisy for some mouthwash because of a bitter taste in his mouth, when he suddenly collapsed on the bed and had a convulsion.

Daisy ran across the road and told Frances Bradshaw that Bob was ill. Not having a phone, she asked if Frances could call Samuel Mallenick, a doctor who lived nearby on Derby Road. Albert Pakes, the municipal doctor who had attended to Alfred Cowle, did not make calls on Sundays.

Leonard Bradshaw, on his way home from work, immediately went to the Sproat house. Before long, several other neighbours were also there, Daisy having raised the alarm in various places – the Walkers, Mia Melville and Emily Stricker, who had been at the house when

Cowle died. Stricker heard that Robert Sproat had been well until he drank a glass of beer. The glass now stood next to the kitchen sink, empty.

Sproat sat propped up in bed, groaning and holding two straps either side of him that were tied to the bedframe. At the foot of the bed was placed a portmanteau and an ironing board to push against if he had another convulsion. Without warning, his head thrust back and his legs shot out straight, his feet pressing against the portmanteau. If anyone tried to touch him, he cried out in agony, 'Please don't, I can't stand it!'

When Dr Mallenick arrived, he found Sproat with a haunted, frightened look on his face. Lying semi-prone on the bed and perspiring profusely, he tried to support himself with his right hand, although he was unable to stay like that for long. He had severe pains in the left side of his abdomen, below the chest. Mallenick was unable to touch him to get a better prognosis, and when Frances Bradshaw tried to slake his thirst she had to moisten cotton wool and put it as close to his lips as she could get.

Not sure what he was dealing with, Mallenick at first suspected a ruptured gastric ulcer. But Sproat's pulse seemed to suggest otherwise. When he learned the patient was a plumber, he considered lead poisoning, although Sproat replied, 'To hang with lead poison. I haven't worked with lead for years.'

While Mallenick was busy examining Sproat, another attack came on. Sproat's body went into a spasm during which he clenched his hands with the thumbs turned in towards his palms. Mallenick thought it might be arteriosclerosis, hardening of the arteries associated with high blood pressure, but this too seemed unlikely. Finally, he considered the possibility of a cerebral haemorrhage.

Mallenick, an Englishman who had been practising medicine for 12 years, had never seen similar symptoms before. He knew that a man suffering from arteriosclerosis could appear quite healthy while in fact he wasn't. The look on Sproat's face, meanwhile, seemed to suggest lead poisoning, which was more common and in some cases could lie dormant for years, with the person showing no symptoms. Strychnine poisoning would also have produced similar symptoms, except that Sproat would have had a better colour in the face.

Mallenick gave Sproat a sedative and called again about half an hour later, and gave him another, although neither seemed to have any effect. Sproat did not sleep but kept on stretching, pressing his feet against the portmanteau, and then going limp. He asked Daisy to send Rhodes to fetch William Johnson, his close friend who was staying at a hotel in town. Johnson arrived and stayed until the early hours of the morning, sitting at Sproat's bedside. The other neighbours had left by then.

'If anything happens to me,' Sproat told Johnson, 'tell Will [his brother] that Daisy must get everything, lock, stock and barrel.'

When William Sproat arrived from Pretoria at four in the morning, he found his brother clutching at the straps tying him to the bed. 'If this pain keeps coming back, I'll be gone,' he muttered. 'No man can stand it.'

Robert Sproat again raised the issue of his estate.

'Will, I've just been talking to Johnson and I've told him that if I didn't see you again, Daisy has got to get everything I've got, lock, stock and barrel. And I know, Will, that you'll see she gets it.'

As the morning light cast a red glow on the ridge behind Terrace Road, Daisy invited William to the kitchen to have some tea. Once he was seated, she told him that he needed to get Robert to make a new will, as the existing one left everything to their mother.

'I can't speak to him now,' William replied, surprised by her conversation. 'Wait till he gets better.'

But Daisy was insistent.

'You will speak to him before you go back to Pretoria,' she said.

After William had his tea, he raised the subject with Robert.

'My will?' he replied. 'I can't make a will now. I'm too ill.'

William said nothing more about it until breakfast, when he told Daisy not to worry and that Robert would get down to writing a will in due course. On hearing that, she left the room and returned with some blank forms.

'I've got a will here,' she said, presenting the papers to William. It was a standard testament. 'He only needs to sign it.'

Once again surprised, William told his brother about the form, whereupon Robert Sproat answered, 'That's all right. Whatever you do is all right.'

'What am I to do?' William asked. 'Is Daisy to get the lot?'

Robert Sproat said, yes, Daisy should get it all.

Later that Monday morning, Emily Stricker looked in at 67 Terrace Road to see how Sproat was doing. Daisy assured her he was much better, then asked Stricker to witness Sproat's will. Stricker suggested waiting until he had recovered, but Daisy wanted the will to be signed at once. When they went into the bedroom, Robert Sproat was prepared to sign the document but first had to be coaxed to release the straps he was holding. While Stricker and William Sproat held him up, he scrawled his name on the document.

In the kitchen, Stricker signed the will as a witness. After she left, Daisy called in as a second witness a man named Edward Osborne, who was doing some building work at the Bradshaws. Osborne knew neither Robert Sproat nor Stricker.

When Pakes, the municipal doctor, arrived at 9 am, he prescribed some powders and booked Sproat off work until 18 October, the following Tuesday. After several days, when he was well enough to move about, Sproat called on Pakes, who prescribed a tonic for him. Sproat took three bottles. He seemed much better, although Daisy wrote to one of her sisters, 'Bob is not at all well.'

By 5 November 1927, a Saturday, Robert Sproat was well enough to spend the whole day at work. The next afternoon, he asked Daisy for a beer, which she brought him. Later he said he did not feel well and took a dose of the tonic Dr Pakes had given him.

Daisy was in the kitchen when Rhodes called to her in a panic, and she ran to find Sproat sprawled on the settee having a convulsion. She sent Rhodes to call Dr Mallenick and went next door to telephone Dr Pakes.

All the neighbours were once again called, and some of them carried Sproat into the bedroom, while Daisy rushed in and out with ice packs. By the time Mallenick arrived, Sproat's face looked ghastly and he had lost consciousness, and Mallenick thought the patient was suffering from a cerebral haemorrhage. Anxious to get backup, he went next door to telephone for another doctor, although he warned everyone that Sproat was in a bad way and he believed the end would come in 'only a question of minutes'. By the time he returned, Sproat was dead.

William Sproat was shocked when he got the news about his

brother, for he had only just got a letter saying he had fully recovered and was back at work. When he and Amy arrived at Terrace Road, Daisy did not appear to him greatly upset.

In the bedroom he was horrified by what he saw. His brother's face was so contorted that he barely recognised him, and Robert had clearly died in terrible agony. When William heard that Robert had taken ill after consuming a glass of beer, he told Daisy that there would have to be a post-mortem.

'Oh, not that,' she replied quickly. 'It will cost seven pounds.'

Taken aback by her answer, he reminded her that without a post-mortem she wouldn't be able to get a death certificate. Daisy insisted that she would get one from Mallenick, and William asked her to show it to him once it was issued. The following morning, she came to breakfast with the certificate signed by Mallenick. The doctor was sure that death had come from some combination of arteriosclerosis, chronic lead poisoning and a cerebral haemorrhage, but gave the last-mentioned as the cause of death.

The rest of the day, a Monday, Daisy spent away from Terrace Road. She ordered mourning clothes, made the funeral arrangements and, at the suggestion of William, cabled the news to Jane Sproat, their mother, in England.

She also sent a telegram to her sister Fanny McLachlan, inviting her to the funeral. McLachlan caught the first train to Johannesburg, and was met by Daisy, who told her about her husband's last hours, and that 'poor Bob' had died of a blood clot on the brain.

That evening, friends called on Daisy to pay their respects. As they sat in the living room, her eye happened to fall on the advertisements page of *The Star*. 'Oh, what a pity,' she said, pointing to the property section. 'Here is a person wanting a house with only one room more than ours or I might have let it from the first of the month.'

Turning to William, she asked his advice about dealing with the estate and begged him to come with her to consult a lawyer the following day.

'Wouldn't it be better to wait till Bob is buried?' he asked, still trying to get over her comment about the rentals in the newspaper. But when Daisy persisted, William reluctantly agreed. Before they went to bed, she produced Sproat's earlier will, the one in favour of Jane, and said it was no longer valid. In front of them all she tore it up.

Robert Sproat was buried in the English section of Brixton Cemetery, right next to Alfie Cowle.

The best place to find a lawyer was Sauer's Chambers, close to the Town Hall, where most of the legal fraternity had moved a few years earlier.

When Daisy walked through its corridors the following day, William Sproat following her, she carefully studied the names on each door. One in particular she saw and then quickly moved on.

'We won't go to this man,' she said. 'He had the last job.' She meant he had handled the estate of Alfred Cowle.

After settling on a solicitor named TE Kinna, they went in and he began questioning her about the estate. Had Robert Sproat left any money, anything of value? Without hesitating, Daisy said that he hadn't – no money, no property, no furniture. William's face must have given away his disbelief, for he knew his brother had left shares and savings worth several thousand pounds.

When Kinna asked if William could vouch for the truth of Daisy's statement, he said he couldn't. He then told Daisy that she would not be able to touch any of Sproat's money until the estate had been wound up in the proper way. On the drive home, William asked why she had misled the lawyer, but she made little of it.

'It doesn't do to tell solicitors everything at once.'

A notice settling the estate of Robert Sproat was posted in the newspapers in the middle of January 1928.

In Cornwall, southwest England, Jane Sproat received a letter a few weeks later that took her completely by surprise. It was from Daisy, the daughter-in-law she had never met, who was begging for financial help. Robert's long illness and the funeral expenses – 'in these days every cup of tea counts', Daisy wrote, referring to entertaining guests after his death – had swallowed up all her savings. Sproat, she added, had also promised Rhodes a trip to Europe, but that wish could not be fulfilled because she didn't have enough money.

Jane Sproat, who thought that Daisy had been well taken care of, forwarded the letter to William Sproat, who knew that she had been. Daisy, as Sproat's sole heir, had received £4 174 plus another £566 from the Municipal Provident and Pension Fund. From the two wills, Cowle's and Sproat's, she had benefited by more than £6 500 in cash and had become the owner of several properties around the city.

When Daisy next called on William and Amy Sproat, William brought up the letter.

'Have you been writing to my mother telling her Bob left you badly off?' he asked.

After first evading the question, Daisy said that Jane must have misunderstood her or misread the letter. William produced the letter, and it was clear what Daisy had meant.

'If you do happen to go to England,' he warned her, 'please do not visit my mother. She is old and would not like to be bothered by you.'

'You can't stop me writing,' Daisy replied.

When Daisy left that day, William and Amy accompanied her to the Pretoria railway station.

'I never want to see you again,' William told her. 'And I don't want you to put your foot in my house again.'

'Why?' she asked.

'Because I have lost all faith in you.'

William Sproat's words left Daisy looking, as he later put it, 'thunderstruck'.

After the train left Pretoria with Daisy on it, he turned to his wife.

'There is more behind this than I know.'

PART 4

BETWEEN DEATHS

1928–1931

CHAPTER 27

Girl on the lake

On the afternoon of Thursday 24 November 1927, barely two weeks after Robert Sproat had been buried in Brixton Cemetery, a young student arrived home from lectures at the University of the Witwatersrand in time for tea with her mother. Irene Kanthack then changed to go out for a walk with their dog, a black cairn terrier. It was about 4.30 pm when she left their house at 35 Oxford Road, Saxonwold.

Her normal walking route went along a path towards the War Memorial in Hermann Eckstein Park, 80 hectares of gardens and avenues and a small zoo – 'a Bois de Boulogne on a smaller scale', Sir Lionel Phillips liked to joke – with one artery ending at a memorial fashioned after the Arc de Triomphe and topped, in April 1915, with a bronze statue of an angel of peace by the Paris-based artist Naoum Aronson. When the sky darkened, at twilight or when black rainclouds gathered, the memorial loomed ominously.

Irene went along the edge of the zoo, down the wide avenues near the lake, and on to the golf course at Parkview. At 6.15 pm, on her way home, she was seen at the back of the zoo by Constable Johannes Bezuidenhout, who was on duty. The sun was falling fast behind dark clouds that threatened to break into a summer storm at any moment.

'You'd better hurry up, miss,' he called out, 'or you'll get wet.'

Swinging her walking stick and followed by her dog, she seemed to be engaged in her thoughts, heading towards Upper Park Drive, alongside the zoo, and then onto a path leading home.

The constable forgot the incident until a bit later, and paid little attention to a tourer-model car, its side screens up, that sped past about five minutes later. After half an hour the storm broke, and Bezuidenhout sought shelter with a colleague, a Constable Van Tonder.

When Francis Edgar Kanthack returned home at 5.30 pm, he was told that his daughter was out walking. He was a high-ranking engineer and former director of irrigation for the Union government who had since opened his own practice. The Kanthacks' son had died tragically in a mountaineering accident on the Isle of Skye, but they still had two daughters. Irene was 18 and popular.

An hour or so later, their terrier ran into the house whimpering. Fearing his daughter had been in an accident, Kanthack phoned the police station to report her disappearance and arranged for an SOS to be broadcast from the Johannesburg radio station.

Listening in on the report was Colonel Alfred Trigger, who had helped to find Dorothea Kraft and still had a short time to serve as head of the criminal division at Marshall Square. He telephoned instructions to several police stations to organise a search party of African constables for an early hour in the morning. Francis Kanthack went with them as they combed the area where Irene was most likely to have walked. Not many people lived there: the houses were far off and there was lots of undergrowth.

More detectives and policemen arrived at the scene, and then a contingent of Boy Scouts, until there were hundreds of people around the lake, while several light planes flew low overhead to help in the search. The lake was dragged. The Friday passed with no trace of the young student being found, although it turned out later that many of the people, as well as police dogs, had passed within feet of her body.

On Saturday morning, a Boy Scout by the name of David Rubin was searching south of the War Memorial. Kicking at a heap of leaves and tree branches, he exposed her body. After he whistled for help, one of the first people to reach him was Constable Bezuidenhout, who had seen Irene last. He recognised the girl immediately.

The police pieced together the events of Kanthack's last moments. It appeared that she had been intercepted at a spot opposite the gate leading into the zoo grounds, a lonely area with trees bordering the roadway on either side. She had run, and a chase had ensued. With a storm about to break, screams and cries for help would have been drowned out by the rain and thunder. A portion of her walking stick was found 300 yards from the nearest house, and it was assumed that she had tried to run there but had been cut off. She hit the attacker with the stick and ran towards Lower Park Drive, which was fenced, perhaps hoping to lose him.

When she struck him a second time with the remaining portion of the stick, it fell or was grabbed from her, and it lay about 100 yards from the first attack. She ran away, retracing her steps to the pathway leading to the War Memorial. At that moment she was felled by a blow to the head and carried into the forest. As she warded off more blows, several of her fingers were cut, and the attacker finally stabbed her below the collarbone. Now dying or dead, she was dragged to a tree stump and covered with branches and leaves.

Robbery didn't seem to be the motive, for her wristwatch was still on her arm. The glass had been smashed, causing the hands to stop at

Among the Boy Scouts who helped scour the park and Zoo Lake for Kanthack was David Rubin (with his hand to his cheek), who found her body.

about 6.35 pm. That had been Thursday and it was now Saturday morning, which meant the killer had been at large for 36 hours. He could be long gone by now.

Not since the Foster Gang had terrorised the city almost 15 years earlier, the newspapers said, had people been more agitated and frightened. There was the usual scramble for guns and ammunition, and mothers forbade their daughters to go for walks unescorted.

Thousands of people gathered for the funeral of the slain woman, and many of the most famous people in the city's political and financial life were in attendance or sent wreaths, including General Smuts, the Dalrymples, Justice Solomon and the Ernest Oppenheimers. The procession to the cemetery was 100 cars long, and in places along the route people stood ten deep.

The police's failure to solve the case led to their being attacked at public meetings and in hundreds of letters to the press. Two Africans were arrested, and then released. More possible evidence turned up: a wooden peg, of the type used by builders, thought to have been the one used to strike Irene; three small handkerchiefs, one stained with blood. A few days later, near the scene, a sheathed knife was found wedged between two saplings six feet above the ground. The police were convinced it was not the weapon used in the killing.

'Find the tourer car,' people said, offering one of countless theories, 'and you'll find the murderer.'

If Constable Bezuidenhout was correct, however, the car had passed him at about 6.20 pm and Irene Kanthack, who was going in the opposite direction, had probably died 15 minutes later. Might the driver have parked and gone back on foot? Perhaps the driver could provide information. A reward of £500 was offered for information leading to an arrest.

Some thought the killer was an African, a 'sex-crazed native on the prowl for an unescorted European woman', but such a man was unlikely to have owned a car. A few days later, an African man working in Hyde Park boasted to his friends that he had murdered 'a person', not saying if it was a man or a woman. He had hidden the body so well, he said, that not even planes or dogs could find it. Some of those he told the story to, although they thought it was another African he had killed, reported him to the police.

Trigger was at first doubtful. It was quite likely that the man had killed someone, but not Kanthack. However, the police chief was then paid a confidential visit by a woman who reminded him that, six months earlier, she had reported the same kind of attack in the same area. The description she gave was similar to that the police had of the African, except for a scar.

She accompanied the police on routine checks for a while, but they found nothing. Even when it was suggested that the police were on a false trail and should rather concentrate on a search for a white murderer, Trigger remained convinced it was an African. He relied on the evidence of the way the body was hidden, placed parallel to a tree and covered with branches and debris like something that had been hunted and killed – plus the evidence from the Hyde Park witnesses and the woman.

But the suspect was released for lack of evidence.

Colonel Trigger was approached by at least two spiritualists, who believed they could add important information. One of them was taken to the park, but his conclusions were completely different to all the evidence the police already had. A second medium, Harry Blank, brought his mother and a friend to a séance, where he said he would call up the spirit of Irene Kanthack.

When asked what happened on the day of the murder, Blank's mother replied, apparently in the voice of Kanthack, 'I was walking past the zoo with my dog when two men stopped me. One said something I didn't like. So I slapped his face.' One of them grabbed her.

'I was frightened and I must have fainted because I don't remember anything more until I woke up where I am now. I was quite surprised to find my throat cut.'

On being asked what the men were wearing, she mentioned several pieces of clothing, including the kind of overall worn by a house painter. It was a very particular piece of information that would come up again later on. In the meantime, though, the case of Irene Kanthack went cold.

CHAPTER 28

Motorbike crazy

The day finally arrived – and Daisy couldn't have been more excited. She was taking her first trip overseas, the kind that Robert Sproat had told her about, with all the luxuries, on the *Arundel Castle*. It was the holiday that she had kept promising Rhodes for years. Only a few months earlier she had told Jane Sproat that she had no money, but

The Union-Castle Line's Arundel Castle, *a 'floating palace', took Daisy and Rhodes from Cape Town to Southampton.*

now she was heading off for several months of travelling by ship and rail, eating and sleeping at hotels, buying things along the way.

Daisy and Rhodes, who were probably lodging with Mary Jane Meaker in Tully Street by now, took the Union Limited to Cape Town and then sailed for Southampton. From there they travelled north, through Wales and Scotland, and then sailed to Ireland before making a final stop in Holland. While they were there, Rhodes celebrated his 17th birthday, and Daisy bought him his first motorcycle, which they brought back home with them. On their return, and after Rhodes encouraged her, Daisy also bought a Chevrolet sedan.

Daisy was giving in to Rhodes more and more, and cars and motorbikes were the only things that he was interested in. He also started having mood swings, seemed to be getting angrier the older he got, especially if he didn't get his way. When things became especially heated, he would threaten to hurt himself, and the threats got worse each time – to jump out of a moving car or put his head through a window.

Sometimes he even turned on Daisy, and she wondered if one day he might even hit her.

CHAPTER 29

Death at Central

By late 1928, after more than two years in Pretoria Central, Herman Bosman was working as an assistant in the 'deficient, inefficiently run' library, although he was hoping to get a transfer to the team breaking stones in the quarry, so he could get out in the sunlight more often.

The cross-shaped prison had two levels. As a first offender, Bosman was kept in the east section on the upper floor, 'two long corridors with iron cells on each side'. Measuring five by seven feet and eight feet high, each cell had only a concrete table, two felt mats on the floor, two grey blankets 'of unpleasant aroma', and nothing that could be used for hanging, in case an inmate thought of harming himself. The ceiling, of wire netting, let in light, and there was a small peephole in the outer wall. The prison uniform was a grey flannel shirt, moleskin knee breeches, a corduroy coat, a red cotton handkerchief, a broad-brimmed felt hat and *veldskoene*, and prisoners regularly had their hair cropped short.

A wake-up bell clanged at 5.30 am, and by 6 the prisoners had to be ready, their blankets rolled up. Breakfast was mealie meal, a piece of bread and tea. At 7, the prisoners fell in for work, at the bookbinders, the printers, the bootmakers, the carpenters, the stonemasons, the plumbers. Dinner was at 5 pm, and at 8 pm a bell rang again, lights were turned out and no talking was allowed till the morning.

Women were kept in a different part of the building.

Bosman's temperament and friendliness made him very popular, 'and I do not think he has an enemy in the Prison'. With him among the first offenders was a man who had been there for 15 years already, William Foster's younger brother, 'the last member of the Foster Gang … a very quiet refined man'. Jimmy Foster kept with him a photograph of the young daughter his brother had released from the cave before he killed himself and his wife.

Bosman had been writing a lot, mostly his reflections on prison and execution. In his first ten days, while he was still facing a sentence of death, he shared one of the 'condemned cells' with a man named Stoffels, on an upper floor close to the room where they were to be hanged.

The gallows took up the width of one wing, with enough room for six executions at a time, even though it was mostly just one person. A lever at the side of the room controlled the trap door, and from a beam were suspended six ropes, with six corresponding pairs of footmarks below them. The length of rope was altered according to the height and weight of each condemned man – or, in the rare case, woman. Before being escorted to the gallows, he or she was offered a tot of brandy. Present at the execution were the hangman, his assistant, the super-intendent of the jail and the chief warder, the doctor and the hospital warder, as well as a minister if requested.

Bosman wrote: 'There was the tramping of feet on the iron stairs and the sound of doors being locked and unlocked, and no sound of voices. No orders had to be given. Each man knew what was expected of him, even Stoffels, who played his part tolerably well, considering the fact that he was not rehearsed in it and was getting no pay for it.

'I heard what sounded like a quick scuffle, then many footfalls. And then a muffled noise in which I recognized Stoffels' voice, but with difficulty, for only part of that noise seemed to come out of his throat. The rest of it seemed to have come out of his belly.

'More heavy footfalls and doors creaking on hinges. And still no rapped-out words of command. Then a mighty slam that shook the whole building, rattling the pannikin on the floor of the cell in which I was. And it was all over. I looked at the warder guarding me on the other side of the grille. His face was a greenish-white.'

A fellow inmate – an older, well read and cultured man who had worked in radio – read some of Bosman's writing and was greatly impressed. When he was released in the early part of 1929, the man took some of Bosman's poems with him, hoping to get them published.

One of them was called 'The Citadel', a nickname for Pretoria Central: *'But Oh! dear God the tears that flow / The anguished grief, the bitter woe / In that stone-builded citadel / The hearts that break ... my heart as well.'* It soon found its way into an incendiary new publication called *The Sjambok*.

The poem was included in a series of sensational articles that *The Sjambok* ran in the middle of 1929 about prison conditions, the daily life of prisoners and the horrors of capital punishment. Nothing like it had ever been printed in the country before.

The editor, Stephen Black, was well known in literary and journalism circles, an iconoclast, a bohemian and extremely talented, although he had also faced bankruptcy after investing in a mine and had been accused of plagiarism. Tall, with a boyish face, even at the age of 50, he had a sharp tongue and a fondness for fedoras. A boxer turned journalist, novelist and then movie scenario writer, Black's real passion was for writing plays, which he directed, staged and acted in.

The weekly newspaper was only several months old when the prison series appeared, but already it was living up to its promise to expose injustice and the seamy side of South African life – on the cover was a big clenched fist holding the eponymous whip – with incendiary stories about corrupt city officials, insurance frauds, bogus medical practices, underhanded lawyers and shady burial concerns.

Black's hand was visible on every page of *The Sjambok*, and, like *Truth*, the exposé-filled London magazine that he fashioned it on, he often used the word 'ramp', meaning a swindle: 'Years ago Johannesburg was reputed to possess "more brains to the square yard than any other place in the world"; but today it might almost claim to produce more ramps per annum than any other city of half a million inhabitants.'

All kinds of people turned up at the magazine's office, offering incredible stories that usually weren't true. One man claimed that – for £250 – he would tell the 'true story' of what had really happened to the Foster Gang, who hadn't died in the cave in a murder-suicide but were still alive and well.

Soon afterwards, another man – not yet 25, of dark complexion, a house painter – offered to tell his version of what Black called 'the greatest South African mystery of recent years' – the unsolved murder of Irene Kanthack.

CHAPTER 30

Wives and lovers

In the earliest days of the city, it was said that if you stood on the Parktown ridge on a clear day, you could see the Magaliesberg, 40 miles away.

It was here – with the ugly mines out of sight – that the millionaires who owned them had chosen to build their mansions and villas, in all manner of styles, with names borrowed from around the world. It was their Knightsbridge or Mayfair.

Among the mansions, Northwards was particularly special. Designed by Sir Herbert Baker – Cecil Rhodes's favourite architect and the man who had helped create the government buildings of New Delhi – it stood vast and solitary, visible from afar, like the masthead on a ship. Among the women who walked through its grand entrance in the middle of 1929 was the guest of honour, Sarah Gertrude Millin, who was greeted by its owner, Lady Frederika Albu, the Berlin-born wife of the Randlord Sir George Albu.

One can only imagine how self-satisfied Millin must have been at moments like this. She had come a long way. Born in Lithuania, she had been raised in a modest home on the banks of the Vaal River, in 'an isolated spot, with no neighbours but the [diamond] diggers'. Yet here she was, just turned forty, not only mixing with the richest women in Johannesburg but about to address them all. (Within a few months,

Millin and her husband would also have their own villa on the Parktown ridge, barely a stone's throw away, on Pallinghurst Road.) Yes, how far she had come!

Millin and Lady Albu walked into the main hall, the double-volume ceiling making the room seem more immense, a huge oriel window offering a view across Parkview and Saxonwold and up the hill to the War Memorial. Beneath the carpet of treetops, near Zoo Lake, was also where Irene Kanthack's body had been found, a fact that was hard to forget that day, seeing that her mother was one of the guests at Northwards.

The ladies, most of them members of the Women's Reform Club, were already taking their seats in the main hall and the minstrel gallery. Millin's reputation had grown substantially since the appearance of her first novel – publishing articles in newspapers and almost a book a year, befriending politicians and writers abroad – and she was about to do a tour of the US. Dressed conservatively as usual, she made her way to the front of the audience and adjusted her glasses as she took out her speech.

She didn't need the paper, for it was a topic she had written about so often that she knew it off by heart. The title of the speech was 'Spouses and Lovers', but it was really a continuation of her fascination with sex and destruction. Storytellers and artists had, since time immemorial, made much of husbands and wives who lusted after someone else, and yet the 'splendid marvel' of marriage was hardly mentioned.

'How dull has been made the tale of spouses,' she said, 'and how fascinating the tale of lovers!' She believed that those days were numbered, and that artists would soon be painting and writing about the goodness of marriage.

The women applauded, and the sound echoed up into the minstrel gallery and further into the vast Northwards.

CHAPTER 31

The killing of Irene

Dark-haired, blue-eyed and very pretty, Gertie Angelo was the kind of woman on the opposite side of the fence to Sarah Gertrude Millin, one who was involved in a very promiscuous – and extremely destructive – relationship.

For two years she had been having a 'passionate sex affair' with a young man named Billy. But then, in early 1929, he left her, which is when she started telling people a secret that she had kept almost for as long as she had known him. Billy might have had something to do with the murder of Irene Kanthack.

On the night in 1927 that Kanthack had been killed, she told them, Billy had climbed through her bedroom window, dishevelled and in 'a rather funny condition'. He was wearing grey flannel trousers, 'a halfway leather coat' and a leather skull cap, and there were stains on his clothes and his face was dirty.

'Then I noticed blood on his shirt. It was a white one with blue dots. He didn't wear a tie. The shirt had no collar. I opened his jacket though he kept it buttoned up, as I wanted to see why the blood was on his shirt. I found bloodstains all over his chest. He seemed a bit excited and I asked him what was the matter. He then said he had "committed a crime with a girl".'

She said that over a period of six months, Billy had also sent her letters – either through the mail or which she picked up at a tobacconist – confessing to the murder. She had kept all of them.

One of the people Angelo told her story to informed the police at Marshall Square, who decided to send out an undercover cop named Theo Zeederberg to investigate. Not wanting to scare her, he said nothing about being a policeman but instead made up a story about wanting to write a true crime book, and asked if he could borrow the letters to get some inspiration. When she agreed, he took them back to Marshall Square to be examined, although they were found to be 'crudely phrased, badly spelled and punctuated, with sordid and suggestive passages, [and] bore the mark of unreality'.

One of the letters, dated 18 December 1927 and addressing her as 'Dear Hatty', began, 'Just a few lines to let you know that I am in a serious fix, but I hope you will try to work me out if anything has to happen on what I told you must take my part and say you got nothing to do in anything like that although you know I told you I done it and there I trust you to keep up on my part nothing has never been said about Kroonstad murder so that proves you never said anyting yet.

'So I hope nothing will be said about Saxonworld and I hope there will nothing been said if there is I kow exactl where it comes from I admit I was over natured powdered and I fanced the girl so I thought I'll take a chance and so I done it but the girl said she was going to report me to the police so I thought I do a good thing of it so I killed her find out that was the only thing to do so I hope you wont say anytng about on what I been telling you for please don't say a word read the letter and tear it up I turst you by telling you all my career so please don't speak to any of the detectives about it. Yours Fore Ever, BILLY'

The police didn't believe Angelo but suspected that, 'prompted by jealousy', she had written the letters herself or got other people to do it for her. Zeederberg finally disclosed his true identity to her, and she was brought to Marshall Square. She stuck to her version of events, and said she would repeat it in an affidavit. Before she could, however, she fell seriously ill with caustic soda poisoning and was rushed to hospital.

Though Angelo was very weak, and the doctors said she might not survive, the police were allowed to take down her affidavit, believing that a woman at death's door wouldn't lie. But Angelo didn't change her story. She also survived the poisoning.

A portion of one of the letters Gertie Angelo said had been written to her by Billy Vermaak.

On the flimsiest of evidence – mostly Angelo's insistence – the police travelled to Gwelo, Southern Rhodesia, and arrested a 23-year-old painter, Vincent 'Billy' Vermaak. At the end of July 1929 he was brought to Johannesburg for his arraignment.

Even though it was only a preliminary hearing, at the magistrate's court, crowds stood outside waiting to get a glimpse of the suspected killer, who was transported from jail in a Black Maria. One newspaper described him as small, though not 'weedy', and another said he was tall, although they both agreed he was of dark complexion, like a Greek.

The courtroom was packed, mostly with women, 'who eyed the prisoner with hostility and loathing', and another dozen stood at the entrance the whole day waiting for a chance to get in. 'The preparatory examination was one of the most remarkable ever heard in South Africa,' one journalist wrote. The young painter had no lawyer to defend him: 'His smouldering eyes watched the lips of every speaker in court, but he neither interrupted nor took notes.'

Most of the hearing dealt with Angelo's testimony. When she first took the stand, she appeared frail and nervous. She spoke in a low voice and fidgeted a lot. Vermaak had courted her for two years, she said, until March 1929, and then left for his parents' farm in Gwelo.

At about the time of Kanthack's death, at the end of 1927, Vermaak was working near the zoo but came to her father's home in the evenings for meals. She knew nothing about the Kanthack disappearance or murder, she said. One night Billy turned up in soiled and bloodstained clothes. When she asked what had happened, he made his comment about 'committing a crime with a girl'. She asked what he had done to her.

'He told me he had outraged her, and after he had done so she [Kanthack] told him she would report him, so he cut her throat. And after he had done so, the razor slipped and cut her breast. Then he buried her under a tree and put some leaves and sticks over her, and handkerchiefs over her face.' He didn't know who she was, but said she had a black walking stick and a black dog.

Angelo said she had removed the blood smears from Billy's clothing with caustic soda. She was closely questioned about the letters she said were written by him. There were others addressed to a motor mechanic named Fred, which also referred to the crime. She said that Vermaak had warned her that 'something would happen to her' if she revealed his guilt to anyone.

When asked why she kept going out with Vermaak after she learned of the murders, she said she was afraid that if she didn't, he would do the same thing to her as he'd done to Kanthack.

By the second day of the preliminary examination, an even bigger crowd had gathered outside the court and remained there all day. Vermaak, dressed in a blue suit, had by now been assigned a lawyer, Morgan Evans, who said his client deserved a proper defence, for he had been 'accused of the commission of one of the worst crimes Johannesburg has ever known'.

Evans quickly showed Angelo's story to be thin and unreliable – there were many details she could not explain, and she was confused about dates – and the magistrate agreed. Both her and her father's evidence was full of contradictions, and he believed it was all a fabrication. What had prompted them to do it wasn't for him to say, but Vermaak was free to go.

In the courtroom, suddenly, the most amazing thing happened. The very same people who, only a few hours earlier, had been convinced Vermaak was guilty and had glared at him mercilessly now were cheering his acquittal. The applause lasted for a full minute and was so loud that the court orderly couldn't stop it. One woman even offered the young handyman a place to live on her farm for as long as he wanted, but he said he would be returning to Gwelo.

CHAPTER 32

A touch of Sherlock Holmes

Billy Vermaak walked into *The Sjambok* office in the Sanderson Building on President Street only a few weeks after being exonerated of charges in the Irene Kanthack case, and asked to see the editor. Stephen Black, who had called the crime 'the greatest South African mystery of recent years', was curious about the visitor but also deeply suspicious of him. The fact that he had been set free didn't matter; he could still be guilty of killing Kanthack.

The young man said he wanted to tell his side of the story, although Black asked him why he would bother if he had just been exonerated by a judge; and if it was money he wanted, Black wasn't going to pay him anything. Vermaak was hoping a story would induce the authorities to pay him a settlement, for he felt he had been badly treated by the police.

He told Black about the 'passionate sex affair' he had had with Gertie Angelo since he was 21, and that he was very interested in 'the study of sex psychology'. Black expressed his surprise that Vermaak, a house painter, would take up such an unusual sideline. It made him even more suspicious.

Why, he also wanted to know, would Angelo have made up all the letters she gave to the police; Vermaak said he didn't know. He produced a 'wad of greyish quarto paper' on which he had written his story, but Black said that his lawyer would have to look at it first.

*Stephen Black's magazine brought him
into contact with Harry Morris, Herman
Bosman and Arthur Conan Doyle.*

Following the visit, Black set about his own exhaustive inquiry into Kanthack's death. He interviewed dozens of people who claimed to have clues and information, 'cross-examined them with the expertness of a trained investigator' and invited them to swear to their evidence in affidavits for the police. He also roped in the famed author of the Sherlock Holmes stories.

Sir Arthur Conan Doyle, who was travelling through Africa for five months lecturing on spiritualism, became greatly interested in the case after Black told him about it. He was convinced that the murderer was not an African, and he started focusing on another potential suspect, a white man who had been boarding in the city centre.

It appeared that the day after Kanthack's murder, the suspect, whose name was known to the police, was seen by the caretaker of a block of flats, the Saxonia on Diagonal Street, washing a bloodstained garment in the bathroom. The caretaker became suspicious and later opened one of his tenant's letters that arrived while he was out. In the letter, a woman in nearby Vrededorp warned him that the police had found some hair in Kanthack's hand and now intended to exhume her body.

Conan Doyle went to examine the room, even though the tenant had already left. He paid the rent for a month, hoping to persuade the police to come and inspect the room too and to take photographs. If they could find the tenant and keep him under surveillance, it might lead to something that connected him to Kanthack. Black, at the same time, discovered that Vermaak had at one point stayed in the very same building, the Saxonia, and that the room he had stayed in had pornographic pictures on the walls.

Black soon became convinced that Kanthack had, in fact, been assaulted by two men who knew her, taken away in a car and then, after she had been killed, her body brought back to the park at Zoo Lake.

The police at Marshall Square were not taking Black's or Conan Doyle's theories seriously. It didn't help that, after their experience with Gertie Angelo, much of the evidence was based on a letter of dubious origin, the one that the caretaker at the Saxonia had seen. They returned to the original theory held by Colonel Trigger, that the guilty man was an African.

Conan Doyle left the country, discouraged by the lack of cooperation from the police, while the detectives were similarly unimpressed by him. 'The famous British writer's methods were fairly unorthodox and we detectives sometimes had to smile at his flights of the imagination and far-fetched theories,' wrote Zeederberg, the detective who had got the letters out of Gertie Angelo. 'The man who could solve murder mysteries so easily on paper, was bogged down in the reality of the murder in the plantation.'

Black's magazine carried one last article on the murder, in late September 1929, ending with words that, after all his investigations, must have been very unsatisfactory to him: 'Miss Kanthack's murderers must be punished!'

Black, meanwhile, had other things to think about – most importantly, how much longer his crusading journalism could last. He was being repeatedly sued, and every week the future of the magazine was in jeopardy.

For all the ramps that he might have been exposing for the public's benefit, his enemies were multiplying. Charges of perjury, libel and defamation kept being made against him. It wasn't unusual to see the editor in his fedora walking up the steps of the Criminal Sessions with his lawyer, a man with curly hair, a slightly dishevelled waistcoat under his black robe and round spectacles – Harry Morris.

Whether it was because Black's cases were so controversial, and seemingly unwinnable, or because he had a soft spot for Black's crusades – the same way he had a soft spot for the con man Andrew Gibson – Morris got him through several trials with just a small fine or the case dismissed.

But it was clear that his client's good luck could only last so long. It would only take one judge with a low tolerance for repeat offenders, followed by one big verdict and one big fine, to ruin Black.

CHAPTER 33

The next bestseller

As 1929 was drawing to a close, and only two months after the catastrophic Wall Street Crash, Sarah Gertrude Millin sailed from New York after finishing a whirlwind tour of the US. It was the kind of trip that many authors could only dream of.

She had met President Herbert Hoover in Washington, overnighted with the Roosevelts in upstate New York – Eleanor Roosevelt liked her novels – and was a guest at the home of the man some considered to be the country's finest novelist, Theodore Dreiser. At Yale, her novel *Mary Glenn* was being used by the drama class; *God's Stepchildren* was recommended reading for the psychology students at Harvard; and at Columbia 'she was entertained by the women professors'. She was still being praised by well-known authors. Aldous Huxley, asked for his opinion of women novelists, said, 'The only woman who is doing anything is Mrs Sarah Gertrude Millin, the South African novelist. She can write.'

But the truth was that Millin needed another bestseller. None of her novels were coming close to the fame of *God's Stepchildren*, which had been on the bestseller lists for six months – and that had been six years earlier! Her publisher in New York had suggested to her that she consider doing a work of nonfiction, and he put forward a possible subject. She agreed.

When she returned to Johannesburg in 1930, she began to write a biography of Africa's most famous and controversial man, the mining magnate Cecil John Rhodes.

CHAPTER 34

Malaria

Cecil John Rhodes's namesake in Johannesburg, the young Rhodes Cecil Cowle, continued to be a thorough disappointment. When he seemed to have reached bottom, he sank even further.

From Hilton College, he had gone to the private Marist Brothers, then to a trade school, and now he was a dropout. He hadn't even qualified as a plumber. At the age of 18, he got a job at a hardware store, but that was only after being pressed by Daisy, who probably found the job for him. Before long, he left that job and then got work on the construction site of the new Park Station. After three months he left, telling her that he didn't like that job either.

Daisy helped him out with money, especially to run his motorbike, and when he wanted a new one that went faster, she bought it for £125. Then she got him a pianola, although he wasn't interested in taking music lessons. He pestered her to buy a new car to replace her Chevrolet. In January 1930, she traded it in, with £300 extra, for a Nash 400 four-door sedan.

Rhodes wanted his mother to get a sportier two-door model, but he was appeased for the moment. She knew it wouldn't last long, and confided to those closest to her, like her cousin Mia Melville, that the situation was depressing. If he couldn't hold down a job, and was unqualified to do anything, it was clear that she would have to take care of him for the rest of his life. He threw tantrums when he didn't get his own way, and he seemed to be getting more physical and sometimes even violent, threatening to hurt himself – or Daisy.

Shortly after she bought the Nash, things started looking up for Daisy.

In early 1930, she met Sidney Clarence de Melker, who worked on the Simmer & Jack Mine, in Germiston. A widower of 46 – closer to her age than Cowle or Sproat had been – he lived with his daughter, Eileen. He was also slightly famous, having played on the pioneering Springbok rugby team that had toured England, Ireland and France in 1906–1907, and people still recognised him on the street. Like Cowle and Sproat, De Melker was a plumber.

By April, things had got so serious between them that he introduced Daisy to Eileen, who, in turn, met Rhodes. The two were almost the same age, 19, and they appeared to get on well. Daisy also liked Eileen. But the likelihood remained that Rhodes could mess up everything for her.

After Easter, Daisy took Rhodes to Rhodesia, where they stayed with her sister Gertrude Puzey in Bulawayo. The idea was to try and get him a job on the railways, a state-run facility where men short on talent and ambition could find sheltered employment. More importantly, it was away from Johannesburg. When that didn't work, they travelled south to Bremersdorp, in Swaziland, where Rhodes got a job with the transport division of the railways.

Daisy returned to Johannesburg, where she continued seeing De Melker. Rhodes travelled back to visit her twice over the next few months. It was clear he didn't like it in Bremersdorp and that the job with the railways wouldn't last long. Daisy sent him money, to keep his motor-bike running, as well as tuckboxes, bedding, a gramophone and records.

Over those months, Rhodes contracted malaria – twice – which left him very ill and in bed for weeks. It was an illness that would soon play an important and deadly role.

In June, on his 19th birthday, Daisy went to visit him. With her she took a blank will form, the same kind she had produced for Robert Sproat. The document made her his sole heir, even though there was little more in his estate than the £100 policy that she had taken out for him with the African Life Assurance Society in 1918. Without any resistance, Rhodes signed the document.

CHAPTER 35

At *The Sjambok*

The City of Gold had changed in the four years he had been locked up, its latest appellation being nothing less than 'the Miracle of Empire', with a 'thrusting self-conscious brashness'. Herman Charles Bosman was released from Pretoria Central in August 1930, six years before his sentence was complete.

Mines and industries were spreading in every direction, and higher buildings had gone up in the city centre – Astor Mansions, the Belvista Flats and the Barbican, taking their cue from the Art Deco craze in New York. The latest incarnation of Park Station was almost complete, with friezes of elephants peering over the reception hall, and the city was getting its first big airport on the eastern edge of town. At the bioscopes the new sensation was Marlene Dietrich in *The Blue Angel*, while there were new bars to explore, and pretty girls crowded the dance studios along Joubert Street.

Dressed in a suit, with his Borsalino hat sitting at a jaunty angle, 'like a ship with a heavy list', Bosman went to *The Sjambok* office in early summer 1930, where he met the man who had published his poems from prison. He liked what Stephen Black was doing, cocking a snook at the establishment and publishing his stories about capital punishment. The most recent had been titled 'Strangled for 14 Minutes by Law', about the dragged-out execution of an African man in a Rhodesian prison.

*Herman Charles Bosman shortly after he was
released from prison.*

Bosman told Black that he had been writing short stories, and it was agreed that *The Sjambok* would start publishing them. He didn't want to use the name he had gone to prison with, so the stories would go under his pseudonym, 'Herman Malan'.

They would also be some of the last articles the magazine published.

CHAPTER 36

'Make her happy'

Rhodes Cowle, still most unhappily stationed in Bremersdorp, wrote to Eileen de Melker, the daughter of Daisy's fiancé, Sidney, at the end of August 1930. They had become friendly, and the letter was chatty, for the most part. He'd had a recurring bout of malaria, he told her, had played in a football match and the country had been visited by the Governor General.

But he ended the letter with words of concern about Daisy. 'I had a long letter from my mother saying how ill she has been. Also she says that the doctors are worried because they cannot get the poison out of her system. It sounds that there is no hope in her letter and I am getting worried every day about my mother and also in my mind that something is going to happen. If there is nothing about her getting better by the end of next week, I will be coming up. So try and do your best and make her get better quick and make her happy, which you are doing now for me. You understand I have only a mother left in the world and some boys do not know who their best friend is; that their best friend is their mother. I think a lot of my mother.

'I have done what I can for my mother and I know that my mother had done a lot for me and I appreciate it very much. I don't know what I will do if anything happens to her and I hope that nothing will happen as long as I am alive.'

Daisy, who did not seem at all like the person described in her son's letters, was gaily making preparations to marry Sidney de Melker and move to a new part of the city, although once again she would be living in the shadow of a mine dump.

De Melker and his daughter lived in Simmer East, near the Simmer & Jack Mine, where he worked. Like Robinson Deep in the west, where Daisy had lived for so many years, the Simmer & Jack Mine was owned by Gold Fields, the company started by Cecil John Rhodes. There was a third mine, Sub-Nigel, forming a trio known as Faith, Hope and Charity.

The closest town was Germiston, named after the birthplace of one of the mine's founders, and which was now home to the Rand Refinery, where more than half the world's gold bullion was smelted annually, and where Johannesburg's first major airport was about to open. Germiston also had a notable courthouse, which, despite its modest red-brick fabric, featured a rather distinctive and unusual-looking Greek temple entrance.

In January 1931, Daisy married De Melker, packed up her belongings in Mrs Meaker's house in Turffontein and went to live at 19 Simmer East Cottages. That was the address where things really started to fall apart.

CHAPTER 37

Herman versus Sarah Gertrude

It was poetic justice, and if anyone should have realised that, it was Stephen Black.

Things had been going badly since the end of 1930, but there were two cases in particular. In the first, Black had repeatedly attacked a lawyer who, he intimated, 'carried on a low and disreputable form of practice'. The prosecutor, who happened to be Sarah Millin's husband, Philip, said Black had waged a vendetta against his client: 'This is a paper which avowedly has for its object scourging and the infliction of pain.'

The judge agreed, and said Black, in his 'cruelty', had done his utmost to bring down the lawyer who was suing him, and he awarded damages of £1 350.

Several months later, things got worse. Black had been making some astonishing claims (inflated figures, fraudulent statements, broken promises, shady histories) about two brothers, Sydney Hayden and David Heydenreich, who owned a fast-growing chain of cinemas called Kinemas. They sued him not for the usual few thousand pounds of previous cases but for an astonishing £195 000.

In March 1931, Black and Harry Morris walked up the steps of the green-domed Supreme Court building one last time. Within a day, an agreement was reached whereby Black and his publishers and printers would pay all the costs, as well as £1 500 and £1 000 to each of the brothers. Black also had to publish an apology on the front page of *The Sjambok*'s next issue as well as in 25 newspapers in South Africa, Rhodesia, London and New York.

The fine wasn't anything near the £195 000 the brothers wanted, but it was enough to sink the magazine. Several weeks later Black closed his doors, although he swore that once he had taken some time off, he would open a new magazine. But in a few months, he would be dead.

Herman Bosman was more than ready to pounce.

He and a friend, a fellow writer named Aegidius Jean Blignaut, had been talking about starting their own magazine. Since Bosman's release from prison, the two men had become a conspicuous and handsome pair at bars and were popular with the ladies. Blignaut was a dead ringer for the Hollywood actor Ronald Colman.

They admired Black greatly, as well as his crusades and his sharp tongue, even talked to him briefly about joining forces – although the legal actions facing Black dissuaded them. In the same month that *The Sjambok* closed, Bosman and Blignaut opened a copycat version called *The New LSD* – based on an earlier magazine Black had edited, *The LSD*. It survived for only a few issues. Then on 18 July 1931, they began *The New Sjambok*. 'We are the defender of the poor and the despised and the downtrodden,' they wrote, 'we are the joy of the honest and the just.'

Many people thought it was a new venture by Black, even though it was smaller, more modest, with little money behind it. Often it was just the two of them in their office on Bree Street, sometimes bringing out an entire paper in a night. They weren't especially good journalists, and the magazine only lasted for three months. But they quickly managed to upset a lot of people, landing up in court on charges of libel, *crimen injuria* and 'publishing obscene or objectionable material, even blasphemy'.

Bosman, now using the name Herman Malan, carried on running articles about capital punishment, prison conditions and corruption in the jails. In 'What God and the Hangman Know', he told of an African man who was still alive after being hanged: 'How he died under the gallows is something that only God and the hangman know, and they say that by this time God has probably forgotten.'

He had also taken an intense dislike to certain people, whom he criticised mercilessly. These included the celebrated poet Roy Campbell and the author William Plomer, as well as Oscar Wilde and George Bernard Shaw, whom he called an intellectual poseur. A special disdain was nurtured for Sarah Gertrude Millin; Bosman described her as 'neurotic', 'complacent, dull-witted and well fed' and said she had 'missed everything in life – which is love'. At one point his 'incessant barbs' brought her to the verge of a nervous breakdown, and her husband threatened to sue the magazine for libel.

In November 1931, in one of *The New Sjambok*'s last issues, Bosman published a review of Millin's novel *An Artist in the Family*, which he described as 'bedraggled inanities': 'She is like a store-keeper, boasting that his wares are the cheapest in town.' If she didn't mine her husband's law books for stories, 'Sarah would dry up altogether. Come to think of it – that wouldn't be a bad thing for South African literature ... Sarah's work is a lot of nonsense, worse than John Galsworthy. No poetry in it.'

Little could Bosman have imagined that he and Millin would soon choose the very same subject to write about: a woman who had just married for the third time and the events that were about to unfold inside her home at 19 Simmer East Cottages.

CHAPTER 38

Tantrums

By Easter 1931, after he had been in Bremersdorp for almost a year, Rhodes Cowle was fed up with the place. He returned to Johannesburg, where he immediately came down with another bout of malaria, which laid him up for three weeks.

Around him, everything was new: the house in Simmer East, a new stepfather and a stepsister, Eileen, who had a cat named Fifi. Even the doctor, Eric Mackenzie, who saw to him during the malaria attack, he had never seen before.

When he was well enough, he got a job driving a laundry van – probably found for him by Daisy – but after a few months he was let go under 'discreditable circumstances', although he told Daisy that the work bored him. Then she got him into a training school for a gold mine, but he didn't stay there for long either. Whenever she mentioned getting another job, he became angry.

Rhodes had been known to have tantrums in the past, but they seemed to be getting worse, maybe triggered by the move from Terrace Road or having to share the house with others. When it got particularly bad, he threatened to hurt himself, or even to commit suicide, by taking poison or driving into a tree or an oncoming tram, or by riding his motorbike off the road at Stanhope Dip.

The tantrums always happened when Sidney de Melker wasn't at home. If Rhodes's stepfather had known about them, he 'would have packed him off somewhere'.

Rhodes's stepsister, Eileen, liked him, but she could see he was spoiled. If he wanted something, he got it. If he didn't get his way, he butted his head against a wall and once through a windowpane. He tried to jump from a moving car.

In front of Eileen and his cousin Francis McLachlan, who they called Ginger and was staying with them for a month, Rhodes threatened Daisy with a jug or vase, or he pushed her and held her by the throat, shouting angrily, 'I won't stand it any longer.' One time he went up close to Daisy, breathed in her face and told her he had taken poison. She burst into tears.

Daisy wrote to Ginger's mother that she wished Rhodes was as nice as her son: 'I am rather disappointed in Rhodes and he really makes me very worried and ill. ... Rhodes's one ambition seems to be to see how nasty he can be towards me. His one object in life seems to be to have a two-seater car.

Rhodes Cecil Cowle at Victoria Lake in about 1931.

'I have done my best. Yet I am played out with worrying over him. This letter is just me to you with an open heart that is broken. I feel that if it were not for Sid and Eileen I would sell up everything I possess and go right away. That is how I feel. If anything should happen to Sid, I'd do it. I'd just sell up and take Eileen to Ireland and leave her with her aunts there and come back here ...'

Away from Simmer East, Rhodes was another person. In his spare time, he played football on an open field near the house. He had met a girl named Doreen Legg at a party in Primrose East.

Things improved when a job was found for him at the Motor Car Greasing and Oiling Company on Kerk Street, in the city centre, owned by Robert Short. Short knew the young man as Rhodes Sproat. As coincidence would have it, the offices of Herman Bosman's magazine were only a few blocks away. Each day, Daisy gave Rhodes a blue flask of coffee and a 'scoff tin' of sandwiches she had prepared for him.

Short found Rhodes to be a 'bright boy, conscientious and never off work because of indisposition'. His job was to clean and grease car engines.

Rhodes confided to Short that he expected to inherit money when he turned 21, in June of 1932, and asked about the terms under which he could buy a car. He fully expected to inherit money from the estate of his father, Alfred Cowle, and he told several people as much. Rhodes didn't realise that there was no money left to inherit.

CHAPTER 39

Yellow dress and a handkerchief

O n Sundays, Harry Morris and his wife had big lunches, with as many as 12 guests seated around the table.

By 1931, the family had moved to a newly built house in Houghton, one ridge over from Parktown, and almost as luxurious. Harry called the house Elangeni, Zulu for 'where the sun shines'.

His schedule was rigorous – in bed by 7.30 pm and asleep by 9 pm every day except Friday and Saturday, up at 6 am to drink 'poisonous black coffee and light up the unfinished cigarettes from the previous day' as he started working – so Sunday lunches were a special event.

With his usual wit, Harry entertained the guests, telling them stories from the courts, which meant 'the discussion would be of murder, death, accident and any other gloomy subject that could be thought of'.

None of those stories would compare to one that Harry would soon be part of, for it involved not one or two unwinnable elements but a full house – theft, a dubious suicide, an incriminating confession, a murder and a renowned ballistics expert he would have to outsmart.

*

Almost 300 miles away, in Pietermaritzburg, a taxi driver named Arthur Kimber, a jovial, heavy-set man of 40, and his assistant Charles

Mills drove to the rank opposite the Town Hall. Kimber, a father of three girls, had three taxis, one of which he drove himself. It was 6.45 pm on 21 September 1931.

After Mills left with a fare, Kimber went to a tobacconist to buy cigarettes. He didn't have much money on him, maybe one pound. At about 7.30 pm the taxi rank phone rang. Kimber, who was first in line, answered. A few minutes later, a man and woman walked from the direction of the Town Hall, entered his taxi, and were driven away.

At 8.10 pm, James Simpson, who was out motoring with his wife, passed Kimber's taxi at Polly Shortt's Hill, five miles away. He did not notice the passengers in it. Another taxi travelling by slowed down and the driver saw two passengers in the rear seat, a woman wearing a pale yellow dress and a brown hat and a man in a dark suit and light felt hat.

Three-quarters of an hour later, Kimber's taxi was found abandoned in town, on King Edward Avenue, some two miles from the Town Hall. The headlights were on and there was blood on the front seat, as well as a cartridge case and a bullet. Also, on the back seat was a man's pale blue silk handkerchief with the letter *M* embroidered on it.

Just after sunrise, Kimber's body was found along the road between the Mpushini Bridge and Ashburton Store, seven miles from town. There were two bullet holes in his head. The district surgeon believed that he had turned to the passengers, who shot him in the left temple and then again in the right side as he slumped over. Kimber was carried away, it appeared, not dragged. Since he weighed 200 pounds, it would have taken a very strong person to do that. His wallet was gone, suggesting that robbery was the motive.

The police in other parts of the country were already pursuing a young couple who had left a trail of unpaid bills and bounced cheques in different places, including the Carlton Hotel in Johannesburg. In Pietermaritzburg they had stayed at the Royal Hotel until 25 September, three days after the murder, whereupon they left for Cape Town. Their names were Richard 'Dicky' Louis Mallalieu and Gwen Tolputt.

Tall, fair, good-looking and only 21, Dicky had been educated at Cheltenham College, in England, and was the son of Frederick William Mallalieu, the former Liberal MP for Colne Valley, West Yorkshire, a seat now held by his son Lance. Dicky had come to South Africa in 1929 as a member of the Oxford Group, a Christian society, and decided to

Dicky Mallalieu and Gwen Tolputt outside court shortly after they were arrested.

stay and farm sheep in the Tarkastad district. He and a friend, Lawrence 'Lance' Hollins, who worked on a neighbouring farm, went to Tarkastad on weekends and shared a room at the Royal Hotel.

Dicky Mallalieu fell for Gwen Tolputt, the adopted daughter of a small-town doctor, even though some said she 'looked older [than him] and [they] saw little if any evidence of the attraction she exercised for Mallalieu'. In April 1931, he asked for her hand, but her parents talked him out of it. A month later, on 24 May, he returned to the hotel room he shared with his friend Hollins, and found him dead. In a note he said to Mallalieu: 'I implore you don't play the fool with love. It may lead you into the most damnable circumstances.' Even though some people talked of murder, Hollins's death was ruled a suicide.

The couple didn't wait long before they eloped and went on the lam, flitting from city to city and hotel to hotel where they bounced cheques and stole a car, until the law started closing in on them. By the time they reached Pietermaritzburg in September, they had passports to flee the country but still needed money for passage.

In the second week of October, the crime reporter Benjamin Bennett, who was working in Cape Town, got a tip-off that the police were about to arrest the couple at the city's Union Hotel, where they were registered as Mr and Mrs Mallalieu, even though they were not yet married. Not wanting a photograph of them to appear in the papers before they were put in a line-up, the arrest was kept a secret, as was the fact that they were being put on a train to Pietermaritzburg under armed guard.

Everything tied Mallalieu and Tolputt to the crime. The yellow dress and the handkerchief. The bullets came from a Spanish-made Astra pistol, a model that Mallalieu owned. The most damning evidence of all came from Tolputt, who, after they were jailed, confessed to another prisoner that they had committed the crime. While Kimber lay on the ground badly wounded, she said, she had encouraged Mallalieu to put a second bullet in his head. Which he did.

The trial was scheduled to take several weeks, with numerous witnesses lined up to testify. The Crown's most important witness was Captain Montague Barraclough, the inspector of Small Arms and Machine Guns of the Union Defence Force. As the premier ballistics expert in the country, he would testify that the bullets found in the taxi and in the room where Hollins had died all came from the same gun – Dicky's. There was no way he could be found not guilty.

The case had Harry Morris's name written all over it – fraud, theft, murder, a confession and a well-known gun expert – and he was quickly contacted by Mallalieu's solicitors. The trial was scheduled to be heard in March 1932.

CHAPTER 40

To kill a cat

On 25 February 1932, the phone rang at Spilkin's Pharmacy in Kenilworth, Johannesburg. The owner, Abraham Spilkin, answered and the woman caller asked if he had something with which she could kill a stray cat. Spilkin explained that he had some poison, but she would need to pick it up in person; he also gave her the option of bringing in the cat so he could do the job for her. She said it would be impractical to bring in the cat, so she would come to him herself.

About two hours later, a woman whom Spilkin recognised as Mrs Cowle walked into the pharmacy. She hadn't been there for some time, maybe several years, in fact. He measured out some powder and she signed the poison register, which was required by law, and then she left.

Two days later, Rhodes had a fight at work with an African employee named Richard. Rhodes objected to him riding a bicycle inside the building, and knocked him to the ground. Richard hit back and Rhodes fell against a bench, giving him a swollen black eye and a bruise above his heart. After he got home, Daisy phoned Short and complained about what had happened.

On Wednesday 2 March 1932, Rhodes left for the garage with coffee and sandwiches prepared as usual by Daisy. The coffee, with milk and sugar, was in a blue flask. He usually had his coffee break and lunch with a fellow worker, James Henry Webster. At the 11 am break he ate the sandwiches and offered Webster some of his coffee. Webster drank first, followed by Rhodes.

At lunch time, they ate together again. Rhodes finished his coffee and sandwiches, while Webster ate half a dozen bananas. About an hour and a half later, while in a pit under a car, Rhodes complained of a burning pain in his stomach and said he felt intermittently lame. He pressed at his side and repeatedly stretched. He stayed at work until 5 pm and went to a scheduled rugby practice afterwards, believing vigorous exercise would help get rid of the pain.

Webster had similar symptoms, although he thought it was because of all the bananas he had eaten. When he got home, he was so lame he could barely get off his bicycle. His mother helped him to his room, and gave him pills and salts to try to clear out his system. At 10 pm he tried in vain to vomit, but managed to do so later on. By daybreak he was feeling better.

At the De Melker home, Rhodes sat down to supper at 8 pm, despite not feeling well. On the morning of Thursday 3 March, he told his family that he felt 'not too grand' but could not stay at home because he had to appear in court on a charge of running a red traffic light. After going to court and receiving a fine, he went to work. His boss Robert Short, thinking Rhodes looked ill and might have influenza, wanted him to go home, but Rhodes insisted on completing the greasing of a car before he left.

When Eileen de Melker saw Rhodes arrive home unexpectedly at lunch time, she thought he was still suffering from the fight he'd had at work. Rhodes suspected it was another attack of malaria coming on. Daisy served them a lunch of cold meat, fried vegetables and tea, but Rhodes only picked at his food and then went to bed. In the afternoon, he called over the fence to his friend Alexander Faules and asked him to tell Doreen Legg he wanted to see her.

At midnight Rhodes left his bed to go outside, where he was violently sick. Daisy followed him and inquired whether she could do anything to help. He said no and returned to bed. On the Friday morning he was pale and looked exhausted, but he had breakfast with Eileen before she left the house.

That afternoon Daisy called Dr Donald Mackenzie, whose brother,

Eric, had attended Rhodes during his last malaria attack. When the doctor arrived, at 4.30 pm, Daisy told him that Rhodes had been ailing for some days but had taken to his bed only the day before. She mentioned that he had also suffered from convulsions as a child.

Mackenzie was struck by Rhodes's total disinterest in his condition, which was unusual for a patient. As Rhodes was examined, he was conscious but had his head turned away and his eyes closed. His temperature was about 101 °F (about 33 °C), but his heart and lungs appeared to be functioning normally. Mackenzie asked him to describe his complaint. Rhodes put his hands to the back of his neck and said he had a pain there and a headache. Daisy said that Rhodes had caught malaria a while back, but Mackenzie found no signs of tenderness in his abdomen.

As Mackenzie was leaving, Daisy asked him what he thought the problem might be, and he said he wasn't sure but perhaps a type of influenza. He wrote out a prescription for a powder containing intestinal antiseptic, and a second mixture to combat the fever, and assured Daisy that Rhodes would be much better by morning.

After supper on Friday, two days after the onset of the symptoms, Eileen sat with Rhodes in his room and gave him a little ginger ale before he told her to switch off the light. When she tiptoed from the room he was sleeping, and Daisy took up the vigil. By the morning of Saturday 5 March, Rhodes's condition had greatly worsened. Daisy made him some custard, but she told Eileen that he had refused to eat it, and so she had eaten it herself.

A neighbour, Mrs Julenda Brunton, came by and sat with Rhodes as Daisy moved in and out of the room. Brunton offered him soup and health salts, as well as brandy that she found in a cup in his room, then suggested placing a hot bag on his stomach. Rhodes cried and foamed at the mouth. Since Daisy didn't have a telephone, Brunton went back to her own house to call Dr Mackenzie, who was unavailable, so she asked Daisy if she should call her own family doctor, Eamon Lamont Ferguson. Daisy said to call anyone – 'The boy's bad.'

Ferguson found Rhodes in bed, almost motionless, his complexion violet. He had also started having severe convulsions intermittently. Ferguson could see that Rhodes was going to die for lack of air, so he gave him a few drops of chloroform to relieve the spasms, but before long Rhodes lost consciousness.

Mackenzie had, in the meantime, arrived. The doctors began artificial respiration on Rhodes, and someone was sent to a pharmacy for strychnine and adrenalin. Mackenzie gave Rhodes three injections around his heart and one in his arm, and started artificial respiration, but he could see that 'the boy was finished'. Within minutes Rhodes was dead.

Mrs Brunton was about to tie a handkerchief around his head to keep his chin up, but someone said he shouldn't be touched until the police arrived.

After the body had been taken away to the mortuary, Mackenzie carried out the post-mortem and found that Rhodes's spleen was enlarged, his liver and brain somewhat congested, and the walls of his stomach inflamed. He gave the cause of death as cerebral malaria.

The funeral took place on Sunday 6 March, and Rhodes was buried next to his father, Alfred Cowle, and stepfather, Robert Sproat, at Brixton Cemetery. It was only three months before his 21st birthday.

The following day, Daisy began organising the estate. She went to Robert Short's garage to collect Rhodes's wages for the first half of the previous week. She told him that her son had died of cerebral malaria, although Short found her strangely unemotional. The next day she visited the office of George Walter Ross at the African Life Assurance Society to claim the money from the endowment policy on Rhodes's life. She received £100; if Rhodes had lived three more months, he would have received five times that amount.

In the following days, Daisy cried a lot, especially when she went with Eileen to see her son's grave. She told Annie Dankworth, a friend who lived two doors down, that Rhodes was haunting her. She heard noises at night, and once a banging in the dining room. When she went to investigate, she saw him standing next to the sideboard wearing a policeman's uniform.

CHAPTER 41

Small arms and machine guns

As Rhodes Cowle was being buried, Harry Morris was on the overnight train from Johannesburg to Pietermaritzburg, to lead the defence of Dicky Mallalieu. Even before opening arguments began, on 8 March 1932, luck was on Harry's side.

It had been agreed to try his client and Gwen Tolputt separately (Morris was not representing her), and, to the Crown's further displeasure, the judge also said Tolputt's confession to the murder while in jail could not be entered as evidence in Mallalieu's trial.

But there were still the bullets from the Astra gun, which appeared to tie Mallalieu to the crime. The casings – from Kimber's taxi and Hollins's hotel room – bore the same 'SB' mark (which stood for Sellier & Bellot, the Czech manufacturer) as well as identical ejector imprints. No two firing pins, the prosecutor said, left exactly the same impression on a cartridge case, but any single weapon always left an identical print. When empty cases were automatically ejected, they also bore characteristic markings, though their depth might vary slightly according to how violently they had been ejected.

Before questioning got to the Astra, as one crime reporter recalled, Morris swatted witnesses aside with ease: 'Definite assertions appeared to be assumptions. Recollections faded into after-thoughts. Rumour and hearsay had been intermingled with facts. He was able to show some of the witnesses were incapable of telling the whole truth even if, or when, they wanted to.'

Then came Captain Montague Barraclough, who was just the kind of expert witness Harry loved to take on – and decimate. The most respected ballistics expert in the country – in fact, he was the only one – his evidence was rarely challenged. For the trial, Barraclough had taken hundreds of photographs – close-ups of bullets, casings, indentations, headstamps, scratch marks and ejector imprints – which Morris, of course, had studied until he knew every mark, scratch and discrepancy.

Barraclough, on taking the stand, was handed the two sets of bullets and casings – from Kimber and Hollins – as well as others that had been used in tests conducted with Mallalieu's Astra pistol. All of them, he said, had similar characteristics and identical markings. He added that in all his experience as a ballistics expert, he had seen similar marks produced on bullets and cartridges only by pistols of the same make and calibre. This the jury could see in the multiple photographs he had taken.

Tests had also been carried out on six other Astras, Barraclough said. Pointing out the markings on their cases, he declared that they were different 'all the way through', and there was absolutely no possibility of any similarity between them.

Morris rose slowly to his feet. He quickly fanned out his gown and smoothed his silk waistcoat. Starting courteously, to put Barraclough at his ease, he asked some preliminary questions about ballistics treatises, and the mechanism and peculiarities of firearms and ammunition. Then the attack began.

'You have *never*,' he emphasised, 'been opposed by another firearms expert in South Africa?'

Barraclough agreed.

'And none of those who have previously cross-examined you knew much about the subject?'

'Not that I am aware of.'

Morris turned to the corner where a table had been set up for Barraclough's numerous photographs. Momentarily feigning despair as he faced the formidable pile, intimating to the jury that, like them, he found it daunting to make sense of it all, the truth was that Morris knew every line on every image.

Casually, he walked to the table and picked up a photograph that was meant to depict the bases of two different cartridge cases. He knew, after hours of pretrial scrutiny, however, that they were in fact exactly the same base. He asked Barraclough to explain how this had happened.

Barraclough was embarrassed, apologetic. He was wrong, he conceded, and Morris was right. The photograph of the two different bases had been printed but mislaid. The effect of the error, Morris pointed out, was that no photograph comparing the two bases had been made available as an exhibit at the preliminary hearing.

'Because of your carelessness,' he pointed out, 'the defence has been gravely handicapped. The absence of this photograph means that the opportunity for investigating it has passed. The defence cannot get that opportunity again. You realise that, do you not?'

The prosecutor interrupted, saying that he, too, had noticed the error while examining the photographs. New photographs had been taken and the defence had been notified of this during the course of the trial.

'The mistake could be seen with the naked eye,' he said, motioning to Morris. 'My learned friend could see it as well as anybody.'

Morris chuckled.

'Quite so. I saw it,' he replied. 'The only person who did not was ... the expert!'

The words clearly stung Barraclough.

Casually selecting several other photographs of the cartridge cases from the taxi, the hotel room and the test firings, Morris invited Barraclough to examine the exhibit numbers. Two of them had accidentally been transposed.

'That,' Morris said for the jury's benefit, 'was also a handicap to the defence. We submitted the exhibits to our expert in England and now, for the first time, we learn here is a further error, that the exhibits are not what they purport to be.'

He picked up another photograph of the cartridge cases set in a row – two from the taxi, one from Hollins's hotel room and one ejected at the test. Which of them, he asked Barraclough, had a bevelled edge?

'The test cartridge case,' Barraclough replied.

Morris disagreed, saying he believed that bevelling appeared on only one of the cases recovered from the taxi.

'That,' Barraclough replied, 'is an optical illusion.'

'Well,' Morris replied, 'I can't see bevelling where you say it is.'

'The cases were standing on a bed of plasticine, and the bevelled edge sank below the surface.'

Morris plunged his hands under the back of his robe and moved forward.

'Do you suggest that whenever differences are pointed out,' he said impatiently, 'his lordship, the jury and counsel have invariably to be satisfied with your *ipse dixit* [baseless assertion]?'

'No,' Barraclough said. 'That is precisely why I put in these photographs.' Then he added something he shouldn't have: 'I never rely on photographs myself.'

'But *we* do,' Morris exclaimed, 'and we are asked to by the Crown. If you don't attach importance to your photographs, why should the jury?'

Suddenly put on the spot, Barraclough was prepared to agree that the same firing pin or ejector in a pistol could make varying marks, although only in depth. That was an important concession for the defence, who, during pretrial investigation, had made a crucial discovery: using only a rudimentary microscope, it was found that the firing pin indentations were elongated and ran, in relation to the ejector marks, in different directions.

'Do you agree,' Morris put it to Barraclough, 'that if the distance between the firing pin indentations and the ejector marks on two cartridge cases agree with each other to within one ten-thousandth of an inch, the two *may*, but not *must*, have been fired from the same weapon?'

'Correct.'

'Do you agree that if the distances between these points do *not* agree to within one ten-thousandth of an inch, the two cartridges were not fired from the same weapon?'

Again, the answer was yes. Morris waited, took off his spectacles, cleaned them, and put them back on. It was good theatre, and he knew the jury were waiting for his next question.

'Did you,' he asked, 'measure these distances with a micrometer or any other instrument?'

'No,' Barraclough admitted.

'Oh! With what, may I ask, *did* you measure them?'

Crowds waiting outside the Pietermaritzburg Supreme Court on the last day of the Mallalieu trial. The verdict shocked even Harry Morris.

'With my eye.'

'"My eye"!' Morris repeated.

Barraclough had, with those two words, quite possibly destroyed all his previous scientific evidence. The expert had not only admitted errors in photographs and transposed exhibit numbers but was also prepared to decide the fate of an accused man by taking a measurement with his naked eye.

Following up quickly, Morris placed the tracing of one cartridge case base on another to show that the ejector marks coincided but the firing pin indentations did not. What did Barraclough have to say about this?

It was the 'misleading nature' of the photographs, Barraclough said.

If the photographs produced by the Crown were misleading, Morris countered, there could be little justification for putting them before the jury. Morris then asked him why he had tested only six Astras.

'You had the opportunity to examine and test many more firearms. Remember, a man might hang on this evidence.'

'From my point of view,' Barraclough said, 'six pistols were not even required.'

'And from my point of view,' Morris replied, 'I am going to suggest that a great deal more experience was required in this case than the expert appears to have shown!'

Morris sat down, hoarse and weary after cross-examining Barraclough – for seven hours. The ballistics expert left the court incensed, realising he had been made to look a fool.

'That bastard Morris,' he growled, 'accused me of practically everything, except committing the bloody murder.'

Through it all, Bennett wrote, Mallalieu sat 'cool, lucid, unruffled'. As a witness, 'he withstood cross-examination, his answers brief and to the point, his explanations reasonable, admission of his youthful escapades frank and forthright'.

On 23 March 1932, after an exhausting 11-day trial, both the Crown's chief prosecutor and Morris gave lengthy closing addresses. The jury took only one hour to return with a verdict of not guilty. Mallalieu was jubilant and approached Morris with his hand outstretched to thank him, but Morris turned away.

'I don't shake hands with murderers,' he said.

PART 5

POISONS AND
STRATEGIES
1932

CHAPTER 42

Suspicion

In Pretoria, William Sproat was distraught and suspicious. He had by now seen one death too many. Still haunted by the gruesome image of his brother Robert's face on his deathbed five years earlier, the news of Rhodes's sudden passing was all that he needed to spring into action. He went to the police and told them about the series of suspicious deaths at the home of Daisy Cowle/Sproat/de Melker.

On the afternoon of 15 April 1932, a group including Sproat, Dr Donald Mackenzie, three government analysts and pathologists – including Gilbert Frederick Britten – as well as police detective JCH Jansen entered the English section of Brixton Cemetery and exhumed the bodies of Rhodes Cowle, Alfred Cowle and Robert Sproat.

From Rhodes's remains were taken over four pounds of viscera, a piece of backbone and a portion of scalp with some hair attached; from Alfred Cowle, the right femur with adhering tissue, a vertebra from the spinal column and some hair; and from Sproat, portions of his spinal column, brain and scalp and hair. They were taken to the laboratories of the South African Institute for Medical Research.

In the viscera of Rhodes, Britten found 1.3 grains of arsenic and 1.7 grains of arsenious oxide. In his backbone and hair, there were also small quantities of arsenic. In Sproat's and Cowle's vertebrae, both of which had a slightly rosy tint, he found particles of strychnine.

On Wednesday 20 April, detective Jansen arrived at the De Melker house in Simmer East with a second policeman, a wardress and a forensics man. When Daisy de Melker opened the door, Jansen introduced himself and asked if they could come in. They were led to the dining room, where he told her he had a warrant for her arrest, and that she was being charged with the murder of her son, Rhodes Cowle.

'How do you know?' she asked. 'How can you say that?'

He told her they had exhumed his body and found arsenic.

'Mia!' Daisy called out, bringing her hands to her face. Her cousin Mia Melville was visiting her. 'They have come to arrest me. They say I have murdered Rhodes.'

Detective Jansen told her to be calm and said that he would need to search the house before taking her to the police station. No arsenic or other poison was found. Before nightfall Daisy was driven away in a Black Maria.

CHAPTER 43

A star is born

Early on the morning of 21 April, several journalists who had got news of the mother accused of killing her son and two husbands were waiting inside the magistrate's court on President Street in Germiston. So were a lot of members of the public, who had already got wind of the story: 'Every available seat and all the standing room was occupied, a fair number of women being among the inquisitive crowd.' Three young women who kept chattering and giggling were twice warned that they would be thrown out.

Daisy was brought in, 'smartly attired in a black dress with white facings ... a trim little figure, about 5 feet 5 inches in height, of medium build and good appearance, and perfect composure'. She took a seat next to JW Louw, who was with a small firm of solicitors, Wright, Rose-Innes & Louw. He had met her only the previous night, after her arrest, and knew very little about her case. On Daisy's other side sat Sidney de Melker.

Magistrate Douglas Mearns explained that she was being charged by the Crown with the murder of Rhodes Cecil Cowle, her son, by the administration of arsenic; and with the murders of William Alfred Cowle and Robert Sproat, her two husbands, by strychnine. The preliminary hearing would start in the middle of May, when the Crown would produce evidence to establish a prima facie case against her.

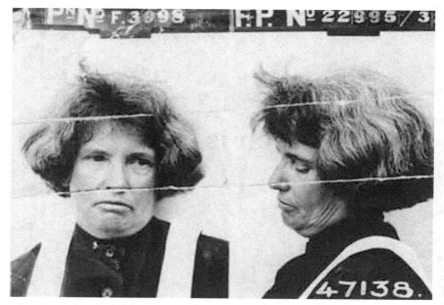

The police mugshot of Daisy taken the night she was arrested.

Once that had been done, the actual trial could take place at the Criminal Sessions.

Daisy left the court escorted by two policemen and a wardress. Outside, a crowd had already gathered, and she smiled when she saw them. A journalist from the *Rand Daily Mail* took a photograph, which appeared in the newspaper the following day, but her face couldn't be seen because one of the policemen had shielded it from view.

On Wednesday 18 May 1932, the magistrate's court in Germiston was a hive of activity, both inside and out. Everyone wanted to get a glimpse of the woman accused of killing her son and first two husbands ('I have had three,' a woman wrote to a local newspaper, 'and I didn't have to kill for them').

'Every inch of space in the court was occupied, women, both young and old, forming a big majority of the attendance. So closely was the Court packed that the main doorway was blocked, impeding the entry of witnesses and others and the magistrate Mr Douglas Mearns ordered the doorway to be cleared.'

After several witnesses were called, the case was adjourned to 1 June.

In the newspapers, the usual comparisons were made with previous sensational murder trials, such as that of Baron Von Veltheim, the con man who shot Woolf Joel in 1898, or the pitiful town clerk Hubrecht de Leeuw, who had bombed the town hall where he worked in 1927. Strangely, they omitted the most obvious comparison: Dorothea Kraft in 1920. She had been the first white woman in the country to be executed, and Daisy de Melker could quite possibly become the second.

Over the next two months, the Crown's lawyers, Syd Goetsche and Sylvester Quinlan, called 60 witnesses. These included neighbours from the three different addresses where Daisy had lived, friends of the victims, Daisy's tenants from Terrace Road and Tully Street, a bricklayer, an agent from the African Life Assurance Society, municipal workers, doctors, pathologists, government chemists and Mary Jane Meaker, whom Daisy and Rhodes had lived with from February 1930 until Daisy married De Melker, in 1931.

Confusion and contradictions reigned. Witnesses testified that the two husbands were healthy, but they were also full of ailments. Rhodes was described as nice, a gentleman, kind, but also vile-tempered, queer in the head, convinced he was about to inherit a fortune and someone who kept threatening to kill himself. Witnesses were often at odds about what they had seen in the final hours. Half a dozen doctors, who at first had diagnosed heart disease, lead poisoning, arteriosclerosis, kidney trouble, cerebral malaria and haemorrhages, now suddenly saw poisoning as a distinct possibility.

Several crucial witnesses had died in the intervening years: Dr Leighton, who had attended Alfred Cowle; a man named Wharton, who was part of Daisy's alibi in the death of Sproat; and even Jane Sproat. Before the trial began, so would Daisy's former landlady Mary Jane Meaker.

There was talk of suddenly changed wills, a custard that was made but never eaten (or maybe it had been), a maid who wasn't allowed to cook, several stray cats, a dead fiancé, a blue Thermos flask that was cleaned so thoroughly it bore deep transverse scratch marks, and a green bottle of Epsom salts.

The prosecution knew that Daisy had motive and opportunity to kill her husbands and son. She had inherited money after each death, and she had been the main caregiver in the house, always cooking the food alone and dispensing the tea, the coffee, the beer, the medicine. But there was still no actual poison or proof that Daisy had ever bought any.

Because Rhodes was the most recent to die, and arsenic was more easily accessible than strychnine, this was what the investigation focused on. The police visited countless pharmacies along the Reef, both east and west of Germiston, but no one could remember ever having sold poison to a woman named Daisy de Melker. And her name appeared in no poison register, which had to be signed upon purchase.

Then the prosecution had an incredible stroke of luck.

A photograph of Daisy finally appeared in a newspaper, this time with her face not shielded but clearly visible. Abraham Spilkin, whose business – Spilkin's Pharmacy – was on the south side of the city in Kenilworth, eight miles away, hadn't been paying attention to the story of the mother accused of killing her son. When he saw her photograph, he was sure she was his former customer DL Cowle, then DL Sproat, but the newspapers identified her as Daisy de Melker.

At first hesitant to disclose what he knew – these were, after all, allegations that could send her to the gallows – he was encouraged by his lawyer to come forward. Spilkin told the prosecutors about the phone call he'd received on 25 February and how he'd explained to the caller, who didn't identify herself, that she'd need to come in to the store to get the poison.

About two hours after the call, a woman Spilkin recognised as DL Cowle had walked into the shop, which she had last visited five or six years earlier. Spilkin remembered her as someone who made small purchases and always paid cash. He measured out 60 grains of white arsenic, about a teaspoonful, which he put in a little cardboard box that he labelled and handed to her. No directions were asked about how to use it.

When Spilkin presented her with the poison register, she signed it as 'DL Sproat of 67 Terrace Road', an address where she had last lived more than four years previously, when Robert Sproat died. No mention was made of the name De Melker or the address at Simmer East.

The day that Abraham Spilkin was to appear in court, prosecutors

Quinlan and Goetsche waited in anticipation to see what Daisy's reaction would be when he came in. She had no idea that he had been found, and his presence had been kept a secret. When he walked into court, 'I saw what nobody else saw,' Quinlan wrote later. 'She seemed almost to recoil with fear and horror. Every drop of blood drained from her face. In those few seconds I knew that she knew that for her it was the end of the road, that there was no way she could escape from Spilkin's deadly evidence.'

What Quinlan didn't yet know was that the man who would be defending Daisy in court, Harry Morris, had just helped another accused murderer, Dicky Mallalieu, escape 'deadly evidence' and an almost certain sentence of death. If anyone could do the same for Daisy, he was the man.

On 5 August, Daisy de Melker was indicted on three charges of murder – for Cowle, Sproat and Rhodes. The trial was expected to start at the Supreme Court – the Criminal Sessions – in October and to last for seven days.

Daisy was taken by her solicitor to consult with Harry Morris.

'The questioning was quite severe,' Issie Maisels remembered, which caused Daisy to get very upset and start crying. Maisels, a tall, young newly qualified barrister, had already been selected to assist Harry on the case. Daisy was taken outside, and then her solicitor returned on his own to apologise, saying she was very highly strung.

Harry couldn't help himself, and added facetiously, 'Not as highly strung, I think, as she is going to be.'

He didn't take on cases like hers for the money, but in Daisy's case the fee would be lower than usual. It was expected that he would earn only £600 for the trial, which was thought would take one week – a gross miscalculation, in the end – which was not even a third of what he had received for defending Dicky Mallalieu. Even for a short case that he had just completed, representing a diamond thief named Jacob Sieff, he got £1 200.

To prepare for Daisy's triple murder trial, he had just over six weeks.

*

The women's jail was in a location that Daisy knew only too well, Hospital Hill.

The ramparts of the Old Fort that she had once walked past to get to work at the Children's Memorial Hospital were now her place of incarceration. Inside were two small jails, the bigger one being for men. The women's section, added in 1910, was built in the shape of a panopticon: from a central point, the cell blocks radiated out so that a single officer could easily watch all the prisoners at the same time. The female prisoners, like the male ones, were there for criminal and political reasons, but in segregated areas.

After the preliminary hearing, Daisy asked for a notebook and she started writing. Perhaps it was seeing the crowds that gathered at the court daily that first started her thinking about her celebrity. As Benjamin Bennett, one of the most avid crime reporters to watch Daisy over the next few months, noted: 'While awaiting trial Mrs de Melker had referred jocularly to the "forthcoming bioscope performance" in which she was to star.'

THE DE MELKER TRIAL.
Left: Mr. Robert Sproat, who died in November, 1927, and (right) Mr. William Alfred Cowle, who died in January, 1923.

The first glimpse the public got of Robert Sproat and Alfred Cowle came out during her trial.

CHAPTER 44

The poster girl

Of the many thousands of people across the country waiting every day to read the latest news about Daisy, especially during the preliminary hearing, were two writers who saw her from very different angles – Sarah Gertrude Millin and Herman Charles Bosman.

For Millin, Daisy had a special fascination. She was the exact opposite of the women Millin admired. She had an ability to lure men with, what many presumed, was her sexuality, even though that might not have been spoken of in public.

'What chiefly interested me about this woman,' Millin wrote, 'was the attraction that, despite her apparent unattraction, she seemed to have. She was really ugly. She was small, thin, with tousled grey hair, claw-like fingers, a faded skin, large spectacles, a mouth like a fish, and a cleft palate.'

Bosman, if he had known that Millin was interested in the case, might have used it to attack her, and to accuse her once again of being so bankrupt of ideas that she was looking to Daisy for her next novel. He wouldn't have been entirely wrong.

But he was already motivated by something else. If found guilty, Daisy faced execution, and that was something he wanted to stop happening at all costs. He wanted to stop that happening. His fight against capital punishment had found a poster girl.

CHAPTER 45

Of all the forms of death

It didn't take long for Harry Morris and Issie Maisels to form an opinion of Daisy, and it was almost entirely damning.

Besides being struck by her unsightliness – the younger of the two barristers judged her the ugliest woman he had ever seen – Maisels thought her incapable of emotion. To Morris she seemed ruthless, remorseless and pitiless. If she had been a man, he remarked to his assistant, she could have been a general, while her pale blue eyes were an attribute he always thought not uncommon in murderers.

But there was another, completely different side to Daisy that Morris couldn't avoid noticing. She had a good sense of humour – she even laughed when Morris mistakenly suggested for her neuralgia not aspirin but arsenic – and a knack for making friends with most of the people she met, even the policemen and warders guarding her.

'Daisy was a paradox. She was an over-sexed woman who "had no time for men". All her victims were males. Her intimate friends were women. Not only did she like them, but they liked her.'

His client's guilt or innocence was unimportant, as it was in all the cases Harry took. He had to deal with the facts that he was given, the evidence presented, the conclusions that would be drawn and anything the prosecution raised to make Daisy appear likely to have killed the three men, and to have done so with premeditation.

Morris quickly detected a pattern about the three deaths.

First, there was the fact that Daisy always made sure to call in the neighbours, whom she then asked to take control of the situation, especially as death was getting closer.

Second, she always had more than one doctor at the scene, sometimes as many as three, creating confusion and multiple diagnoses. Morris had a suspicion that Daisy had gained the belief that most doctors were not good at diagnosing poisoning: 'Of the six medical men called in on the various occasions only one expressed a suspicion of poison.'

Third, each of the victims had an underlying illness or malady at the time of death: Cowle's kidney and stomach trouble, Sproat's recent trip to the dentist for two tooth extractions, and Rhodes's fight at work and his bouts of malaria. (That was a similarity he'd had with Daisy's fiancé, Bert Fuller, who died while suffering from a complication of malaria, but questions about Fuller's death had not been raised – at least not yet.)

Finally, Daisy had done everything possible to avoid post-mortems being carried out that might raise questions about the cause of death.

Morris knew he could create confusion and doubt about many of these things, but the arsenic Daisy had bought from Spilkin was the biggest problem. Daisy told him that the poison was for a stray cat, and that she had sprinkled some powder on a piece of meat and left it out; once the cat was dead, she had put its body in a rubbish bin. Yet she hadn't mentioned the incident to anyone else at the time. In addition, she had travelled ten miles across the city to buy it, instead of going to her local chemist, a Mr GF Pirie. As for signing the register at Spilkin's Pharmacy as 'DL Sproat' instead of De Melker and using her old address at 67 Terrace Road, she said it was simply 'force of habit'.

Morris explained to her, as he did to all his clients, that she had the option of a trial with or without a jury. The jury would be all men, and public opinion against her was getting stronger every day. The slaying of two husbands was one thing, but one's own flesh and blood? And the fact that poison was involved made it even worse.

A quotation Maisels recalled having read – most recently it had been used in the 1924 trial of the French inventor Jean-Pierre Vaquier for using arsenic to kill his lover's husband – was from the 18th-century jurist Sir William Blackstone: 'Of all forms of death by which human nature may be overcome the most detestable is that of poison because it can of all others be the least prevented, either by manhood or forethought.'

The two poisons Morris had to consider had very different uses and effects.

Strychnine was by far the worse. Not only was it lethal, with no known antidote, it produced the most theatrical and excruciatingly painful symptoms of any known toxin. A vegetable alkaloid, strychnine had a strikingly bitter taste, even when only a single minute grain was added to a gallon of water. To distinguish it from other powders that were colourless and innocuous, a dye was sometimes added.

After strychnine was ingested, death came in as little as five minutes, but first there was a feeling of suffocation and dread. The victim swallowed with difficulty, followed by twitching and violent convulsions. The arms and hands flexed, the jaw clamped tightly shut, the eyeballs protruded, the pupils dilated and the spasm of the facial muscles produced hideous contortions. As the abdominal and thoracic muscles contracted, the body arched so violently that sometimes only the head and heels stayed on the ground, while the midriff vaulted upwards dramatically. There was usually little loss of consciousness and the mind stayed alert, making the suffering more intense and the spasms agonising. After a few seconds the convulsion passed and the muscles relaxed. The patient suddenly looked better, though fatigued, and normal breathing resumed. But another attack could be triggered by the slightest touch or even on hearing a noise. Death came from asphyxiation or, after so many convulsions, exhaustion.

Its mere mention caused headlines, as had happened just ten years earlier, when, on 20 June 1921, a commotion broke out at the entrance of Harrods in London, where a well-dressed elderly man collapsed and was writhing in pain outside the famous department store.

Sir Alfred James Newton, a former Lord Mayor of London and a director of Harrods, had suddenly taken ill as his car was pulling up outside the building. Surrounded by onlookers, he died before a doctor arrived. An autopsy found the cause of death was strychnine poisoning. Shortly before the attack Sir Alfred, who was 75 and had a weak heart, had complained about a bitter taste in his medication, which he took for indigestion. The powder, made up at Harrods' own dispensary, was meant to include only sodium bicarbonate, bismuth and water, but was, upon analysis, found to contain enough poison to kill 'a considerable number of people'.

While a medicinal dose of strychnine was barely visible to the naked eye – only one-sixteenth to one-sixty-fourth of a single grain – the 24 doses in the bottle contained 17 grains, enough to kill more than 60 people. A subsequent inquest found no one responsible for Sir Alfred's death, but the public's fascination grew, as it always did with a possible case of poisoning, and especially when the poison was strychnine.

In an early study of 186 cases, almost half the people who had consumed strychnine died in less than an hour. Twenty-two lasted for over four hours. Often it happened by mistake, for example a doctor's wife who took strychnine instead of morphine, or chemists who accidentally put too much strychnine in medicines. In one case, a doctor mistakenly drank strychnine instead of gin while in his surgery. On realising his mistake, he injected himself with morphine, although it wasn't an antidote, and he died that evening.

An infamous user of strychnine, 'the arch-poisoner', the Prince of Poisoners, a man Charles Dickens called 'the greatest villain that ever stood in the Old Bailey', was an English doctor by the name of William Palmer. In 1855, Palmer used strychnine to kill a gambling friend, John Parson Cook, whose money he started stealing as he slowly poisoned him. It was later suspected that Palmer had also poisoned his brother and his mother-in-law, as well as four of his five children, who died of convulsions before their first birthdays.

When Palmer was arrested, crowds flocked to the Old Bailey every day, and during the trial the gallery was filled with the fashionable set of Mayfair. The spectacle caused *The Times* to remark, 'We are compelled to ask ourselves if this vulgar curiosity, this display of fashion on a tragic occasion is in accordance with the spirit in which justice should be administered.'

When Palmer was executed, at an outdoor hanging in 1856, the public once again turned out in great numbers – 60 000, it was estimated – with many of them shouting just one word: 'Poisoner!'

Arsenic, because it wasn't as deadly, was more commonly used and easier to purchase. Odourless and colourless, it was not unusual to find it in medicines and commercial products, overexposure to which could, unintentionally, lead to death.

Arsenic, albeit in infinitesimally small amounts, was used in the treatment of malaria, asthma, chorea, eczema and psoriasis, and in 1910 an arsenic-based drug called Salvarsan became known as the 'magic bullet' for treating syphilis. Paints and fabrics often contained arsenic, as did a pigment called copper acetoarsenite, also known as Paris Green or Vienna Green.

A medicinal dose of arsenic varied from one-sixtieth to one-twentieth of a grain, a fatal dose from two to four grains. The interval before death varied from 18 hours to a more lingering three days, although it could be as short as an hour or as long as a week or even a month.

For the poisoner, arsenic had the benefit of creating symptoms – nausea, diarrhoea, abdominal pains – that could easily be mistaken for any number of other ailments, leading to a misdiagnosis.

In the 19th century especially, arsenic had been the poison of choice for many women who wanted to do away with their husbands or children. Gustave Flaubert's heroine Emma Bovary famously chose arsenic in order to kill herself, and the author described its effects on her in painstakingly gory detail.

In 1849, Rebecca Smith, a regular user of arsenic to kill her children, went on trial and became the last woman in England executed for infanticide. The 43-year-old Smith had borne 11 children in 18 years, and had poisoned most of them by rubbing arsenic into her nipples before feeding them.

CHAPTER 46

The frogs

To slightly complicate matters, especially on the question of how much poison was needed to kill someone, a seemingly unimportant event took place one Saturday morning in August 1932.

The man who set it in motion was John Mitchell Watt, a graduate of the University of Edinburgh who had been a professor of pharmacology at the University of the Witwatersrand since 1921, and had just co-written a book about the medicinal and poisonous plants of southern and eastern Africa. If anyone knew poisons, it was Watt.

A well-known book on toxicology by the American chemist Ralph Waldo Webster maintained that to prove the existence of poison as evidence, only a biological test was necessary. Local analysts, meanwhile, only used the chemical test. Out of curiosity, Watt decided to carry out both tests on samples of strychnine to see whether they delivered the same result.

After obtaining samples of Sproat and Alfred Cowle from the analyst Gilbert Britten, Watt began. He mixed one-tenth of a milligram of strychnine in a solution that was given to a small frog, resulting in convulsions; a chemical test with the same solution also produced a positive result. When the solution was reduced to one-hundredth of a milligram, however, and given to a similar-size frog, it produced no convulsions but a chemical test did.

Watt didn't realise it then, but his curiosity had just complicated the prosecution's case against Daisy de Melker.

Harry Morris didn't have someone of Watt's calibre on his team, for the professor was the single most esteemed poison expert in the country. So, as Morris had done with Captain Barraclough, the ballistics man who had testified against Dicky Mallalieu, he would be his own expert.

He consulted two doctors, a pathologist and a general practitioner, and also got advice from a junior lecturer in Watt's own department. Mostly, however, he read – books such as Ralph Waldo Webster's *Diagnostic Methods: Chemical, Bacteriological and Microscopical* and *Legal Medicine and Toxicology by Many Specialists*.

Morris learned how long it took for various poisons to have an effect. Which were metallic, which vegetable? What were their alkaline compounds? How many compounds were there in arsenic? What was the similarity between strychnine and brucine, a closely related alkaloid commonly found in the *Strychnos nux-vomica* tree? In what products did you find brucine? And veratrin? Furthermore, was it strychnine that had caused the back to arch in Sproat and Cowle, or were there other possibilities? And was Rhodes's enlarged spleen caused by arsenic, or by something else? Was it possibly his malaria, and were there overlapping symptoms?

Morris acquainted himself with the different tests for determining poisons, ones that Gilbert Britten had carried out and that he knew Watt would be doing: the Stas-Otto process, the fading purple test, Maudelin's reagent and the Malaquin test, which created a rose-red ring on the surface if strychnine was present.

Repeatedly going over the testimony from the preliminary hearing, Morris noticed two important omissions: no one who had testified about the deaths of either Sproat or Cowle had mentioned bitterness, a striking characteristic of strychnine, and only one person had said anything about a contorted face.

So, if the men hadn't died of poison, what had killed them? Morris, thanks to Daisy, had other very likely possibilities. Cowle could have died from chronic nephritis and a cerebral haemorrhage, Sproat from arteriosclerosis and Rhodes from malaria or, as a last resort, suicide.

CHAPTER 47

Rule of similar fact evidence

Tall, handsome and well groomed, Cyril Jarvis strode across the great lobby of the Supreme Court while people rushed in all directions as they would in a busy railway station, the sound of their voices echoing back from the domed roof high above them.

As chief prosecutor for the Crown, he was feeling optimistic. The discovery, during the preliminary hearing, that Daisy had bought arsenic from the pharmacist Abraham Spilkin, directly linking her to her son's death, was a major break for the prosecution. Numerous hurdles remained, however, all of them surrounding the deaths of her two husbands, Alfred Cowle and Robert Sproat.

Despite the traces of strychnine found in both men's spines long after they were buried, no actual strychnine had been found in Daisy's possession. There had also been no post-mortem on Sproat at the time of death, making a conclusive decision on the cause of death five years earlier almost impossible. But Jarvis had on his side John Mitchell Watt, who, with all of his experience of poisons, was ready to testify that Cowle (most definitely) and Sproat (quite possibly) had died after ingesting strychnine.

Without the actual strychnine, Jarvis was going to link the similarity of the two deaths using a law that had been applied elsewhere in the Empire, not always with success. Known as the 'rule of similar fact evidence', it allowed evidence of a suspect's propensity to commit similar crimes to be admissible in court. If the deaths of multiple people linked to the accused were so similar, they could lend support to each other. Two infamous cases that Jarvis would rely on were the 'Brides in the Bath', one of Edward Marshall Hall's most famous cases, and, from Australia, the 'Baby Farming case'.

In 1915, Marshall Hall's client, George Joseph Smith, was accused of drowning his new wife in a small bathtub. Smith, a bigamist, had married seven women in as many years, two of whom had died in exactly the same way. The prosecution used the two other deaths by drowning in bathtubs to establish the pattern of Smith's crimes. He was found guilty of murdering the three women and sentenced to hang. It was one of Hall's less successful cases but still remained famous.

In 1893, more than two decades earlier, in Sydney, Australia, a couple named John and Sarah Makin were charged with murdering a baby they had been fostering, and then burying his body in their backyard. The couple had 'beguiled' the mother with a story that Sarah had lost her own babies and they desperately wanted another child of their own.

During the Makins' trial, the Crown led evidence that the remains of other children had been found buried behind a house that the couple had previously occupied, and at least five women testified that they had given their children to the Makins under similar circumstances, never to see them again.

Before pronouncing judgment, Sir Matthew Henry Stephen said that he would let a panel of his seniors decide whether or not the inclusion of the other evidence was unfairly prejudicial. The panel decided that even though the application of the rule of similar fact evidence was not free of challenges, the extra facts were important: 'Under these circumstances their Lordships cannot see that it was irrelevant to the issue to be tried by the jury that several other infants had been received from their mothers on like representations, and upon payment of a sum inadequate for the support of the child for more than a very limited period, or that the bodies of infants had been found buried in a similar manner in the gardens of several houses occupied by the prisoners.'

Both Makins were found guilty, and John Makin was executed.

Cyril Jarvis knew it was a long shot to use the rule to connect Daisy to the deaths, but he hoped that it, together with Watt's experiment, would tip the scales.

CHAPTER 48

A gallows made for you

By September 1932, a month before the trial started, the public hostility towards Daisy was getting out of control. Nasty and macabre ditties could be heard on the street, many of them based on the popular song 'Daisy Bell (Bicycle Built for Two)': *'Daisy, Daisy, give me some arsenic do / I've gone crazy to give all my dough to you. / You can then make another marriage / When I'm safe in the black carriage. / But soon you'll flop – through a six-foot drop / Of a gallows that's made for you.'*

Even though songs and rhymes wouldn't decide Daisy's fate, Harry Morris knew how important a role public opinion played in any trial. He only had to recall the murderer Dicky Mallalieu, whose good looks and reputation had counted for a lot in his acquittal.

Mallalieu was handsome and dashing, and had gone on a wild and adventurous jaunt around the country. Meanwhile, his victim, Arthur Kimber, was an overweight taxi driver who dutifully paid his bills regularly and went to his job on time every day.

Unlike Mallalieu, Daisy had nothing on her side: She was unattractive, and the crimes she was accused of committing required a unique level of evil. Because of the ever-worsening public sentiment, Daisy had chosen not to have a jury but only a judge. Her fate lay in the hands of her lawyer, Harry Morris, and the man who would preside over the hearing, Justice Leopold Greenberg.

PART 6

SETTING DAISY FREE

17 October

CHAPTER 49

Before fashionable ladies

Despite the early hour, hundreds of people were already gathered on the lawn and steps outside the Supreme Court on the first day of what newspapers were calling 'the poison trial'. Many had been there since the previous night, hoping to get a seat in the public gallery. On Pritchard and Von Brandis streets, spectators hung out of the windows waiting to get a view of the Black Maria when it arrived with the accused, Daisy de Melker.

Around the world – in London, Shanghai, New York – newspapers ran stories about the upcoming trial. In *Vanity Fair* Daisy was compared to the American murderer Winnie Ruth Judd, although the cases had nothing in common other than sensation.

One year earlier, Judd had killed two friends, Agnes Anne LeRoi and Hedvig Samuelson, and dismembered one of them, before transporting both bodies in a trunk and suitcases by train from Phoenix to Los Angeles. When she was apprehended at Central Station, it was because of the stench coming from her luggage.

Harry Morris arrived in court an hour before the hearing began, as was his custom. At the end of a long table stood Cyril Jarvis, his height suddenly accentuating the differences between him and Harry Morris. The one was tall, handsome, a good dresser, thoughtful, a Rhodes scholar; the other short, bespectacled, pugnacious, slightly dishevelled, with no aspirations to being an intellectual.

But Jarvis wasn't fooled. The chief prosecutor, like Harry's other opponents, had repeatedly seen him cast a spell over witnesses, jury-men, the public gallery, even the judge, until, imperceptibly, the mood in court changed, and a watertight case sprang a leak, and someone who had obviously been guilty, even of murder, was suddenly discharged with a slap on the wrist.

Jarvis had also received some especially worrying news. William Sproat, one of his key witnesses – the reason they were here today, the man who had started the whole investigation against Daisy – was seriously ill with double pneumonia, and it was unlikely that he would be able to testify.

Behind Jarvis the public gallery was already packed, while another 200 people waited in the vestibule outside for a chance to get in, 'mostly with fashionably dressed women'. Next to the jury box stood a sergeant of the court, making sure that it stayed empty, except for special guests. At one point, two well-dressed women in their early forties came through a side entrance. Both of them motioned a greeting to Harry Morris and Jarvis, and took their seats in the jury box as spectators, the only way a woman would be allowed into it. They were the judge's wife, Jenny Greenberg, and her friend Sarah Gertrude Millin.

Daisy was ushered in, dressed in a black suit with a lace front – the outfit she had worn for the funeral of Rhodes – and a beret, which she took off. She was holding a notebook in front of her, a prop that would be with her every day of the trial. At her back, as she sat on a stool in the teak dock, stood a policeman and, nearby, a wardress.

The moment Justice Leopold Greenberg entered, everyone rose.

The youngest judge ever appointed to the Supreme Court, at the age of 39, Greenberg was known for his even-handed decisions and his sharp wit. Because there was no jury, he had opted to choose two assistants – AA Stanford and JM Graham, both senior magistrates with considerable experience – whom he could consult and who themselves could also ask questions of the witnesses. It suddenly struck Issie Maisels that Daisy's fate was in the hands of three Jews: himself, Morris and Greenberg.

Each time Daisy was asked to plead, and with an almost resolute tone, her response was the same: 'Not guilty.'

Jarvis, in his opening address, said that the Crown would call 59 witnesses. He would show that Alfred Cowle and Robert Sproat had died of strychnine poisoning, the motive being the money that Daisy would inherit under their wills. She had given arsenic to Rhodes Cowle because relations with him had not been good since her marriage to Sidney de Melker. There were regular quarrels, and Rhodes had become impossible.

Jarvis began by describing Daisy's background – a roaming life that took her to Rhodesia, Cape Town, Durban and, finally, Johannesburg – and the sudden deaths that went wherever she did: first her fiancé Bert Fuller and then her four children. Daisy, masked behind a pair of large owl-like spectacles, had opened the notebook in her lap and began writing in it almost from the moment the first witness was called.

CHAPTER 50

Day one

They came through quickly at first – the undertaker, the municipal pension agent, an insurance man – before the first mention of poison was made.

A pharmacist from Rhodesia, who had known Daisy as a child, explained how easy it had been to get strychnine there until only the previous year, 1931. Daisy's eldest brother, John, who had come down for the trial, said that when she came to live with him from the age of ten, in 1896, he had bought strychnine that was 'whiteish' in colour when he went out hunting, which he used to destroy wolves, but he had kept it 'under lock and key' and then destroyed it afterwards. Jarvis asked him a question about Daisy's engagement to Bert Fuller, and Judge Greenberg interrupted.

'There is no charge of [her] murdering Fuller,' he reminded the prosecutor, who nodded.

'It is evidence of accessibility to poison,' Jarvis explained.

'Is it the suggestion of the Crown,' Greenberg put it to him, 'that she had this strychnine in the early part of the century and kept it till 1923?'

'It is possible.'

Two of Daisy's sisters, Fanny McLachlan and Gertrude Puzey, were called next. Even though neither had seen the accused much over the years, they said she seemed to have a normal marriage, especially to Cowle, and was affectionate towards her son.

From the evidence table, Jarvis retrieved several letters that the accused had written to McLachlan, and read extracts showing Rhodes's reason for conflict: 'His ambition seems to be to see how nasty he can be towards me ... His one object in life seems to be to have a two-seater car.'

Morris got McLachlan to admit they were not only a happy couple but a very happy one, and that Daisy had grieved bitterly after Cowle's death. She believed Daisy gave in to her son too easily.

'Did your son Ginger make any report about Rhodes's conduct while he was staying with the De Melkers?'

Her son had told her of various incidents, such as Rhodes swallowing poisonous liniment to upset Daisy.

CHAPTER 51

The neighbours

The picture they all drew, one after another, was of terrible death-bed scenes that none of them could forget. The descriptions went back and forth, from Alfred Cowle to Robert Sproat, as each witness remembered something else – the sick man's fear of being touched, the pain, the crying out for help, the rigidity, the request to hold his ankles as an attack struck, their own inability to pick up the body, the sudden end.

Ethel Balderow, who had been warned by Daisy that she might call her for help during the night because of Cowle's health, raised the suspicion that both husbands were healthy until they suddenly became ill and died. Robert Sproat, who she found 'a very fine man', told her on the afternoon before he died that he 'felt queer'.

Harry Morris didn't let that comment go unchecked, and asked: 'Did he give you any details as to what his feelings were?'

'He didn't know what was the matter with him. I asked him why he didn't call a doctor. He laughed and said he was not used to doctors.'

Morris put it to Balderow that she was making up some of her testi-mony from what she had read in the newspapers and had heard other people say, because it differed from what she had said in the first hearing.

'Did you read any of the newspaper reports of the preparatory examination?'

'Yes,' she replied, 'I read them all.'

'Come over, my husband is dying!'

That was the cry Margaret Walker said Daisy made to her the day that Cowle died, in January 1923.

'What was his appearance?' Jarvis asked Walker.

'He was in terrible agony. Sometimes he was rigid and at times he lay doubled up.'

'Did he make any sounds?'

'When anybody touched him, he told them to leave him.'

She drew a very similar picture for the end of Robert Sproat. Recalling the day that she and her husband, Archibald, passed him as they walked to church, she said he had been in the garden working, but that after they returned home at 12.30 pm, Daisy had called them over. Sproat was lying in bed, 'in terrible agony'. Though he had more colour than Cowle, he seemed to be suffering from the same thing.

'She told me that her husband had been all right until he took a glass of beer.'

Harry Morris asked her what struck her most about Sproat's condition. *The agony.* For Cowle? *The agony.*

'You say you saw Cowle huddled up at the time. What do you mean by that?'

'His legs were pulled up and his arms were pulled up.'

'Did Cowle say anything while you were there?'

'Just "Leave me, leave me."'

'Did you notice the same symptom in Sproat's case?'

'Yes, he told people not to touch him.'

'What was Cowle's usual complexion?'

'I never paid any attention to it.'

'Will you be surprised to hear that Cowle suffered from kidney disease?'

'I didn't pay any attention.'

Morris fanned his robe in preparation to strike down the credibility of the witness.

'You really are not in a position to form any opinion as to whether he was healthy or not,' he put it to the witness.

'I take it if a man goes to his work every day, he is healthy.'

'There are many industrious men who are not healthy,' Morris said. 'But the same applied to Sproat. You formed your opinion of his health in the same way?'

'Yes,' she replied.

Leonard Bradshaw, who had helped carry Cowle from the kitchen where he collapsed to his bedroom, wasn't there when his friend finally died, but he was for the end of Robert Sproat. He recalled asking Dr Mallenick what the matter was, and the doctor said, 'It's only a couple of minutes before he will be dead. He's bleeding at the brain.' After Sproat died, he and his wife went to console Daisy. 'She just said, "I've done what I could for him."'

His wife, Frances, remembered the horrific state of each man on his deathbed. Cowle foamed at the mouth.

'He asked me for water, but when I brought it, he could not take it. He was trembling. His face went very blue. When he died, he had just got over a rigid period. Then he fell back.'

With Sproat it was so sudden that she remarked to Dr Pakes, 'He can't be dead; he spoke to me only a second ago.'

Of all the neighbours who hovered over the deathbed scenes in Terrace Road, Emily Stricker saw more than the others. It was she, after all, whom Daisy had called aside to witness Sproat's will. She recalled the day it happened, when Sproat's health had improved but he was still very weak.

'When I came back into the kitchen,' Stricker told the court, 'Mrs de Melker and the brother [William] were still talking about the will. She gave him a will form and dictated what to put into it. He wrote. When the dictation was finished, I said, "Don't you think it will be better to leave it until he [Robert] is better?" Mrs de Melker said no, she wanted it signed now. The brother and I went into the bedroom and Robert Sproat signed the will. He was quite willing, but it took a long time. We had to lift him from the pillows and hold him. After that we went into the kitchen. Mrs de Melker asked me to sign as a witness, and I did so.'

*

As Daisy was escorted out of the court and through the basement of the building to the Black Maria waiting outside, policemen gathered to stop people from getting too close to her as she came out of the rear entrance. Seeing the crowd brought on a smile.

'Just look at this,' she said to those guards nearest her. 'They're all here to see me.'

CHAPTER 52

The doctors

At different times in his job as the main physician for the Municipal Provident and Pension Fund of Johannesburg, Dr Albert Pakes told the court on the third day, 19 October, he had attended to all three Cowles – Alfred, Daisy and Rhodes.

In January 1923, he was called urgently to Terrace Road and found Alfred Cowle on a bed in a back room. Dr Leighton – who had since died – had been there before him.

'Was Cowle able to speak in a way you could understand?' Jarvis asked him.

'Yes, but he was rather afraid to do so.'

Pakes drew his opinion of Cowle's condition from what he was told by the patient and those at his sickbed, which included Dr Leighton's belief that it was a hysterical attack. His own conclusion was opisthotonos, a condition in which the body is rigid and lies arched back. Cowle died during the few minutes that Pakes had gone home to fetch some chloroform and medical instruments.

Recalling that Cowle had told him about taking Epsom salts prior to feeling ill, he asked Daisy for the bottle, which she brought him. He told her that under the circumstances, he couldn't issue a death certificate, and when the police arrived she should hand over the bottle for analysis.

'Did you form an opinion as to the cause of death?' Jarvis asked.

'Yes. I had formed the opinion that it was strychnine poisoning.'

The fact that Cowle was conscious, he said, together with the arching of his body, suggested one of two things – tetanus or strychnine. He had ruled out the possibility of hysteria and chronic nephritis. When he discovered the absence of lockjaw, a sign of tetanus, he immediately thought it was strychnine.

'Did you have anything in your mind about foul play?'

'No.'

'Did you say anything at the time as to your opinion about this?'

'Yes, I said I thought that it was strychnine poisoning.'

'Did you take any subsequent action regarding the matter?'

Pakes said that when he learned the results of the post-mortem – chronic nephritis or cerebral haemorrhage – he assumed that the bottle of Epsom salts had been analysed, and he accepted the findings.

'Had I known my instructions were not carried out, I should have doubted it very much indeed.'

Four years later, on the evening of 16 October 1927, Pakes again received an urgent summons from Terrace Road – this time for Robert Sproat. Like Cowle, Sproat went into a spasm in front of Pakes, clenching his hands with his thumbs turned into the palms.

'He was holding on to something, I do not remember what.'

Harry Morris stood up behind the long lawyers' table, pausing for a moment before he started. Pakes was a serious problem for him, especially his diagnosis of strychnine poisoning, even though he had only made it known much later.

As was Harry's manner – to set a witness at ease – he began with several simple questions, such as how much strychnine constituted a fatal dose (a half to two grains) and, once consumed, how long it took to die (five minutes to four hours).

'When you saw the arching, did you at that moment consider the five possible causes?'

Pakes said that he had thought of only four – tetanus, hysteria, chronic nephritis or strychnine poisoning – and only later of the fifth, spinal meningitis.

'Before you left the house, you came to the definite conclusion that this was a case of strychnine poisoning?'

'Yes.'

When Morris asked why Pakes had not immediately contacted the first doctor who had seen Cowle, Dr Leighton, he said he thought it was more important to get home to fetch chloroform and a stomach tube.

'You knew time was precious?'

'Yes.'

'You knew that if it was strychnine poisoning, the patient might die any minute?'

'Yes.'

'While you were there, did you mention to anyone that it was strychnine poisoning?'

'I said I took a very serious view of the case. Whether I said it was strychnine poisoning or not I cannot remember.'

'If you thought it was strychnine poisoning, was it not your duty to tell the patient and warn him to be careful?'

'It is not the custom for a medical practitioner to blurt out his opinions in front of everybody, least of all the patient.'

'Didn't you consider it your duty to inform the patient's wife?'

'No.'

'Why didn't you tell them?'

'Because the medical profession has certain rules of etiquette.'

Morris moved towards the counsel table as he continued talking, then turned back to Pakes.

'Is that part of the etiquette?'

'Certainly.'

Morris feigned a look of astonishment. He brought his arms up at the back of his robe and left them there, crossed, before he began again, turning to the judge and his two assessors.

'I want to get the whole of this indictment against the medical profession,' he said, his voice louder than normal. 'When a doctor suspects a man to be suffering from strychnine poisoning, it is not his duty to inform the patient or his wife?' He rounded on Pakes. 'Is that part of the etiquette of the medical profession?'

'Yes.'

'Then save us from our doctors.'

There was laughter in the gallery.

In Samuel Mallenick, the second doctor to take the stand, Harry Morris found a much more useful witness than Pakes, someone who might actually help his case, for he remained convinced that Sproat had died of a heart attack.

Mallenick told Jarvis that after attending to Robert Sproat during both his illnesses, he had been left puzzled, and had consulted numerous medical books and papers trying to find answers. The symptoms he saw on his first visit – pain on the left side of the stomach and heavy perspiration – he interpreted as a ruptured gastric ulcer. On discovering that the patient was a plumber, however, he thought maybe it was lead colic, even though Sproat insisted he hadn't used lead for years.

'I had no other cause to attribute his condition to. I had excluded gastric ulcer. The lead colic, however, did not fit in with the rigidity.'

When he was called in to see Sproat the second time, the patient was already in a very bad way and Mallenick thought it was a cerebral haemorrhage.

'Did you make up your mind as to what was the cause of death?' Jarvis asked.

'I had made up my mind two weeks earlier that he was suffering from arteriosclerosis brought on by chronic lead poisoning.'

Jarvis asked whether the symptoms he found could conform with strychnine poisoning. They could, Mallenick replied, except that strychnine caused a dilation of the capillaries of the skin, creating a face that was flushed instead of anaemic.

'If traces of strychnine were found in the spinal column five years after death,' Jarvis said, 'would that affect your view as to the cause of death?'

Mallenick said that if he had to choose between poison, strychnine or lead, two reasons pointed to its being lead – the patient's anaemia and the greater prevalence of lead poisoning.

Judge Greenberg asked if the traces of strychnine in the spinal columns did not upset those probabilities.

'I suppose so, but death might just as well be due to one as the other.'

'Do you mean,' Jarvis said, 'that you could find strychnine in a system which would not have anything to do with death?'

'Yes.'

The final 48 hours of Rhodes's life were described by the two doctors who visited him as he lay dying, Donald Mackenzie and Eamon Ferguson.

Mackenzie, who saw Rhodes twice, recounted how he had come to the house on the Friday afternoon, finding the patient suffering from a headache and high temperature but with almost total disinterest in his illness. The doctor thought it might be a type of flu common at that time of the year.

'Did you notice anything in Mrs de Melker's demeanour?' Jarvis asked.

'No, I just told her that I did not think Rhodes was very seriously ill, and I thought that when I returned in the morning he would be better.'

Early the next day, 5 March, Mackenzie was called to the house but was in surgery at the time. He later received a call cancelling the visit, as Eamon Ferguson had been contacted, but then, just before midday, he was summoned to come urgently. When he arrived, he found Ferguson with Rhodes, who was unconscious.

Ferguson told the court that when he arrived at the house that morning, the patient's face was violet red and he was having severe convulsions. He could see Rhodes was going to suffocate, so he gave him a few drops of chloroform to relieve the spasms, but then Rhodes lost consciousness.

Because Rhodes was Mackenzie's patient, he said the first doctor should be called immediately. After Mackenzie arrived, with Rhodes already unconscious and dying from asphyxia, the doctors began artificial respiration.

Jarvis asked Mackenzie: 'Did you say anything to those present, including Mrs de Melker, after the boy had died?'

'I told Mr de Melker that the case completely baffled me, and that there would have to be a post-mortem examination. As I said that, Mrs de Melker turned and looked toward us but said nothing.'

After the post-mortem, Mackenzie gave the cause of death as cerebral malaria, for two reasons – the enlarged spleen and the previous reference by Mrs de Melker to malaria – but, he added, he did not have all the facts.

'Taking the finding of arsenic in the body into consideration,' Jarvis put it to him, 'what would you say about the cause of death now?'

'I think that the cause of death was consistent with acute arsenic poisoning.'

Mackenzie, like Pakes, immediately became a target for Harry Morris, especially after changing his mind about Rhodes's cause of death. Instead of malaria, he now said it had quite possibly been arsenic poisoning.

Harry quickly pointed out Mackenzie's trail of mistakes. First, he had identified influenza and said Rhodes would be better the next day. At the same time, he had failed to detect an enlarged spleen, even though it had been found during the post-mortem.

'An enlarged spleen is a symptom of malaria?' Morris put it to the doctor.

'It is a *result* of malaria,' Mackenzie corrected him.

'Is it ever a result of arsenical poisoning?'

'It could be.'

'Have you authority for that?'

'It is common sense.'

Judge Greenberg asked Mackenzie why he said that.

'In arsenical poisoning you get an inflamed condition of the stomach, and in any inflammatory condition, the spleen can enlarge.'

Greenberg asked if Mackenzie could rule out the possibility that Rhodes had died of malaria or some gastro-intestinal trouble rather than from arsenic poisoning.

'I am prepared to say that, taking everything into consideration, it is much more likely that death was due to arsenic.'

'But is possibly also due to one of these other conditions?'

Mackenzie nodded. 'It is possible.'

CHAPTER 53

The unknown substance

On the evidence table below the judge and his two assessors lay objects that drew the morbid stares of people in the public gallery: most notably, there were portions of vertebrae from Robert Sproat and Alfred Cowle.

The government analyst Gilbert Britten, who had discovered the traces of strychnine and arsenic in the viscera, brains and bones of the victims, said the quantity of poison he had found in all three men was sizeable. Even though there was arsenic in Epsom salts and other commercial medicines, it was in such minute quantities that one would need to consume 800 pounds of Epsom salts for it to be toxic.

'Having regard to the weight of the viscera [of Rhodes],' he said, 'I regard the arsenic found as being an exceptionally large quantity.'

As for the strychnine in the spinal columns of Alfred Cowle and Robert Sproat, even though it was only a small quantity, that in itself was remarkable, for it was a substance that disappeared over time. Jarvis asked him what he would deduce from finding the poison in a body after five years.

'That an exceptionally large quantity must have been administered.'

'Do you mean a fatal dose?' Judge Greenberg asked.

'Certainly not a medicinal dose,' Britten replied. 'There must have been at least a fatal toxic dose.'

Britten had also carried out tests on medicines in the De Melker house, as well as on the hair and nails of Rhodes's friend James Webster. These had delivered positive results for arsenic in Webster's fingernails up to 27 September, more than six months after Rhodes's death. Britten had also tested 25 other samples of hair sent in different envelopes, and all the results came back negative.

After the dozens of hours of reading and interviewing he had done, the mounds of extraneous information he had gone through, Harry Morris now homed in on his first real victim – Gilbert Britten. Not only did he inundate the analyst with questions that he was unable to answer – the more obscure, the better – but he also identified things that Britten had neglected to do.

What was the toxic effect of different compounds of arsenic (Britten was unsure) and *had he tested both the proximal and distal ends of Rhodes's hair* (he hadn't) and *were there tests of the paper packets the hair and fingernails came in for traces of arsenic* (no, again).

'Is it possible that they could contain arsenic?'

'It is highly improbable, but possible.'

'Are you in a position to say that the arsenic found was not superficially deposited on the specimen?'

'It was found there, but I am not prepared to say how it came there.'

If, Morris asked, arsenic had accidentally found its way into the experiment, say, on the copper foil or platinum wire used in the Reinsch test, would that have thrown off the results? Britten said he had tested the equipment for arsenic beforehand, and had found none.

It was during an exchange about his tests for strychnine that Britten admitted that even though he was sure the pink colour of the bones had not been caused by clothing or something in the soil or blood, there hadn't been enough of the coloration to carry out a chemical test. Indeed, during the extraction part of the Stas-Otto process, the pigment was destroyed.

Like a cat, Morris pounced. How did Britten know then that it was not an 'unknown substance' – maybe even some form of bacteria – that had given him a reaction for strychnine?

'I am positive of it,' Britten replied.

'You do not pose as an expert on bacteriology?'

'I have not had experience of it.'

'There is no pigment or bacteriological matter which will give a strychnine reaction?'

'I do not know of any.'

Anyone who had watched a Morris trial before could see the signs. The tide against his client was slowly turning.

CHAPTER 54

Fascination

Each morning for that first week, the two well-dressed women had arrived in court; Jenny Greenberg and Sarah Gertrude Millin were politely shown to the jury box by the sergeant of the court.

Across the room from them, in the gallery, members of the public frantically rushed for seats, leaving behind hundreds of others outside, hoping, usually in vain, to get in if someone gave up a seat during the day. In the heat, several people standing in the sun had already fainted.

The divide in court was conspicuous: the well-dressed pair sitting in the spacious jury box versus everyone else crammed into the public gallery; the two individual constants versus the ever-changing mass, like two managers at a theatre watching the daily churn of their audience. But one thing was always the same – almost every spectator was a woman, staring in fascination and disgust at the woman in the dock.

When, after Britten's testimony, proceedings were adjourned until the following Monday, Daisy was escorted out by the guards and the solitary wardress, and they were met by a cordon of policemen gathered outside to stop the crowd from getting too close to her and the Black Maria. The two well-dressed women, the judge's wife and the author, exited unnoticed out of a side door.

24 October

CHAPTER 55

The novel and the film

Sarah Gertrude Millin left her sprawling stone house on the Westcliff ridge – she and Philip had moved higher up the ridge in tandem with her increasing fame – and drove a few hundred yards down Pallinghurst Road to Stone Lodge, a similarly grand English-looking home owned by Judge Leopold Greenberg and his wife. After picking up Jenny Greenberg, they drove into central Johannesburg for the start of the second week of Daisy's trial.

Millin had started attending the trial out of curiosity, but by the end of the first week she had decided to stay. As she had done before with news events that caught her fancy – the Bulhoek Massacre of 1921, the Red Revolt of 1922 – she had decided to write a novel based on the case. But this one would be much closer to her, more personal.

Even though Millin would have denied it, she and Daisy were more alike than one would have thought by looking at them. Separated by only two years in age – Millin was 44, Daisy 46 – they both came from large immigrant families of modest income. Millin was one of seven children, Daisy one of eleven. They grew up far from the bustle of any city but later ended up in the biggest of them all.

But Millin, unlike Daisy, never had children, had achieved great fame around the world and had married well. Since her first novel, in 1920, she had written nine more, and she corresponded with a score of famous people in England and the US, including John Galsworthy, Theodore Dreiser, Mahatma Gandhi, Francis Brett Young and Sir Ernest Oppenheimer. She had met the American president, Herbert Hoover, and was friends with Eleanor Roosevelt and General Smuts.

Daisy, on the other hand, had achieved little. In spite of her 'apparent unattraction', however, she had managed to acquire at least one lover and three husbands. And this in particular bothered Millin greatly. 'I thought of all the meritorious, agreeable women who, in their lives, had never found a man to love them,' she wrote later, 'and I asked myself why this ugly, cruel, avaricious, death-dealing woman had so easily engaged the interest of men.'

It hadn't escaped Millin's attention that Daisy's dead son was named after the man whose biography she was busy writing.

CHAPTER 56

The question of the custard

By the time Millin and Greenberg arrived at the court, the crowd outside had swelled to its biggest yet. Scores of people had waited through the Sunday night and then sold their seats for up to 30 shillings apiece. Even after the gallery was full, another 200 people stood waiting in the vestibule, hoping in vain to get a seat later on. Word spread that the first witness would be Daisy's stepdaughter.

As Eileen de Melker walked to the witness stand, Daisy smiled at her. The young woman spoke softly at first, telling the court of her first meeting with her stepmother and Rhodes early in 1930. She described a mother who was attentive to her son, and a boy whom she thought nice but spoiled.

'He was always wanting his own way. Often when he passed the remark that he had seen something in town for his motorbike which he wanted, he would get it.'

Two days before he died, a Thursday, when he came home from Short's garage feeling ill, Eileen thought he might be suffering from malaria again, or from the fight he'd had at work. At midnight the following day, she said, after hearing him get up from his bed, she went to him and saw him vomit. Daisy took him to bed and asked if he wanted anything, but he didn't. The following day he still seemed unwell, but by Saturday morning he seemed brighter and said he was going to work. At 11 am Eileen was called home urgently, and when she got there she found Rhodes already unconscious.

'Do you remember some custard being made?' Jarvis asked her.

'Yes, Mrs de Melker baked him a custard the morning he died.'

'Did Mrs de Melker give it to him?'

'She had it herself.'

When he asked why, she replied that he'd apparently not wanted it. She hadn't witnessed any of this herself but was relying on what Daisy told her.

'At supper that evening [after Rhodes died] she said, "Fancy, I made this for Rhodes, and now he's gone, and I am having it."'

Rhodes's violent outbursts had got progressively worse from the time he moved into the De Melker house. When Daisy told him he had to return to his work – he was still at the laundry then – he lost his temper.

'Did that happen very often?'

'Very often.'

He sometimes lifted objects threateningly at Daisy, like a vase or a jug, but he actually hit her 'quite frequently'.

'What was her attitude?'

'She tried to pacify him.'

'Did she use violence towards him?'

'She had to give a certain amount of strength to protect herself, but not otherwise.'

'Was she always patient with him?'

'Yes, she was always ready to forgive.'

Rhodes often threatened to kill himself, Eileen said, sometimes by wrecking his motorcycle against a pole or by jumping in front of a train. The threats were so frequent that they began to ignore him.

'I said he hadn't the grit to do it,' she admitted.

The fits didn't change her feelings for him, and she remained fond of him as a brother.

'I was sorry for him for having a rotten temper.'

'Did he ever do anything violent to you?'

'He once hit me across the face.'

Loud whispers in the gallery ignited until they spread across the room, then stopped just as suddenly when Judge Greenberg looked across to them.

*A photograph of Rhodes Cowle published in
the newspapers at the height of the trial.*

Harry Morris rose for the cross-examination.

To him Eileen said that Rhodes's temper got even worse after his bout of malaria in 1931. He once attacked his mother so ferociously that Ginger McLachlan, Daisy's nephew, had to get him off her.

'What was the cause of it?'

'He didn't want to go to work.'

'When Rhodes spoke to you about running into the pole, did he tell you how he was going to do that?'

'On his motorcycle. He told us he'd be found dead in Stanhope Dip.'

Recounting the time Rhodes swallowed poisonous liniment, she said it was a Saturday and he had got back from work late. After eating dinner, he asked her to help him with his bike. When she refused, he accused her of not liking him any more and walked out. On his return, he breathed the liniment smell into her face and said, 'I've threatened to take it, and now I have done it.' When he saw he'd upset her and made her cry, he said, 'It's all right, I haven't taken very much.'

A louder outburst of whispering than usual came from the gallery, causing Morris to appeal to Judge Greenberg.

'If this kind of thing is going to go on,' he said, 'I will have to make an application for the court to be cleared.'

Morris stood for a moment facing his assistant, Issie Maisels, across the lawyers' table and then, the court quiet again, moved back to Eileen de Melker. Could she, he asked, give examples of Rhodes's tantrums.

Once he had got upset when she had been invited to play tennis but he hadn't, so smashed his tennis racket to pieces. Another time he had come home to find something wrong with his bicycle, so he started chopping it up with an axe.

CHAPTER 57

A nice boy

During Eileen's testimony, each mention of a particularly violent act by Rhodes, especially towards herself, caused Daisy to quietly sob, and the wardress would bring her something to drink.

Over the next few days, a stream of witnesses who had known Rhodes were called to the stand: his 'girl', Doreen Legg; her mother, Elizabeth; his friend James Webster; Webster's mother; his employer, the garage owner Robert Short.

They all described him as a nice boy, a gentleman, easy to talk to, a hard worker, conscientious, polite, likeable. All of them had been told of his expectation to come into money on his 21st birthday, money he believed had been left to him by his father, Alfred Cowle, and with which he would buy a car.

But Harry Morris quickly cast doubt on each witness's evidence as unreliable, foolish, gullible, biased. None so much as Julenda Brunton, Daisy's neighbour in Simmer East, a prime example of the kind of witness Morris described as someone who remembered 'a little of what [she] saw and heard, something of what others said, and a good deal of what [she] imagined'.

Brunton made her role at Rhodes's deathbed sound pivotal. It was she who called her own doctor, Eamon Ferguson, when Dr Mackenzie couldn't be reached; she, not Daisy, who spent many of Rhodes's last hours by his side; she, not his mother, who ministered to him with soup and brandy.

'Isn't it extraordinary,' Morris said, his tone exaggerated, 'that the mother should be standing there while you were assisting her son?'

'As soon as I get into a sick room,' Brunton admitted, 'I help the person.'

'He asked *you*,' Morris emphasised the last word, 'although his mother was standing by?'

'Yes.'

'Aren't you imagining things?'

'Oh, no. I held the basin for him.'

'Mrs de Melker will say that it is entirely untrue that you held anything for Rhodes.'

'Oh.'

'The bottle of salts you put next to him had the figure of a nude lady on it?'

'Yes.'

'What conversation did you have with Rhodes about that?'

'I put the bottle next to his bed and said, "There's a nice girl to look at." He turned to me and said, "I have nothing to do with girls." I said, "What about your mother?" He answered, "I have finished with her too."'

Brunton said Daisy was standing close by, but she didn't react to Rhodes's words.

'Mrs de Melker will say that no such conversation took place in her presence.'

'I can swear to it.'

Brunton's most damning testimony was that Daisy had asked her to get Ferguson to issue a death certificate, even though he hadn't been there in the final hours. A death certificate, however, would mean avoiding a post-mortem and any questions. Morris asked Brunton why she hadn't pointed out that this was unethical.

'I did just as I was asked.'

'Mrs de Melker will say that your story is untrue.'

'But what does Dr Ferguson say?'

'Never mind about that. Will you be surprised to hear that before you are supposed to have asked Dr Ferguson for a death certificate, the post-mortem had been agreed upon and settled?'

'No, it wasn't.'

'This idea of ringing up Dr Ferguson for a death certificate was your own idea,' Morris accused her. 'I put it to you that Mrs de Melker had nothing to do with it.'

Brunton, clearly flustered by being repeatedly contradicted, said: 'You're trying to tie me into a knot, Mr Morris. Be fair. If you can't be fair to the living, be fair to the dead.'

Morris turned to Greenberg.

'I don't think we'll take any notice of this,' he told the judge.

'No, I don't think so,' Greenberg replied.

'Now, we've had enough of this,' he told Brunton.

'And I've had enough of you, Mr Morris,' she replied.

CHAPTER 58

The pharmacist Spilkin

As soon as the man entered the courtroom and walked forward to the bench, Daisy leaned forward. She did this only with several key witnesses, the ones whose testimony she had a particular interest in.

Abraham Spilkin recalled the day in February that Daisy had come to buy poison, which she said was to kill a cat. Jarvis asked him if he always provided poison to people wanting to kill cats.

'I usually suggest that we would rather do the job ourselves. I did in this case as well.'

'What did she say to this?'

'She said she was a long way off, but I told her that if she came in, I'd let her have the poison.'

She arrived a few hours later, and after he made up 60 grains of white poison that he put in a small box and labelled 'arsenic', he told her to sign the poison register. When she signed as DL Sproat, Spilkin said that he was surprised.

'I'd known her as Mrs Cowle. She told me that she had remarried and that her name was Sproat.'

Spilkin said Daisy hadn't asked for directions about how to use the poison.

'Apart from labelling the arsenic, did you mention what poison it was?'

'No, I don't think I did.'

Harry Morris, facing perhaps the single worst witness for his client, the one who could link Daisy to poison, tried his best to make Spilkin look silly.

'Did it occur to you as rather foolish to ask a woman to bring a cat from Bertrams to Kenilworth?' he asked.

'We always try to avoid selling poison where we can.'

He didn't think anyone would send a cat that distance anyway, he said. In reply to Morris, he said that he had sold a fair amount of poison to destroy cats and dogs.

'Your register shows quite a large number of such cases?'

'Over five years, not so many.'

'She will say she also bought some aspirin at the time. Do you recall that?'

'No.'

'When you sold her that arsenic you entertained no suspicions?'

'No.'

Judge Greenberg had a question: 'Didn't you think it strange that she should come from Bertrams to Kenilworth to buy a small amount of poison?'

'Chemists are not allowed to sell poison except to people they know. She had known me for some time, and I took it that was the reason.'

CHAPTER 59

Scribblings

As Daisy watched Spilkin leave the stand, Sarah Gertrude Millin kept her eyes on Daisy, constantly taking notes for her planned novel.

During the month-long trial, people spent the night outside the Supreme Court in the hope of getting a seat in court the next day. Many of them sold their places.

Each day, she wrote, the accused woman came to court in an unchanging uniform, 'the same black dress with the same lace front. After a time, I looked at the stale lace front with nausea.' When Daisy left the court and waved to the crowd, it was 'as if she was a cinema star', with the accompanying vanity. When one newspaper photograph annoyed her, she commented: 'I'm much better looking than that ... Let the papers come and take a better [picture] of me.'

Inside the court, Millin and reporter Benjamin Bennett saw the forceful presence Daisy exerted over those around her – even the policemen and wardresses – and that 'all the people connected with the case quite liked her'. When Daisy found out that the woman sitting next to Millin was Jenny Greenberg, she took to smiling at her.

Daisy, meanwhile, was also taking notes, or, as one visitor remarked, 'writing, writing, writing, as if she were reporting the proceedings for the press instead of being tried for her life'. At the end of each day, the two women similarly cut out articles from the day's newspapers and kept them in a bundle, Sarah for her novel and Daisy the scenario for her 'forthcoming bioscope performance'.

Little did they know that someone else was working on his own controversial record of Daisy's trial, and it was about to hit the streets of Johannesburg in a very big way.

CHAPTER 60

'They'll never forget her'

In the small apartment in the city centre that they shared, Herman Charles Bosman and Aegidius Jean Blignaut worked through the night, as they often did, to bring out the eight-page booklet.

'The Life Story of Mrs. de Melker' was nothing short of a paean to Daisy, even though neither of its authors had attended a single day of the trial, as well as a denunciation of all the women who had frantically sought a seat in court.

Bosman wrote that thousands of women, 'actuated by a sordid curiosity', came every day to see Daisy on trial. The accused woman 'flung a contemptuous glance at the uninspiring assortment of inquisitive spinsters and bedraggled housewives and then sat back and forgot about them. But they'll never forget her.'

These women were jealous, Bosman declared, unable to get even one husband when she had got three. Daisy possessed such 'great strength of character and invincible faith in her own superiority', she was influencing even the 'hard-faced females' who stood guard outside her jail cell.

'It is no exaggeration to say the entire prison was ruled by Mrs de Melker. Like an honoured guest, she gave the place tone. More than one wardress set about improving her table manners, trying to drink her tea in the refined and genteel way she had seen Mrs de Melker do it. A wardress was afraid to indulge in the usual coarse abuse of prisoners in case Mrs de Melker should overhear it and think her unladylike. Even the speech of the wardresses altered. From the loud crudities and solecisms of slum parlance they modulated their voices to what they regarded as Mrs de Melker's aristocratic tones.'

The pamphlet quickly sold out 200 000 copies, and the two men began working on a follow-up.

31 October

CHAPTER 61

The poison expert

Making his way through the crowd of women outside the Supreme Court on the morning of Monday 31 October was a handsome man in his forties, his hair neatly trimmed, his suit light-coloured, two heavy volumes clasped under his left arm, and in his right hand a beige hat.

The poison expert, Professor John Mitchell Watt, the prosecution's key witness, began his testimony by saying that even though he hadn't seen any of the bodies, he based his conclusions on the medical information acquired from the dead men's doctors and post-mortems. He believed Sproat's and Cowle's deaths were most likely caused by strychnine poisoning, and that of Rhodes by arsenic.

Holding up two small bottles, each containing a grain of poison, one strychnine, the other arsenic, he explained the characteristics of each. Strychnine's strikingly bitter taste could perhaps be masked by similar bitterness, say Epsom salts, but not by beer or even heavily sugared tea. Arsenic was easier to disguise, but the result was unpredictable.

'It is absolutely impossible in regard to arsenic to prophesy what will be the result of a given dose in any individual.'

Asked about the possibility of Rhodes having consumed more than one dose of poison – such as in the custard Daisy had made for him – Watt said it was possible but not imperative. When Cyril Jarvis reminded him that the young man was well enough by the Friday to go back to work, Watt said, 'People have been known to do much more when suffering from arsenical poisoning.'

What about the possibility of dying from malaria, Jarvis asked, which the post-mortem stated was a possibility. Watt, who had served for four years with the Royal Army Medical Corps in Asia and had treated thousands of cases of malaria, said it was impossible.

*

The journalists who squeezed into the gallery paid particular attention to Watt. Every day they wrote down the testimony, word for word, scribbling like crazy, long tracts, speeches, arguments. Daisy's story was the biggest court case they had seen, and each day it was selling more papers, getting bigger headlines and generating more columns.

The reporter Benjamin Bennett, who had been covering crime for a decade, believed they were watching the 'greatest law battle' unfold. Every day they saw the lawyers for each side bring scores of books on jurisprudence to court and refer to them repeatedly: 'On the one hand is the grim majesty of the law sparing no trouble or expense to establish the guilt of the prisoner beyond reasonable doubt; on the other, the duels with doctors, the thrust and parry with scientists and witnesses accused of allowing memory, theory and imagination to prejudice them against her.'

The 'duels' and the 'thrust and parry' belonged, of course, to Harry Morris, who was about to unleash them on Watt. In the same way that the ballistics expert Captain Montague Barraclough had provided Morris with the perfect target in the Mallalieu case – with his photographs that he had numbered incorrectly – Watt had made the mistake of carrying out the strychnine test on frogs in his laboratory.

The discrepancy between chemical and biological tests to determine the presence of the poison – even though it was very slight – had already been raised during the questioning of the analyst Gilbert Britten. Asked by Judge Greenberg why there were some people still calling for chemical and biological tests, Britten said that chemists were happy with just the one, but doctors wanted the other.

'Didn't that [Watt's results] shake your faith in the chemical test?' Greenberg asked him.

'No, I was quite confident.'

'Is there a case known to you where death was due to strychnine but tests have failed to produce a biological result?'

'No.'

'Do you still adhere to your conclusion that strychnine was found in the bones of Robert Sproat and Alfred Cowle?'

'Yes,' Britten had replied.

Harry Morris, when he stood to address Professor Watt, began without his usual sweet-talking, not bothering to try to get the witness on his side. This, they both knew, was war. Watt was the expert, his enemy, and from the outset his questions came like the rat-a-tat of a machine gun.

'Why did you make that [biological] test?' *Because at that stage, I think I was reading* [Ralph Waldo] *Webster on toxicology and another author who expressed the opinion that the biological test is essential.* 'You read that passage, with which you disagreed?' *Yes.* 'You didn't disagree then?' *I neither agreed nor differed.* 'How did you come to differ from him?' *After I had discussed it with my chemical assistant and with the chemist at the government laboratory, they assured me that the chemical tests were definite with regard to the recognition of strychnine. I accepted their view. I did not have sufficient knowledge to criticise their view.* 'Then Webster may be right?' *I don't know.* 'Do you regard Webster as an authority?' *Do you regard as an authority a man whose every opinion I would accept?* 'Would you accept his opinion?' *Not necessarily.*

Morris's movements about the courtroom were a concert of hand gestures, moving his arms in front of him and behind, adjusting his spectacles, wiping them, sometimes clearing his robe from his path as he would some unwanted obstacle. Each time he quoted a passage from a textbook on toxicology, whether it was Webster or anyone else, Watt seemed to disagree with it.

'What an iconoclast you are!' Morris remarked, unable to help himself.

When Watt contradicted two famous European professors of pharmacology, from Heidelberg and Vienna, who believed that the immediate cause of death in cases of strychnine poisoning was asphyxia and exhaustion, Watt again disagreed.

'Of course [you do],' Morris said, 'these two places are merely little towns in Europe, I believe.'

Every now and then Daisy – 'writing, writing' – looked up from her 'scenario' to lean forward and pay extra attention to Morris and Watt's exchange.

'Have you ever attended a case of strychnine poisoning?' *No, not on human beings.* 'Have you seen the post-mortem appearance of anybody who had died of strychnine, or have you held a post-mortem?' *No.* 'And the same applies to arsenic?' *I have never seen a case of acute arsenic poisoning, and I haven't seen a post-mortem.* 'And lead poison?' *I have seen cases of lead poisoning.* 'Have you had any special experience of kidney diseases?' *Just a general experience.* 'In giving evidence with regard to these two poisons, you have drawn largely if not entirely from books and not from personal experience?' *Yes, except in so far as I have utilised my own knowledge of the effects of these substances.* 'Your knowledge derived from your reading?' *No.* 'Is there any matter in regard to which you have given evidence that is within your own personal experience?' *Quite a bit.* 'What subjects?' *The effects of strychnine on the animal body, and one's general knowledge.* 'The rest of which is derived from books?' *My knowledge of the effects of these things is based on a good deal more than reading.*

Given that Watt himself had said one of the most striking features of strychnine was a bitterness almost impossible to hide, Morris continued, did he not find it remarkable that in three different instances, Sproat's first and second illnesses and Cowle's death, it wasn't mentioned once.

'They maybe have [been mentioned], but it was not said in evidence.'

'But that symptom should not have escaped the doctors.'

'It is such a minor aspect that it may have.'

Furthermore, said Harry, there had been no mention made by bystanders of a hideous contortion of the facial muscles.

'Does [that not] strike you as curious?'

Greenberg corrected him.

'There *is* some evidence,' he said. 'Mrs Sproat said that after her brother-in-law's death, his face was contorted.'

'One gets the impression from the evidence that there is some suggestion of contortion,' added Watt.

'But it is a striking feature,' said Morris. 'It impresses.'

'Yes.'

There were a number of cases on record, Morris put it to Watt, where a person had accidentally been poisoned by strychnine in the medicines or drugs they were taking. *Yes, but it was mostly with children, and concerned medicine in tablet form.* And what about repeated medicinal doses that contained strychnine? *They might be secreted in the liver, but would not cause death.* Was there record of someone dying from not shaking a bottle containing strychnine tonic and then taking the toxic last dose? *Yes, it had happened.*

When Harry finally turned to the death of Rhodes, he focused on all the ways that arsenic could have entered his system.

Wasn't arsenic, he put it to Watt, a natural constituent of the human body? The professor, after being pressed, replied: 'I believe that some people have claimed to have discovered traces of arsenic in certain tissues. The reverse is also maintained by the same sort of people.'

Morris referred to a case in which the victim had tried to commit suicide years earlier, and it was believed the arsenic had formed a cyst in his stomach. For a long time it had sat undetected. Could the same have happened to Rhodes? Watt was unconvinced.

What about arsenic in other forms – in certain fruits and vegetables? *I don't know.* Was arsenic used for spraying fruits and vegetables? *I think so.* In soap and hair wash? *I don't know.* Was it used for malaria? *Not in the treatment, only as a tonic afterwards.* Was arsenic present in Salvarsan and Neosalvarsan? *Yes.* Was Neosalvarsan used for malaria? *Not to my knowledge, but for venereal disease.* Arsenic could be absorbed through the skin? *Yes.* Arsenic had a different effect on different people? *Yes.*

'If both Rhodes and Webster had arsenic on Wednesday morning,' Morris put it to him, 'will you agree that there is a marked difference between the two of them?'

'Very.'

'Don't you attach any importance to the fact that on the one hand Webster took to his bed between five and six that night and Rhodes was out visiting friends and did not go to bed till about ten o'clock?'

'It is a difference.'

'But it does not call for comments?'

'Not particularly.'

'But Rhodes is supposed to have had a double dose and he is unaffected?'

'He was not unaffected.'

'Isn't it unusual that if Webster had arsenic at ten o'clock that morning, he did not exhibit any symptoms till 5.30 that afternoon?'

'It is uncommon.'

'And it is uncommon that he should be completely recovered by the next morning?'

'That is so.'

'Particularly if the arsenic were taken on an empty stomach,' Morris added.

'Yes.'

'You find the same unusual feature in the case of Rhodes. The next morning, he is able to go and attend court. Does not that argue a degree of recovery?'

'I do not think that we have any comparative evidence as to what he was like the previous evening and then again in the morning.'

Morris asked Watt if he wouldn't agree that Webster's case was unusual. Watt was hesitant to concede at first, but then said that he had never come across a case of lameness in the arms as a result of arsenic, which had happened with Webster.

And yet, Morris continued, Watt believed that Webster had consumed arsenic? *Yes.* Where did he derive that from? *From his own general knowledge of arsenic.* Not from books? *No.* This then, Morris put it to him facetiously, was a contribution to the learning on arsenic? Watt agreed.

Morris's questioning had raised a question from Stanford, one of Judge Greenberg's assistants.

'Did the symptoms exhibited by Webster influence you at all in coming to your conclusion in the case of Rhodes Cowle?'

'No.'

'So,' Morris put it to the professor, 'there is nothing certain about arsenic?'

'Nothing except that it kills.'

'And even that's not certain. What about Webster?'

'Yes,' Watt agreed. 'I should have qualified my statement.'

CHAPTER 62

Death threats

Over the course of two days, Watt was on the stand for 15 hours. When it was over, and Morris left the chamber by a side entrance, his step was agile as usual, his smile always there, but those close to him knew that he was exhausted.

Public opinion against Daisy only grew stronger and more hostile each day, and every point that Morris scored in her favour was met with mounting antagonism.

'As [Morris] stands between the accused and his accusers,' a friend wrote, 'he is oppressed by a sense of isolation and loneliness.'

Morris had been receiving anonymous letters threatening to kill him and Daisy if he succeeded in getting her freed, which each day became more likely.

'She was told that if she was not hanged she would die. So was I,' he later wrote. 'Her conviction seemed to be the only escape from death.'

CHAPTER 63

Testimony from his sickbed

Early on Friday 4 November, the last day of the third week, the grand staircase and grounds of the Supreme Court were eerily quiet, the few lone pedestrians on Pritchard Street passing the domed building. The crowds that had consistently gathered outside during the day, camping there at night, were suddenly gone.

Little more than a mile away, at the panopticon prison on the ridge, a Black Maria was waiting to pick up Daisy de Melker and drive her to Pretoria. Well before 10 am they pulled up at the Arcadia Nursing Home, where she was brought through a back entrance to avoid the journalists gathered outside. Policemen stayed on guard after she entered the building.

The others were already there. Dressed in civilian clothes were Judge Greenberg, magistrates Stanford and Graham, Cyril Jarvis, Issie Maisels and a court stenographer, all of whom had taken seats around the bed of a man recovering from pneumonia. Harry Morris had stayed in Johannesburg, preparing to question Daisy the following week, and so Maisels was to do the cross-examination. For a single day, the trial had moved location to take the testimony of its most important witness – William Sproat. A nurse and doctor were in attendance throughout the proceedings.

A screen had been erected in the room, and Daisy was escorted to one side of it and kept out of sight of the man whose suspicion had brought her to this place. As in court, she sat with her two notepads on her knees, and began writing from the moment Sproat started talking.

His voice weak and often full of emotion, he said his brother Robert, who was seven years his senior, had come to South Africa from England in 1903, and he had joined him nine years later. In 1923, on their voyage back from visiting their mother, William met his future wife, Amy, who was on her way to Australia. In early 1927, Robert and Daisy, themselves only married a year, accompanied him to Durban to greet Amy on her arrival from Australia and to attend their marriage.

In court the previous week, Amy Sproat had caused a flurry of excitement in the gallery when she spoke of Daisy asking her repeatedly to get Robert to change his will. When Harry Morris asked her if she knew that a lawsuit was being brought to overturn Robert Sproat's will and make Daisy pay back the money – which would benefit her husband – people in the gallery had started clapping. Judge Greenberg had immediately called for order, saying he would not hesitate to clear the court if members of the gallery behaved like that again.

'Was there anything wrong with his health?' Jarvis asked William Sproat, who, propped up on several pillows, looked very poorly himself.

'He was a strong chap,' he replied.

William had not seen a lot of his brother after he married Daisy. When Robert fell ill the first time, in October 1927, William came to see him on Terrace Road.

'I went to his house and found him lying on the bed hanging on to two straps.'

'Did he speak to you?' Jarvis asked.

He recounted how his brother had asked him to ensure that if he died, Daisy got all his estate – 'lock, stock, bolt and barrel'.

'What happened after he spoke to you?'

'One of the people in the room wanted to say goodbye to my brother and put out his hand, but my brother was absolutely terrified of shaking hands. After some time, all the others left, and Mrs de Melker and I were left alone with him. As the morning wore on, she told me that she'd poured me a cup of tea and asked me to come into the kitchen. I followed her, and she mentioned to me that I had to get Bob to make a will as he was leaving everything to his mother. I said, "I cannot speak to him now. Wait till he gets better." But she said, "You will speak to him before you go to Pretoria." After I'd had my tea, I spoke to my brother about it. His reply was, "My will? I cannot make a will now. I'm too ill." So, I said nothing more about it till breakfast time. Then I remarked to Mrs de Melker, "You needn't worry. Bob is still going to write a will." She said, "But he doesn't need to write a will. I've got a will here. He only needs to sign it." I went back to the room and told my brother what his wife had said. He said, "That's all right. Whatever you do is all right." "What am I to do?" I asked. "Is Daisy to get the lot?" He said she had to. A woman called Mrs. Stricker then came in and the will was eventually made out. After a bit of persuasion, we managed to get my brother to let go of the straps and sign his name to the will. When we got back into the kitchen, I told Mrs de Melker that she had better get another witness. She went out to get one.'

Ten days later, he got a letter saying that his brother was quite well and back at work. But barely a week after that, on a Sunday, he was visited by a policewoman who told him Robert had died. When he got to Terrace Road, Daisy met him at the door.

Jarvis asked: 'How did she seem to you?'

'It flashed through my mind at the time that she was not very much upset, but I didn't say very much about it.'

'Did you speak to her again afterwards?'

They had spoken about a post-mortem, which Daisy was dead against because it would cost too much – seven pounds. She said she would get the doctor to issue a death certificate.

'I told her that I would like to see the certificate.'

The next day, a Monday, she had gone out. That night she had made her comment about renting out Terrace Road as soon as possible, to which he had replied, 'I don't think it's right that you should go on looking forward to letting your house before my brother is buried.'

'I felt a little astonished,' he told the people gathered around his hospital bed.

He recounted how, in front of everyone in the living room at Terrace Road, Daisy had torn up Robert's first will, saying it was 'no good', and then asked William to accompany her to see a lawyer the next day to finalise the estate.

At the Sauer Building opposite the Town Hall, where numerous solicitors had their offices, she avoided going to the one who had handled Cowle's estate, but instead chose a man named TE Kinna. When he asked her if Robert had left any money, property or furniture, she said no.

'My face must have changed to a look of consternation because only a few hours before we had been looking into my brother's affairs. The solicitor must have noticed this, and he asked whether I could vouch for the truth of the statement. I told him that it wasn't true.'

The solicitor told Daisy that she wouldn't be able to touch any of the money until Robert's estate had been settled.

'Did you ever see the death certificate?' Jarvis asked.

On the Wednesday, just before breakfast, Dr Samuel Mallenick came by and brought a death certificate. William had read it, but he did not understand the medical terminology.

'But you knew that one of the causes of the death was cerebral haemorrhage?'

'Yes.'

When William got back to Pretoria, he wrote to his mother telling her about Robert's death, adding that she was not to worry about Daisy as she was well provided for. After some time, she wrote back and included a letter that she had received from Daisy, claiming that all her inheritance money had been spent on Robert's illness.

'The next time I saw Mrs de Melker, I said to her, "Daisy, have you been writing to my mother pleading poverty?" She tried to avoid the question, but I told her that I wanted a straightforward answer. She replied that perhaps my mother had misunderstood her.'

Later that day, as he was taking Daisy to the railway station, he told her not to visit his mother when she took a trip to England that she was planning.

'In the end I said to her, "I never want to see you again, and I don't want you to put your foot in my house again." She asked me why and I said to her, "Because I have lost all faith in you." She seemed thunderstruck.'

Issie Maisels, whose height was obvious even as he remained seated in the compact room, began his cross-examination of William Sproat. Though Maisels was only 28, it was obvious why Morris had chosen him

248

as his junior on the case; he was quick and sharp, his voice calm.

'On the occasion when Mrs de Melker came to visit you in Pretoria [after Robert Sproat's death], you had made up your mind by lunch time that she could not be trusted.'

'Yes.'

'Why didn't you order her out of the house then?'

'There would have been trouble. I thought it best to wait until I was calmer.'

Maisels, echoing a promise Harry Morris had made several times in court, said that Daisy would contradict many of the things William Sproat said: about whose idea it had been to send not one cable to Jane Sproat in England but two; that William Sproat had told her to give the money she'd inherited back to his mother ('If she does [say that] then one of us will be telling lies'); that there was animosity between the two of them.

Referring to the lawsuit brought by the Sproat family to have Robert's will declared illegal, meaning Daisy would have to pay back at least £4 000, Maisels asked if William stood to benefit.

'Most of it will go to my young brother,' the witness replied.

Magistrate Stanford, curious that it was William Sproat's wife, Amy, who was the only person to mention the contortion of Robert's visage, asked what he'd noticed about his brother's face upon death: 'I'll never forget it. I would not have recognised him. He looked as if he had died in terrible agony, and his face was drawn down. I'll never forget it.'

*

Soon after midday, the witness exhausted, the questioning came to a close. Outside, where the reporters were still waiting, Daisy was overheard saying, before she entered the Black Maria, 'He's lying like all the others. They're all lying about me.'

The contingent of vehicles drove back to Johannesburg together. By the time they reached Hospital Hill, the police van with Daisy in the back would have turned off to the Old Fort, and she wouldn't have seen the commotion in the city centre. But maybe she heard it.

On the corner of Bree and Hoek streets, and well before dark, thousands of light bulbs had been turned on to illuminate the sign of a brand-new super-cinema, the biggest in Africa, the 3 000-seat Metro. Indeed, the Metro was bigger than most of the great movie houses of London and New York.

So important was the Metro that Arthur Loew, the vice president of film studio Metro-Goldwyn-Mayer (MGM) in the US, would be in the city the following week to officially open it. He had just left Hong Kong on the world's fastest plane, a Lockheed Orion called *Spirit of Fun*.

People had gathered on the sidewalk outside the Metro from early that morning for the first showing, at 1 pm, and they would stay there in their throngs until 2 am the next day. The brand-new film they'd come to see, starring Buster Keaton and Jimmy Durante, couldn't have been more perfectly timed as the trial of the woman accused of killing two husbands who were plumbers drew to a close. It was the story of a man enlisted by a woman to make her husband jealous, and called *The Passionate Plumber*.

*

In a jail cell on Hospital Hill, meanwhile, another performance, one worthy of any movie screen or stage, was taking shape under the dark of night, being rehearsed in her head over and over again. The sequence of events that led her to walk into Spilkin's Pharmacy on 25 February, the troublesome cat, the cakes she had bought, the pepper spray, the garbage can, the motor pit, the ice creams, the bruise on her son's head, the custard, the coffee, the post-mortem. She had to figure it all out perfectly, for on this performance Daisy's life would depend.

7 November

CHAPTER 64

Her performance

It was an enormous gamble, calling her as a witness, he knew that. People like the fraudster Lazar Schmulian and – in England – the murderer Frederick Seddon would have done better had they not insisted on testifying. But Harry Morris believed Daisy would do well.

She had publicly wept over her husbands and son, and had always shown the utmost concern. With a straight face she would contradict the worst testimony against her – from Dr Pakes, William Sproat, Julenda Brunton and the pharmacist Spilkin. Morris would say that she was not a murderer but, on the contrary, a loving and dutiful wife, a housekeeper, a nurse, a hard worker. All he needed to do was to create a shred of doubt.

On Tuesday 8 November, escorted to the witness box by the court orderly, as three policemen stood close by, Daisy sat straight-faced on the high stool. In the packed gallery, in Herman Bosman's words, the 'inquisitive spinsters and bedraggled housewives' watched as she paged through the notebooks on her lap. Morris instructed her not to consult them.

'Did you,' Harry began, 'administer any poison of any shape or form, either to your husbands William Alfred Cowle or Robert Sproat, or your son Rhodes Cecil Cowle?'

Her voice was clear as she said, 'No, I did not.'

'As far as you know, these three persons died of natural causes?'

'As far as I know.'

From that point on, Daisy's performance of a lifetime began. She denied what others had alleged, professed happy marriages, described sickly though even-tempered husbands fond of medicines, recalled doctors at odds with each other, played the understanding widow, used as corroboration several people who had since died, and shed many tears.

'It has been suggested,' Morris put it to her, 'that during your stay [until young adulthood] in Rhodesia, you obtained possession in some way or another of strychnine. Is there any truth in that?'

'None whatever.'

On one holiday back in Rhodesia while she was studying to be a nurse, she became engaged to Bert Fuller, but they had to postpone the wedding because he was called back to work on the mine in Broken Hill. She left for her aunt's boarding-house in Johannesburg, where she was expecting Fuller to visit her and they would get married. When she received a telegram saying he was seriously ill, she left for Bulawayo, where he died in March 1908. She returned to Johannesburg in June.

'When did you become engaged to Cowle?'

'In December 1908.'

They were married by antenuptial contract, but Cowle had no assets of any particular value, she said. She practised as a nurse for a short while. She gave the dates and names and circumstances of deaths of her four infant children. Cowle, she said, was an affectionate father and a most devoted husband, sober of character and industrious, even-tempered but on the melancholy side.

'What kind of health did he enjoy?'

'Very indifferent.'

At both their homes, on Tully Street and Terrace Road, Cowle had pottered about the garden, although he had suffered from kidney trouble for as long as she knew him.

'Do you know whether Cowle ever took tonics?'

'He was always taking tonics.'

'Were those always prescribed by medicinal men?'

'They were prescribed by different doctors, or suggested to him by men he was working with.'

'Did he make any complaint?'

'He often complained that he had terrible pains in the neck and fullness in the chest.'

'Did you make any recommendation to him about seeing a doctor?'

'Often.'

'Did he do so?'

'He was always putting it off.'

On the morning of 11 January 1923, she had given him Epsom salts – at his request – and some tea.

'He measured out his own dose and said he was feeling rotten.' Cowle was doing up the laces on his boots when he threw himself back. 'He shook his head. I ran to him and he got grey. I held his hand and shouted to Rhodes, "Come and help me!" Rhodes and a friend came running in.'

The first doctor to arrive was Leighton, who, conveniently for Daisy, had since died. There were repeated convulsions.

'You heard the evidence of Dr Pakes and Professor Watt. Did the convulsions take the form described by Dr Pakes? The arching of the body and throwing back of the head?'

'I never noticed any arching. If there had been any, I would have noticed it.'

'Did Dr Leighton make any remark about the convulsions?'

'He asked me if Cowle had been in the habit of having them. I said, no, they were much like my children's convulsions.'

'Did Dr Leighton tell you whether he diagnosed anything in particular?'

'He said, "You remind me of a man with shell shock."'

'What is your recollection of these convulsions?'

'He was not huddled up.'

'At any time was Cowle foaming from the mouth?'

'Not to my knowledge.'

'Was there any complaint by Cowle of a bitter taste in his mouth?'

'No.'

'In these convulsions, did he clench his hands?'

'He held the bedclothes.'

'What was the conversation with Dr Pakes about the salts?'

'He asked me what my husband had had that morning. I told him about the salts and brought them. They were in a jar of greenish glass. Dr Pakes looked at it, said "Oh", and put it on the table.'

'Did he say anything about handing it to the police?'

'Not to me.'

'Were the salts there when the police came?'

'Yes.'

'Were you asked for the salts?'

'No.'

'Did Dr Pakes make any observation about strychnine poisoning?'

'He may have done so in the bedroom.'

'Did you hear him?'

'I think I did hear him say something about it.'

'Was he speaking to you?'

'I think he was speaking in general.'

Judge Greenberg's interest was suddenly aroused: 'You say you heard him?'

'I have a faint recollection of someone saying something about strychnine, but I can't remember who said it.'

'Was it while Dr Pakes was there?'

'Yes.'

Between Cowle's death and her marriage to Sproat, she became a portress at the Children's Memorial Hospital.

'It is suggested,' Morris said, 'that during this period you had access to poison. Is that so?'

'No.'

'Have you ever been in possession of strychnine during any period of your life?'

'No.'

'Had you anything to do with the handling of poisons or chemicals?'

'Nothing whatever.'

Moving on to death number two, Morris asked what kind of married life Daisy had with Sproat.

'Very happy indeed. He was thrifty, sober and even-tempered. He was in constant employment and we had no financial trouble whatsoever.'

The day before his first illness, Sproat came home after having two teeth extracted by a dentist in town. He complained of a bad taste in his mouth. She attended to him and he went to sleep for a while. When he woke up, he complained that his face felt drawn.

She said that Sproat often used to complain of terrible indigestion and he took all kinds of medicines. The day after the dentist, he seemed all right, and on the Sunday they went for their usual drive. In the evening they were sitting on the verandah, Sproat reading the *Sunday Times*. He went into the house and called to her to bring him some mouthwash but suddenly collapsed in the bedroom.

'Do you know of anything which caused this sudden change in his condition?'

'No.'

Dr Mallenick, who attended to Sproat, had given him two hypodermic injections, half an hour apart.

'What were the injections for?'

'The last two were to make Bob sleep.'

'Did they have any effect?'

'No.'

It was during his second visit that Dr Mallenick thought Sproat was suffering from lead poisoning. Sproat told him it was not possible for he did not work with the metal, but Daisy said that he had in fact been doing lead work recently.

'What kind of work was it?'

'He was soldering up a lot of copper posts for me. They were all in sections and there was a lot of lead work on them.'

'That night, did you sleep much?'

'No. Bob did not sleep at all. Billy Johnson was sitting on a chair and sometimes held Bob's hand. William Sproat arrived later. I sent for him.'

Sproat returned to work two weeks later, on a Tuesday. On the following Sunday he took ill for the second time. He woke up saying he did not feel too well. At 11.30 am he took a dose of a tonic Dr Pakes had given him. She was in the kitchen when she heard Rhodes call to her excitedly.

'Did you see any such fit or arching or spasms as Dr Pakes has described?

'No. I didn't.'

As for the contentious will that Daisy seemed so eager to be included

MRS. DAISY DE MELKER

Daisy complained that the photographs in the newspapers didn't do her justice.

in, Morris asked her if she had on a number of occasions told Amy Sproat that Bob had not made a will.

'I may have, but I don't remember doing so on a number of occasions.'

How had it happened that she had a blank will on her while Robert Sproat lay on his deathbed?

'A friend of ours, a Mr Wharton, asked me to get some for him. When I met him, he said he had already fixed it up. So, I kept the will forms.'

'When was that?'

'It must have been before 13 September 1927, because Mr Wharton died then.'

'William Sproat says that Robert Sproat signed the will under much persuasion. Will you tell the court the circumstances in which the will was signed?'

'He signed the will without any persuasion at all.'

'Mr Sproat said that you remarked to him it was not necessary to tell the lawyers [TE Kinna, whom they visited after Sproat's death] everything and you were not going to disclose the whole of Sproat's assets.'

'That was his remark entirely.'

'Is there any truth in the statement that you told the lawyer that Sproat left no assets?'

'There is not.'

'Did you give all the information that was necessary about the assets?'

'Yes.'

'When you visited William Sproat in Pretoria, was there any discussion about a letter you wrote to Sproat's mother?'

'Never.'

'Did you write to Sproat's mother?'

'Often.'

'Did you make any application to her for funds?'

'Never.'

CHAPTER 65

A suicide

The young man in the photograph was not unhandsome, his de-meanour more smouldering than sulky, a broad face with sensuous lips and thick hair neatly combed back, dark eyebrows, white open-necked shirt, as if he was about to go sailing on Victoria Lake in Germiston. It was this picture of Rhodes Cowle that the *Rand Daily Mail* published during Daisy's testimony, when public sympathy for the three victims was at its peak.

Despite how he looked, Daisy said on her second day of testimony, Rhodes was not strong. Besides convulsions up to the age of six, there was whooping cough, measles, German measles, diphtheria, mumps, flu and – twice – scarlet fever. He kept having flare-ups of malaria after first contracting it on the way to Swaziland in 1930.

She went through the things she'd bought him – the motorbikes, a better car for the family, a trip overseas – and the series of jobs she'd found him – plumber, salesman, construction worker and finally trans-port worker in Bremersdorp.

He returned to Simmer East in March 1931, and was ill with malarial fever for several weeks. Daisy said that she herself had suffered badly from malaria, and had also seen people dying from it; in two cases their symptoms were similar to those displayed by Rhodes near the end of his life. After his recovery in 1931, he worked at a laundry for a short time but was dismissed. Then she put him in a training school at a gold mine, but he refused to stay there.

'Was Rhodes a beneficiary under the will of his father?' Morris asked.

'No.'

'Is there any truth in Rhodes's pretensions that he was going to get something when he came of age?'

'It was just his talk.'

'What was Rhodes like physically?'

'He looked a strong healthy boy.'

'Constitutionally?'

'He was of very indifferent health.'

'And mentally?'

'At times he was very queer.'

'What was his disposition as a child?'

'Sometimes he would be lively and sometimes depressed. This became more marked later in his life. Rhodes very often made dreadful threats and told me he was going to commit suicide ... On one occasion he put his head through the dining room window.'

'You mean the closed window.'

'Yes.'

'Did he hurt himself?'

'No, he broke the window.'

'What led to that outburst?'

'Just a bit of temper.'

Rhodes had also tried to put his head through the panel of a door and then through his own bedroom window. The liniment he had swallowed, which was meant for external use on his sprained shoulder, was clearly marked 'Poison'.

'What was his object in drinking this?'

'He said to poison himself.'

'What led to it?'

'Another fit of temper ... He wanted to take the car to work and I objected.'

'Did you take these threats and attempts seriously?'

'Not at first.'

'And ultimately?'

'He worried me.'

Morris turned to the fateful, critical day in February when she had gone to Spilkin's Pharmacy to buy poison. Of her entire performance in court, it was the next few minutes that would count most. Her alibi was that the poison had been to kill a cat, but the only witness who could corroborate that was Gordon Melville, Mia's husband; he testified that Daisy had told him at least two months before Rhodes died that she wanted to poison some cats. To no one else did she mention killing a cat or even that she wanted to.

'What was your experience with stray cats?' Morris asked her.

'We often had them round. At night they kept us awake. When I would leave my fancy work on the verandah, I would return to find the cats sleeping on it and sleeping among the plants. They annoyed me intensely.'

'Was your house the only one plagued with stray cats?'

'No. I often heard other people chasing cats.'

'For how long had this been going on?'

'A few months.'

'Eileen had a cat called Fifi.'

'Yes.'

'Do you know whether Fifi was in any way responsible for the presence of the other cats?'

'Chiefly.'

'Were these cats always healthy ones?'

'No, miserable cats.'

'What steps did you take to try and get rid of them?'

'On one occasion I got up in the middle of the night and threw pepper on the screen door. But the cats returned after a couple of nights.'

On 25 February, she said, she went to Turffontein to spend the day with Mrs Meaker – who had died since the preliminary hearing – but before reaching her house stopped at a shop to buy cakes and sweets.

'Then I saw a mangy cat on the table. When I left home in the morning, I had no idea of ringing up Spilkin, but seeing the mangy cat brought to my mind the cats of Simmer East. Then I thought I would ring up Spilkin. When I got through to Spilkin, I said, "Do you know who's speaking?" He said, "Yes, Mrs Sproat." "I want to know if you will do me a favour," I said. "Will you be in this afternoon? Can I come along?" He said yes. With that I put the receiver down.'

'How long had you known Spilkin?'

'Some years.'

'Did you know him when you were Mrs Cowle?'

'Yes.'

'Did Spilkin know you as Mrs Sproat?'

'Yes.'

'At any time when you were Mrs Sproat, did you deal at Spilkin's shop?'

'Often.'

She mentioned one occasion when, as Mrs Sproat and a widow, she made a purchase at Spilkin's.

'That was the day of the snowstorm,' she added.

'When Spilkin saw you on the day of the snowstorm, did he have any difficulty in recognising you?'

'No.'

She denied saying anything to Spilkin on the phone about poison or killing a cat, and said he had never suggested she should bring the cat to him to be killed. On her way back from lunch with Mrs Meaker, she went to the pharmacy.

'What happened in the shop?'

'Spilkin was serving a customer. As I entered, he said, "Good afternoon, Mrs Sproat." I stood back until he had finished serving the gentleman. Then he asked me what he could do for me, and I said that there were some cats that were an awful nuisance at the house. I said I wanted him to give me something to destroy them. He said, "Right-o!" and went to fetch something in the back of the shop.'

'Did you suggest any particular kind of poison?'

'No, I left it to him. He brought a small box with a little white label and some very fine writing on it with him. "This will fix them," he told me.'

'Did you know what was in the box?'

'No.'

'When did you know?'

'When he said in court that it was arsenic.'

Judge Greenberg: 'Didn't he tell you it was arsenic?'

'No.'

Morris continued.

'You signed the poison register DL Sproat. And gave the address as 67 Terrace Road. And Spilkin says he looked up in surprise. Did he do that?'

'No. I just said, "The usual address."'

'Who wrote the address?'

'He did. I just wrote DL Sproat and he said, "All right, I'll write the rest." Before leaving I also bought a bottle of aspirin.'

'Why did you give the name of DL Sproat?'

'Just force of habit.'

'Did you have any other accounts in the name of DL Sproat?'

'Yes. I've been running a number of accounts in that name even after I was married to Mr de Melker.'

'What address did you intend Spilkin to write down?'

'I intended him to write down 19 Simmer East.'

Morris asked if she knew Spilkin had written down her old address.

'No.'

'What time did you get home that afternoon?'

'About 4.15.'

'What did you do with the poison?'

'When I got home there were two cats on the verandah. There was nobody else at home. I went inside and threw my hat on the bed. Then I opened the parcel, quickly took out the little round box, and left it on the kitchen table. I went into the pantry and got a piece of steak. I cut it up and rolled some of the pieces of meat in the white powder. The pieces of meat with poison in I took onto the front verandah.'

'Where was the cat Fifi?'

'Shut in my bedroom, so that she should not get some of the meat.'

'What happened to the cats on the verandah?'

'The cat in the chair ate some of the meat. It remained there for a while. The other cat was still asleep on the floor. When I went out a second time, this cat jumped over the fence and I did not see it again. The other cat flew around the corner and went into the pit for the car in the garage, so I threw the rest of the meat down there.'

'What became of the cat?'

'I found it there the next morning and rolled it in a piece of sacking. Then I threw it in the dustbin.'

On 27 February, Rhodes came home late. He had a mark over his eye and said he had hit his head at work. The next day, Sunday, she found out about his fight with the African labourer Richard, and on the Monday she telephoned the garage to complain. On the Wednesday night, 3 March, after eating some of his supper, Rhodes went out. He made no complaint about his health. When he came back at 10.30 pm, he looked yellow and said he was sick. 'Have you been eating too many ice creams?' she asked. He laughed and said, 'You don't know how many ice creams I have had since Saturday.' She said: 'Ice creams and late nights do not agree with malaria.'

The next morning, the Thursday, he looked pale, but he attended court for a traffic offence and was fined one pound. She was present and paid the fine. He came home at about 12 pm and went to bed in the afternoon. That night he started to retch and vomit, but there was nothing in his condition to be alarmed about. On Friday morning, he seemed drowsy. At lunch time, Daisy said, she asked Eileen de Melker to telephone Dr Mackenzie. She stayed in Rhodes's room all night. About 9.30 the next morning she became alarmed at Rhodes's condition and went across to Mrs Brunton's house to phone for a doctor. She could not get Mackenzie, so Mrs Brunton suggested calling Dr Ferguson.

'It has been suggested that you did not concern yourself at all with Rhodes's illness that Saturday morning.'

'I was in the room nearly all the time and I did all I possibly could for the boy.'

After Rhodes's death, Dr Mackenzie said there would have to be a post-mortem.

'I said certainly. We went to the charge office to tell them, and the body was fetched at 3 pm.'

'That dear old lady, Mrs Brunton,' Morris said, poking fun at the prosecution's hostile witness, 'says you suggested to her that she should get in touch with Dr Ferguson and ask him for a death certificate. Did you make that suggestion?'

'It was she who made that suggestion.'

'Did you ever make any request to her to ring up Dr Ferguson?'

'No. She suggested phoning Dr Ferguson. I took it she didn't like the idea of the boy being hacked up.'

'Who made the custard for Rhodes while he was ill?'

'I made it on the Saturday morning and ate it myself because Rhodes didn't want it.'

'It is suggested that you put arsenic in Rhodes's Thermos flask on the Wednesday morning.'

'No.'

'Did you put arsenic in anything Rhodes had at any time?'

'No. I never had the arsenic to put in.'

*

Even by this, the fourth, week, Daisy's trial provided the newspapers with countless twists and turns, as good as any matinee serial at the bioscope, with headlines fit for purpose: 'What the Analyst Found', 'Poison Register Signed by DL Sproat', 'Evidence Causes a Stir', 'Mrs De Melker in Tears'. The poison, the scientists, the stray cats, the deathbed scenes, the flustered witnesses, the ghost of Rhodes haunting Daisy, the theatrical defence, the sobbing. It was the murder story that kept on giving.

Each of the three writers most involved in the case had their own take on it. The crime reporter Benjamin Bennett, the only true journalist among them, wasn't fooled by Daisy's performance: 'The calls to doctors and neighbours ... the wringing of hands as death hovered over her husbands and son, her tears afterwards – all this that was urged as proof of innocence was consistent also with a cunning to remove suspicion.'

Across the courtroom, in the jury box, Sarah Gertrude Millin thought of how this could all be turned into fiction. In the end, it wouldn't be far from the truth, and about her main character, named Julia, there was 'a fascination, a mystery. Without knowing it, one wanted to get at something in her, this mystery.'

Julia wouldn't be as plain as Daisy, but there would be three deaths, also two husbands and a son, and the reasons why she dispatched each one of them were what many people suspected. The first husband had become a financial burden through ill health, the second had something valuable to leave her and her son knew or suspected too much, and had become 'a penance to her peace of mind'.

Herman Charles Bosman, the third writer, even though he still hadn't set foot in court, was busy putting together his second pamphlet, a mixture of fact and fiction, with Daisy still the heroine of the story.

CHAPTER 66

Denials

When Cyril Jarvis began his cross-examination of Daisy on the morning of 10 November, her voice was tired and quickly grew to a hoarse whisper. Several times the wardress brought her hot milk, and Jarvis paused while she sipped at it.

Starting his questioning again, Jarvis raised all the suspicious occurrences that seemed to dog Daisy's life from the earliest: the death of her fiancé Bert Fuller, inheriting from him, the multiple deaths of her children, the wills she'd brought to Sproat and Rhodes.

'Is it true that you inherited something from Bert Fuller?' he asked.

'He made the will in the course of his illness. His brother told me about it afterwards.'

'When did Bert Fuller die?'

'March 3, the day we were supposed to have been married.'

'Are you quite sure?'

'Yes.'

'You see, I've got Bert Fuller's will here and it's dated March 4.'

There was a pause before she replied.

'We were supposed to have been married on the third and then we put it off to a later date.'

She came to Johannesburg in July 1908, she said, and got her money out of Fuller's estate in December.

Jarvis asked what happened to her twins.

'They were premature and weakly.'

'Did they have any convulsions?'

'I don't think so. The other children all had convulsions at teething.'

Jarvis put it to Daisy that her friend Selina Poplawski had said she'd noticed nothing wrong with Alfred Cowle on the Christmas Day they had come for lunch, yet he was dead only a few days later.

'She did notice and remarked on it,' Daisy insisted.

The morning Cowle died, he had tea that he prepared himself, and drank it after taking some Epsom salts.

'Did you mix the salts for him?' Jarvis asked.

'He mixed it himself, about a teaspoonful. I got it out of the scullery for him.'

After he had another cup of tea, the first attack came on. She said Cowle didn't seem to be in pain, though his face was haggard and drawn. He did not go 'stiff and rigid' or purple in the face, she said, nor was there any arching of his back.

'What led up to Dr Pakes asking the question about the salts?'

'He just asked what Cowle had taken.'

She denied that Pakes had asked for the salts and bottle to be given to the police for analysis.

'Why do you think Dr Pakes wanted to see the salts?'

'Just to see what kind they were.'

'You had a recollection of strychnine being mentioned. Did it not pass through your mind that he might have got it from the salts?'

'No.'

Her voice after an hour could barely be heard, and Judge Greenberg adjourned proceedings for 20 minutes to give her a rest. When she returned to the witness box, he suggested that a platform be erected so that she could sit in an easy chair.

Once she was more comfortable, Jarvis resumed. His questions jumped around from one detail to another, this time about Sproat's first illness, the will he had so hurriedly drawn up and how Daisy had come to have the blank will forms ready for him. She once again mentioned the now-deceased Mr Wharton, for whom she'd picked them up. *Why couldn't his wife have gone?* She was on holiday.

'Who made the first suggestion about this will?'

'William Sproat did, I think. He said he would see to it that I got everything. I said it would be just as well to get Bob to make a will properly.'

'Would it be wrong to say that you dictated what had to be filled in?'

'It was all on the printed form. He just had to fill in the names.'

The Saturday night before his death, Daisy testified, Sproat slept quite well, but on the Sunday morning he seemed languid and tired. He took some tonic. The rest of the day she was busy with the dinner, and Sproat was outside.

'You were not actually in the dining room when Sproat took ill?'

'No, I was in the kitchen. Sproat poured himself out some beer. He must have drunk it, for I saw the empty glass on the table. He had the beer from a bottle from which he'd had some the night before.'

'Did he say anything to you about this beer before having it?'

'No.'

'Did not the idea of it being connected with the beer cross your mind?'

'No.'

The questions about Rhodes threatening her and beating her once again brought tears to Daisy's eyes, and she repeatedly removed her big spectacles to wipe them away.

For his 19th birthday, in June 1930, she went to Swaziland to visit him and took the blank will form for him to sign.

'Why did you tell him to make a will?'

'Because I had seen the trouble friends of mine had when their sons died.'

'Did you think there was a chance of his dying?'

'No.'

'Did you think it essential for a young fellow like Rhodes [to have a will]?'

'Yes.'

'What did he have to leave?'

'Nothing.'

'What did he say when he saw the will form?'

'I filled it in and he signed it.'

'Didn't he express surprise?'

'No.'

'He just took it as a matter of course?'

'Yes.'

'Did you leave the will with him?'

'No, I brought it back.'

Increasingly, Daisy was tying herself in knots. The performance Morris had allowed her to give was wearing thin, mostly when it came to buying the arsenic, what happened afterwards and why she had kept it a secret.

Jarvis asked her about travelling more than ten miles across the city to Spilkin when she had a chemist named GF Pirie who had a shop nearby where she had done business before.

'He didn't know me as well as Spilkin.'

If she had gone to Pirie, Greenberg put it to her, wouldn't it have been a lot closer and quicker. Daisy agreed.

She said she had given Spilkin her old address, 67 Terrace Road, because it was a business address and 'force of habit'.

Jarvis corrected her: 'You said yesterday that you told him, "Just the usual address."'

'No, I said 67 Terrace Road.'

If, as she maintained, Spilkin hadn't explained the procedure to her, how had she known what to do with the arsenic?

'I thought I could just put it in milk or meat. My own common sense told me that cats ate meat ravenously.'

'Were you never interested to see what poison you'd bought?'

'No.'

'Wasn't there a printed label on the box?'

'No, there was not.'

Judge Greenberg: 'Why didn't you tell Spilkin that your name was De Melker?'

'Because he knew me as Sproat, and I was in a hurry to get home.'

After she had put down the poisoned meat for two cats, one of them ran into the motor car pit, she said. About 5.30 pm she went to look and found it was no longer there, nor was the meat. The next day she found the dead cat under a fig tree in the garden.

'Did you tell anyone you had given the cats poison?'

269

'I told Gordon Melville. I had an idea I told Mr de Melker. I may not have.'

'You didn't think it necessary to tell De Melker?'

'No.'

'Did you think it necessary to keep quiet?'

'Yes.'

'Why?'

'I don't know.'

'Poisoning cats was a thing you had never done before?'

'No.'

'It was an exceptional thing?'

'Yes.'

'But you didn't mention to De Melker that you had bought poison from Spilkin?'

'No.'

'Did you tell De Melker the next day that you had found a dead cat and thrown it into the dustbin?'

'No.'

'Why?'

'I don't know.'

'Did you ever tell him before your arrest?'

'Yes. I told them in a general way when they were cleaning the car.'

'That you had poisoned a cat?'

'That I had got rid of them.'

'Up to the time of your arrest, had you any idea that you were suspected of being connected with Rhodes's death?'

'No.'

'Or your husbands' deaths?'

'No.'

The journalist Benjamin Bennett noticed the change.

She had started the trial as a woman full of bravado, 'a suggestion of hardness and cunning that might be associated with one who has planned and executed a coldblooded crime' but was now someone unsure of herself: 'When her answers come, they are the wrong ones for an innocent woman.'

On Friday, 11 November, the end of the fourth week, for the first time something changed about the black-and-white outfit she wore every day. A red poppy had been attached to her lapel to commemorate Armistice Day.

Jarvis was unrelenting as he kept questioning her about Rhodes, the last day he was alive, the lunch and coffee she always prepared for him, the liniment he'd swallowed, other poisons in the house he could have used, the Thermos flask his coffee was in, the last time he threatened to kill himself.

'When he threatened to smash up his motorcycle,' Daisy recalled.

'What gave rise to that?'

'He was annoyed with me. He wanted me to go into town and see some two-seater cars.'

'With the idea of buying one?'

'Yes, for him.'

'Was he expecting to get a motor car?'

'He was always wanting one.'

'Was it ever suggested to him that he would get a car with the money from his endowment policy?'

'No.'

Rhodes lost consciousness on the Saturday morning, before Dr Ferguson arrived, and he never came to again.

'Then he did not say anything to anybody before he died?'

'No.'

'Did he say anything before he went unconscious?'

'No. He just told me not to leave him.'

'Mrs Brunton seems very definite that it was your suggestion that Dr Ferguson should be phoned and asked for a death certificate to avoid a post-mortem. You said it was not so.'

'It was not so.'

'Did Mrs Brunton suggest it to you herself?'

'Yes.'

'When?'

'Soon after Dr Mackenzie left.'

'In what way did she suggest it?'

'She said she would ring up Dr Ferguson, let him know the boy was dead, and see if he would not give a death certificate to avoid a post-mortem.'

Judge Greenberg: 'Where was that statement made and when?'

'I went back into the bedroom where Mrs Rowan and Mrs Brunton were. I said, "Don't touch the body. There's going to be a post-mortem." Mrs Brunton followed me out on to the verandah and it was then that she said it.'

'Who else was present?'

'Mr de Melker.'

'What was your state of mind towards a port-mortem?'

'I was quite willing.'

'Is there any reason you can suggest why Mrs Brunton should make up this evidence against you?'

'No.'

'Did Mrs Brunton come back and tell you the result of her conversation over the phone?'

'Yes, after we came back from the police station. She told me that Dr Ferguson had said he was surprised to hear the boy had died and that it was a good thing there was going to be a post-mortem, as it might save thousands of others.'

'Had you any thought in your mind before Detective Jansen came that you were going to be arrested?'

'No.'

'When he came to arrest you, it must have been a terrible shock?'

'It was.'

'Do you agree with what he says about your arrest?'

'Not with all.'

'Where do you suggest he was wrong?'

'I was terribly shocked and upset.'

'Jansen said, "I have come to arrest you for the murder of your son." He said this at the door. What did you say to that?'

'"Me?"'

'And then?'

'They were all talking. They followed me in. I called Mrs Melville and said, "Mia, they are accusing me of murdering Rhodes." Then I sat down and felt faint.'

'Didn't you ask how it was suggested you had murdered Rhodes?'

'No.'

'Didn't Jansen say it was by arsenic?'

'I was so taken aback, I was speechless.'

'Are you definite he didn't say that?'

'He may have.'

'Is it not possible he said that arsenic was found in the body?'

'Impossible.'

'What was the first time you remember arsenic being mentioned?'

'When I saw the constable writing it down in the book at the charge office.'

'What was written in the book that suggested arsenic to you?'

'I saw him write "administered" and I heard Jansen whisper in Dutch, "*Daar is nog een.*" [There is another one.] I didn't know if there was someone else he was arresting. I never associated it with myself.'

'He must have asked for a statement. You were in the dark about it?'

'Yes.'

'And you didn't think of finding out? I cannot understand the lack of desire on your part to know how it was suggested you had done this, innocent or not.'

'I could not understand it myself.'

'Did you want to know?'

'I tried not to think. I concluded it was poison when Jansen said he wanted to search for poison.'

'When did your purchase of arsenic of February 25 occur to you in connection with the charge?'

'I never knew I had purchased arsenic on February 25.'

'Well, poison. Did that occur to you?'

'Yes, when I spoke to [the lawyer] Mr Louw the day after my arrest.'

'You did not have in your mind the possibility of Rhodes having got any of that poison?'

'No.'

CHAPTER 67

Spirit of Fun

Like clockwork, the crowds gathered on the pavements along Pritchard Street that Friday to see the Black Maria drive off with Daisy locked inside – she had been under cross-examination by Jarvis for a total of 18 hours. Suddenly, the sky above them was filled with a mighty roar.

Peering into the sunlight, they saw a small plane head west towards the Rand Airport. The papers the next day explained that the plane was the *Spirit of Fun*. On board the world's fastest plane was MGM's Arthur Loew, who had flown 56 hours from Hong Kong over eight days to open the giant Metro cinema. *The Passionate Plumber* had by now made way for *Inspiration*, starring Greta Garbo.

Daisy, reading the newspapers every day, would have seen the story of the Hollywood producer placed right next to the ones about the trial. There was another story of how Loew, who boasted that it was he who had actually discovered Greta Garbo in Sweden and taken her to Hollywood, might have found another Garbo in Johannesburg. She was going to do screen tests at the African Film Productions studio in Killarney to be sent to Louis B Mayer of MGM, and she was being called 'the Rand Garbo'. To the Daisy who loved movies, who imagined her own life on screen, who was writing a scenario, this was perhaps as close to Hollywood as she would ever get.

The head of MGM in America, Arthur Loew (second from right), arrived on Spirit of Fun *at the Rand Airport just as trial was closing. The plane crashed at Victoria Falls a few days later.*

If Daisy had only known that it was her story, and not Loew's, that was being featured in papers around the world. Each one of them focused on some or other highlight of the past month: Julenda Brunton pointing to a nude girl on a medicine bottle before Rhodes died; the maid Dora Makhosi, who had worked for the De Melkers for ten months, saying she cleaned the house but Daisy had never let her do any of the cooking; Amy Sproat's explosive testimony about Daisy making Robert Sproat draw up a new will; Dr Mallenick siding with the defence, saying Sproat had died not of poison but of natural causes; the sighting of Rhodes's ghost in the De Melker house.

Now all that remained were the closing arguments of Cyril Jarvis and Harry Morris.

CHAPTER 68

Last words

The trial of Daisy de Melker, Cyril Jarvis began, was unique in the courts of South Africa, if not the world. There were three counts of murder, and each one had to be dealt with separately, but it was clear that there was 'evidence at all stages of the case which is common to one or two counts or to all three'.

Not long after Jarvis began his peroration – and it would take three days to complete – Greenberg showed what appeared to be a growing resistance to his arguments. It was a good sign for the defence. When the prosecutor said that Dr Pakes seemed to be sure Cowle's death was a result of strychnine poisoning, Greenberg replied that, to the contrary, Pakes did not appear to have formed anything like a definite opinion of strychnine. He either did not know as much at the time as he learned later on or 'his mental state now makes him think he knew more then'.

'It does not mean that he deliberately gave misleading evidence,' added Greenberg, 'but the conviction in his mind that it was strychnine might have affected his recollection. There is the possibility that at first he held that opinion very vaguely.'

Be that as it may, continued Jarvis, there was strychnine found in the body, and who other than Daisy had the likeliest chance of causing it to be there? She was alone in the house with Cowle and Rhodes; she prepared their food; and she gave Cowle the Epsom salts, which, just like strychnine, were bitter.

'But the case did not depend on this matter alone,' Jarvis said, and there were others also convinced of strychnine poisoning, in particular Professor Watt and the government pathologist Gilbert Britten.

Once again Greenberg interrupted him, saying that other people may not have drawn the same conclusion as Watt. Supposing – he put it to the prosecutor – that some of the symptoms, including those for opisthotonos, were excluded. How was the court to decide that Cowle's death must have been from strychnine poisoning?

'One of the strongest reasons is still left,' Jarvis said, 'the absence of any other cause of death.'

Greenberg asked Jarvis what he made of Mrs Balderow's claim that she had been told by Daisy a month or two earlier to be prepared for something happening at the Cowle home, to expect a call in the night.

'The publicity given by the accused might merely have been preparation for death.'

'Wouldn't it have been easier to call a neighbour over in the evening of the seizure?'

'It was a step to ensure a neighbour would be able to say there had been a previous seizure of that kind,' Jarvis said. 'Poisoning – unlike a murder committed with a weapon in a sudden passion – is a crime which must be thought out, which must be planned; the means must be considered and the opportunity created or sought for.'

The evidence of Pakes came up again an hour later, when Jarvis was reviewing the death of Cowle – and once again it gave Judge Greenberg pause.

If Pakes, who had attended to both husbands, had recognised strychnine poisoning, he asked Jarvis, would he not have been struck by the significance of how similar the second death was to the first?

'It depends on the degree of similarity of the features.'

'[Pakes] said the Cowle case made a very deep impression on his mind,' Greenberg put it to him. 'He said that as soon as he was asked about it, he remembered it ... Here are symptoms which you say are symptoms of strychnine poisoning. The sign [of similarity] never struck him. Is not that rather strange?'

Referring to Sproat's first illness, the judge was curious why Daisy would have tried to kill him even though his will had not yet been made out in her favour. In his opinion, Jarvis replied, it was quite possible that Daisy, with her medical knowledge, had administered just enough poison to take Sproat to the point of death where he would make a will.

Addressing the issue of Daisy having blank will forms on hand for Sproat to sign, Jarvis said he was reluctant to accept her explanation that she had got them for a 'Mr Wharton'. Wharton had also conveniently died in the intervening years – 'as in the case of most of the doctors who had attended on Cowle' – so he couldn't corroborate any of the testimony.

'On the face of it, it is rather extraordinary that a person should ask somebody else to obtain will forms for him in town.'

Greenberg said Daisy had explained that Wharton's work made it hard for him, and that she had also bought vests for him.

'There is nothing particularly embarrassing in asking a married woman to buy vests,' Jarvis said in disbelief, '[but] one might comb the universe and have some difficulty in finding a person who had bought will forms for another.'

And finally, Jarvis came to his strongest evidence – Rhodes – who, Harry Morris was arguing, had died either of malaria or, after many threats to do so, by his own hand.

'These threats – as far as witnesses who had no apparent motive for telling anything but the truth are concerned – seem to be of a rather vague kind. One might rather get the impression of Rhodes as being a young man who was fond of talking about himself, rather moody and "ratty" – and there might have been good reason for this. But taking the picture as a whole, is it not that of a captious, spoilt boy, not too fond of work, and giving vent to utterances which are a bit on the startling side?'

Outside of the liniment episode, he said, Rhodes didn't really try to kill himself. Indeed, he could have swallowed the whole bottle of liniment if he'd wanted to. He could have ridden in front of a train or into a tree a long time ago.

Daisy, meanwhile, had motive and opportunity for getting rid of her son. He was a thoroughly disagreeable, moody, sulky boy who treated her as no boy should treat his mother; and she was the one who fed him and made him coffee to take to work daily. She could also quite easily have given Rhodes a second dose of arsenic on the Saturday morning in the custard. She had also presented him with a will he hadn't asked for.

'He might agree to sign it,' Jarvis said, 'but that he would express no surprise at the idea of making a will is rather extraordinary.'

Judge Greenberg, who had been silent for a while, spoke again, siding, if not with Daisy, then questioning the evidence against her. *Could Selina Poplawski maybe have been mistaken when she said she heard Daisy say that Rhodes would never get this £500 endowment policy?*

'They were in a travelling car, after all,' he added.

Could Julenda Brunton maybe have been wrong when she claimed she was alone at Rhodes's deathbed?

'If the accused had administered the poison,' Greenberg put it to Jarvis, 'might she not have wanted to be in attendance to hear whether anything suspicious was said?'

Greenberg also – quite astonishingly – raised possible reasons why Daisy might have signed the wrong name in the poison register.

'If Mrs de Melker wanted to give a name which would mask her identity,' he said, 'why didn't she give Spilkin the name by which he knew her [Cowle]? ... According to Spilkin, she had spoken to him as Mrs Cowle that morning, and it would be fresh in her memory. Why should she not have adhered to that name? ... If it was involuntary, then there is nothing sinister in her giving him the wrong name.'

'The sinister part,' replied Jarvis, 'is in not giving the name of De Melker. Her own chemist Pirie was close at hand, and no one else in the house knew of it. Mr de Melker had no knowledge of it until the preparatory exam.'

Jarvis said Spilkin must have realised how serious it was to give evidence that would damn the accused. In the light of that evidence, and Daisy's denial of it, one could come to no other conclusion than the poison had not been bought for a sick cat but for some other purpose she had in mind.

'What do you say was the motive?' asked Greenberg.

'I say the motive would privately be monetary.'

'For a mere £100?' Greenberg asked.

Jarvis nodded, adding, 'In cases recorded there are instances of mothers dealing with children in this way for a monetary motive infinitely less than £100.'

'Assuming guilt on the third count [of Rhodes], does it throw any light on the second count [Sproat]?' Greenberg asked.

Jarvis, once again referring to the rule of similar fact evidence, like the 'Brides in the Bath' case, was adamant that it did.

'The similar circumstances warrant application to the other case,' he said. 'The fact that there was death by poisoning in one case would be used to strengthen the decision that there was poisoning in the second case. The person benefits in similar circumstances. In one instance death is due to poisoning. In the other instance when you get near to poisoning and the person benefits and the circumstances are sufficiently similar, you are entitled to say it strengthens the case that it was also poisoning.'

Greenberg was unconvinced, calling it 'a dangerous and ambiguous guide'.

'What is perfectly clear in this case is that, taking it as a whole, the case is one of circumstantial evidence. It must of necessity be based on circumstantial evidence. Cases of this kind where poisoning is alleged almost invariably are. Poisoning is not done with witnesses present. It is the easiest of all types of crime to succeed in doing with the presence of witnesses.

'If there is a gap through which the accused is entitled to escape,' said Jarvis, 'then, of course, she must escape. But if the net of evidence is woven so close and so coherent in texture that no evidence on her part can enable her to react through, then there must be a conviction.'

It was impossible to imagine at the start of the case, in the small court with the Greek temple entrance in Germiston, six months earlier, but the odds were now more than even that Daisy would be acquitted.

CHAPTER 69

An ocean of investigation

At 3.30 pm that afternoon, after Jarvis had ended his closing argument after 13 hours, Harry Morris began his, which would take even longer.

Daisy's case, he began with his rasping voice, was an 'ocean of investigation' that he had set out upon. But now that it was coming to a close, he focused his attention on one particular facet, the third and final death – Rhodes Cecil Cowle. Unlike Jarvis, Morris did not go through the charges chronologically, and some read this as a further sign that he was quite sure Daisy would be acquitted of the first two.

'The Crown has not proved that either Rhodes or his fellow worker Webster had suffered from arsenical poison.'

Webster, who had eaten half a dozen bananas, simply had indigestion, Morris said. He dismissed Professor Watt's evidence about the poison in both victims as 'lopsided', for he hadn't considered the bananas that Webster had eaten for lunch. Watt, furthermore, had never in his life seen a case of arsenic poisoning.

'My suggestion is that Webster was suffering from an ordinary stomach ache, which was cured by household remedies.'

As for the arsenic in Webster's hair and nails, Morris added, the analyst Gilbert Britten had done his work in a very slipshod fashion.

'I am not suggesting this boy [Webster] is a liar, but that under the influence of suggestion he has got a story which he is confusing with the facts. He has transferred to Rhodes, quite unconsciously, symptoms from which he himself was suffering.'

Morris said that Rhodes died of malaria or some other natural condition. Dr Mackenzie himself had declared cerebral malaria the cause of death.

'Dr Watt says that is not so,' countered Greenberg.

Morris, once again dismissing Watt's conclusion, continued. Several recurring bouts of malaria from 1930 onwards had affected the young man badly, and 'Mrs de Melker said that he then appeared to have changed entirely and was not only queer but became worse.'

If indeed he had ingested poison, Morris said, then it was almost certainly by his own hand, and for one of various reasons.

'First, that Rhodes took arsenic as a result of physical or mental depression; secondly that he took it in a vain hope that it would cure him of a disease which he probably thought was malaria. My submission on the evidence is that Rhodes started and ended his life with a diseased mind.'

Greenberg asked why, if Rhodes was so intent on killing himself, he had stopped drinking the liniment.

'Because, fundamentally, he was a coward,' Morris said, and then referred to Rhodes's repeated threats and failed attempts to put his head through doors and windows.

'Is it not remarkable,' Greenberg put it to him, 'that these paroxysms only took place in his home?' They were limited to the house and limited to the time when Mr de Melker was away.'

Morris said that Rhodes's frequent references to the fact that he was getting money or a car from his endowment led one to the conclusion that he was also suffering from a modified form of megalomania.

Greenberg asked if there was not in Rhodes's mind the idea that he had some sort of claim to his father's estate.

'Would that, standing by itself, be a motive for murdering him?' Morris countered.

'Must one not consider the possibility?' Greenberg said. Perhaps Rhodes was using threats in connection with the deaths of Cowle and Sproat.

Morris said there were rumours and gossip that this was the case, but Rhodes had also been a lot younger at the time of his father's death, possibly too young to even remember the circumstances.

'My suggestion is that every individual is a potential suicide. As the philosopher says, "When the cares of life are greater than the terrors of death, you have that suicidal condition." Rhodes had a motive for wanting to end his life. Mrs de Melker apparently had no motive.'

Judge Greenberg asked Morris where Rhodes got the poison from.

'That is a difficulty,' he replied. 'But it seems to me that there is no insuperable obstacle to his having got poison. He may have got it indirectly.'

Greenberg wasn't convinced.

'One cannot shut one's eyes to the publicity this case has received, and if any chemist had supplied him with poison, is it conceivable he would not have come forward?'

Morris shook his head. To the contrary, he said, he doubted whether any chemist or person who knew of a purchase of poison would come forward to help the defence and Daisy. That person might be silent 'under a conviction of fear'.

Whenever he could, he drew a sympathetic portrait of the woman the entire country hated, pointing out how she had quickly summoned neighbours and doctors, showed generosity to her son and lavished love on him, shed many tears afterwards, all pointing to the impossibility of having been able to murder him.

Only a few days before his death, Daisy had remonstrated with the garage proprietor Robert Short about the fight Rhodes had been in with another employee; she had also made a 'tidy', a birthday gift, for his girlfriend, Doreen Legg; and she had accompanied him to court and paid his traffic fine.

'It was so highly improbable as to render it impossible that Mrs de Melker had administered poison to him.'

It was the Crown's suggestion, he said, that on Friday 4 March, she had 'prepared her victim for the sacrifice, but then she invites an eyewitness [Mia Melville] to the slaughter'. The young man could easily have said something to her if he believed his mother was trying to kill him. 'I submit that [Daisy's] conduct is inconsistent with a criminal purpose. The same goes with the calling of Dr Mackenzie.'

'If she hadn't done so,' Greenberg argued, 'would it not have given rise to adverse criticism?'

'It seems to be inexplicable that at the period she was ready to commit murder, she called in a doctor.'

But if she hadn't, Greenberg carried on, she might have had trouble getting a death certificate, which was something 'she was acquainted with in her earlier history'.

'But the fact remains that on Friday, Dr Mackenzie had diagnosed a perfectly good cause of death. Gastric flu. This calling in of three doctors seems inconsistent with the diabolical plot she is suggested to have conceived on February 25.'

*

By the beginning of the last day of his closing argument, Morris's energy was flagging badly, more than anyone could see, but he hid it well. Now, more than ever, he must have felt, as he was later described, 'oppressed by a sense of isolation and loneliness'.

He had been through the details of each death, the illnesses and afflictions of the husbands, the original diagnoses of the doctors, the improbability of Pakes being able to recall Cowle's death after nine years, sudden changes to diagnoses, the lack of motive. Cowle was the father of Daisy's children, and was steady, industrious, even-tempered and always employed. She might have inherited money and property upon his death, but she would also be deprived of a wage earner. As for the suggestion that Daisy administered just enough the first time to make Sproat ill so he could change his will, that was impossible.

'If the medical witnesses in this case are any criterion as to the knowledge of poison, then her knowledge must have been infinitesimal.'

Morris dismissed the Crown's witnesses as being heavily against his client. First, the multiplicity of the charges against her weighed on their minds. Second, a number of facts might have influenced them, especially when the charge was so heinous and despicable. Finally, they perhaps developed a bias in favour of the charge, a need to stand by one another.

'What is the Crown case? It is that a mother bound her son, and her only son, to his bed with the paralysing fetters of arsenic; that she then remorselessly and callously and cruelly slaughtered him; that she stood by and watched while he writhed in the agony of poison; that she even derived some satisfaction from it? That cannot be. It is an utter negation of her twenty years of care, attention, and solicitude. It is contrary to the maternal instinct which is protective and not destructive, and contrary to human nature.'

CHAPTER 70

Tickets to see the end

From early that week, a story about another woman had been vying with Daisy's for the headlines. Amy Johnson, the celebrated British pilot, was to take part in a solo transcontinental air race.

Early on 14 November, as closing arguments at the trial were starting, Johnson took off from Lympne, in Kent. It took Jarvis and Morris almost the same time to make their arguments as it did for Johnson to fly across Africa. As her aircraft, *Desert Cloud*, was passing west of Johannesburg four days later, Harry Morris was uttering his final words about the impossibility of Daisy slaughtering her only son. He had been speaking for almost 16 hours, and the trial had already stretched over 39 days. The court adjourned for the weekend.

On the following Monday, with clouds massing over Johannesburg for a summer storm earlier than usual in the day, the crush around the Criminal Sessions was more severe than ever. As always, people camped outside the previous night, and there was a booming trade in places in the queue, the price depending on how close to the court entrance they were, ranging from 5s to £1 15s (the price for an ounce of gold that day was £6 7s). All around one could hear bets being taken on the verdict.

Women outnumbered men by five to one, and Sarah Gertrude Millin and Jenny Greenberg had been joined by Ethel Hayman, the wife of another barrister. The other jury seats were taken by 'fashionably dressed women', the wives of barristers and court officials. Squeezed into the press box with Benjamin Bennett were 13 other journalists. The news would be published across the world, in *The Boston Globe* and *The New York Times*, *The Scotsman* and *The Times* of London. Policemen stood at every door. Passages and the vestibule were crowded, and the air was noisy with the screams and protests of those who jostled for a seat.

The first thing they would have noticed was that two of the most important actors were missing – Harry Morris and Cyril Jarvis. What could it possibly mean? Did Morris already know he had won, and so didn't feel it necessary to be there? Had Jarvis lost the most sensational of murder trials? Or was it the other way around?

The truth was simpler. Jarvis had the flu, and Morris, exhausted, had asked Greenberg if he could be excused. It had been the longest and most challenging trial, not to mention the most poorly paid, he'd ever been in. At his place behind the long lawyers' table sat Issie Maisels.

When Daisy entered the court, dressed, as always, in the black mourning outfit she'd worn for Rhodes's funeral, she looked haggard. She had not changed her clothes in six weeks. She seemed to have aged considerably in that time, the lines around her eyes deep and grey, and the 'aggressive courage' she had started with was nowhere to be seen. Looking at the door through which Greenberg and his assessors were to arrive, she seemed almost unaware of the crowd and mechanically sipped at a glass handed to her by one of the guards.

Judge Greenberg, after the court came to order, began by complimenting Harry Morris on what he had achieved, casting a very real shadow of doubt over at least two of the three murder charges. For the following three hours and 18 minutes, he summed up the case.

It was quite possible that Daisy had poisoned Sproat and Cowle, he said, but there were things that bothered him. To use strychnine, one needed only a minuscule amount to kill someone, and a special machine to measure such a tiny amount. How had Daisy got it right to give Sproat enough not to kill him but just to afflict him, so that he could change his will? Then there was the fact that she had called in Dr Pakes three times, despite the chance that he would notice similar signs in the patients and suspect that poison might have been used.

'If she did intend to poison Sproat,' he said, 'one would have thought that she would have chosen a poison which did not produce similar symptoms.'

She had also called in the same set of neighbours.

'These points are not conclusive,' Greenberg said, 'but they are points which create some doubt on the aspects of the case other than the medical.'

The mood in the court changed quickly. Millin and Greenberg's wife sat still, realising there was a good chance that the accused could be set free. Daisy never took her eyes off the judge, her knuckles as white as the handkerchief she was clenching.

Greenberg dealt with Jarvis's contention, on the basis of the rule of similar fact evidence, that the two counts of strychnine poisoning could 'lend support to each other; that one may fill up the gaps in the other case'. He mentioned three cases that had been raised: the 'Baby Farming case' of 1894, *Makin v Attorney General for New South Wales*; the 'Brides in the Bath' case, *Rex v Smith* of 1915; and *Rex v Armstrong*, of 1922, which involved a man who had made up small packets of arsenic allegedly to kill weeds but strong enough to kill a person, and had used one on his wife and then, eight months later, on someone else. In all three cases, Greenberg said, the courts had found that a prima facie case of murder had been made out against the accused, apart from the additional evidence, but here that did not exist.

'In the present case there were two deaths and the cause of death is not proved independently in either ... The position, therefore, with regard to the first and second counts is that the Crown evidence neither convinces nor does it convict the accused, and the accused must be found not guilty.'

Whispers of horror shot through the gallery like lightning. Maisels heard the people outside the court too, as word of the verdict reached them. Daisy bowed her head. An attendant handed her a glass of water, which she sipped, murmuring her thanks.

'I turn now to the last charge, that of the murder of Rhodes Cecil Cowle on March 5 of this year.'

A peal of thunder rang out above the Supreme Court, almost drowning out his words.

'Rhodes Cowle died of arsenical poisoning and the coffee was the source from which he received the arsenic that caused his first indisposition. The next question is: who was responsible for the presence of arsenic in that coffee?'

'Mr Morris has argued that we are all potential suicides, but the potentiality is reduced to nothing in the case of Rhodes Cowle. The case is stronger against suicide than if there had been no evidence at all. If there were not suicide, did the poison get into the flask through accident on the part of Rhodes? There is nothing in the evidence to suggest that possibility. According to the evidence of the prisoner, there was no arsenic in the house. I cannot see how it could have got there accidentally.'

As for Rhodes's threats to do away with himself, Greenberg didn't believe them: 'Such things might be said by a youth to give him the blasé air of a man of the world, a feeling of superiority, induced in some measure, no doubt, by a recent visit to England. It was inconceivable that he would poison himself and his friend. Neither was there anything to suggest that the poison had got into the flask accidentally.'

Now and again Daisy sank back wearily in her chair, her head resting on a brown coat thrown over its back. At other times she brought her hand to her head and leaned forward to rest on the rail of the dock.

Greenberg spoke then of her relationship with her son.

'I do not wish to make the matter any more painful than I can help, but Rhodes's treatment of his mother was abominable ... He showed the greatest disinclination to work. I think there was every prospect of his becoming a burden on her ... The occupations in which he had been engaged were blind alleys and would not have enabled him to support himself. I do not think he was capable of qualifying himself for a better occupation.'

Daisy pressed her hands to her face, bent forward and sobbed, her whole body shaking. Soon she was composed again. More peals of thunder rumbled and the sky darkened outside, rendering the court dark and rightly subdued. The lights were turned on by an orderly.

Greenberg addressed the question of motive. Where it was sentimental or subjective, he said, it was difficult to prove and even to discover.

'Although the question is of great importance, proof is not always essential.'

He recalled how Rhodes was looking forward to a car on his 21st birthday and how he might well 'make himself a nuisance' if he did not get it. When the judge said Daisy clearly had a fondness for money, she shook her head slowly in disagreement. When he said that with her lay the opportunity of administering the poison, she pressed her hands to her face again and, bending forward, sobbed bitterly. As she did so, some of the women in court stood up to watch her.

'I can see no escape from the conclusion that the accused put arsenic into the flask,' Greenberg announced. 'It is unnecessary to decide whether that was the fatal dose or not. If it was, she is responsible. If it was not, and subsequent doses were given when Rhodes was ill, it is inconceivable anyone else could have done so. The only conclusion I can come to is that the accused is guilty on this charge.'

Daisy raised her head and groped for the railing in front of her. Asked if she had anything to say, she rose uncertainly to her feet and uttered one sentence, 'I am not guilty of poisoning my son.'

As she remained standing, Greenberg continued.

'There is only one sentence I can pass ... That you be taken ... and hanged by the neck until you are dead. And may God have mercy on your soul.'

People in the gallery jumped to their feet to watch one last time as Daisy was led out, although the policemen left her to walk unassisted down the stairs to the holding cells.

Sidney de Melker, Eileen and one of Daisy's sisters were allowed to see her before she was taken outside, a heavy police presence on hand for the last time. As she got into the Black Maria, the sound of a thousand people booing and hissing filled the streets near the Criminal Sessions.

Back at the jail on Hospital Hill, the black dress she had worn for the trial was taken away and in exchange she received the outfit of a white female prisoner, a blue sweater and black woollen stockings with a red stripe just below the knee and a pair of heavy second-hand buckskin shoes several sizes too large for her. Almost resembling a schoolgirl, she was transferred to the place of execution – Pretoria Central.

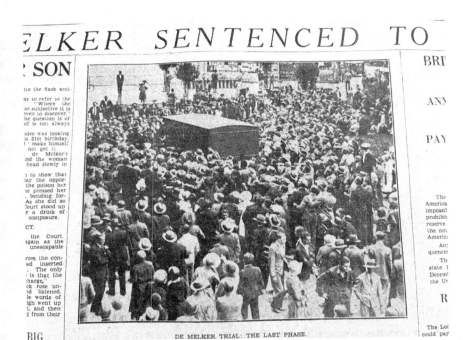

Crowds gathered around the Black Maria as it took Daisy away from court after the verdict.

CHAPTER 71

Abandoning hope

The news, as expected, was printed around the world. In *The Times* of London, Daisy found herself lodged between the 'German Crisis, Nazi Suspicions', the Disarmament Conference in Geneva and talks at the League of Nations about the Japanese invasion of Manchuria. The *Rand Daily Mail* and *The Star* devoted entire pages to Judge Greenberg's decision under banner headlines: 'Text of the De Melker Poison Trial Judgment'. People couldn't get enough.

A week later, a large crowd of women were at the Supreme Court again, hoping to see Daisy one more time, 'but they were doomed to disappointment, as she did not make an appearance'. After a brief hearing, it was ruled that Robert Sproat's will had been irregularly witnessed and was invalid.

A sum of more than £4 000 was ordered to be paid to the executors of Jane Sproat's estate in England. But Daisy had neither money nor property for attachment, for her four properties, worth £3 640, had all been mortgaged. So her estate was sequestrated.

Her name quickly dropped from the headlines. South Africa was about to abandon the gold standard – 15 months after Great Britain, and even though gold production had reached a peak of almost 12 million ounces, valued at £49 million – and was facing the worst drought in living memory. In Germany, President Paul von Hindenburg had started negotiations for a new cabinet with Adolf Hitler.

When Daisy's name came up again, it was because Herman Bosman published his second pamphlet, 'Mrs de Melker Under the Gallows'. In perhaps the first piece of actual reporting he had done for the case, he went to interview Sidney de Melker at the house in Simmer East where Rhodes had died, 'which looked ominous in the dusk. It seemed as if a blight lay over it.' He couldn't see his way to physically going inside.

'If I agitate for a new trial for Mrs de Melker for a reprieve,' he told De Melker, full of bravado and his own sense of self-importance, 'I know it will be granted. The nation must hear me.'

'A new trial?' De Melker replied in astonishment. 'Who is going to pay for a new trial? I haven't got any money.'

And that, for Bosman, was the end of that.

'When I went away from Germiston, I realised how intensely lonely Mrs de Melker was. I also understood, in a terrible kind of way, that now I had given up my idea of intervention, Mrs de Melker could abandon all hope. It all depended on me. And I decided to do nothing about it.'

Almost as a premonition of Daisy's execution, Bosman imagined the last day of another murderess, Dorothea Kraft, who had killed Louis Tumpowski. She 'looked magnificent on the morning of her execution', he wrote lyrically. 'Her long dark hair hung loose down her back, halfway to her ankles. They wanted to give her brandy. She declined with a wave of her hand ...'

Because the gallows were in the men's section of Pretoria Central, Kraft walked 'a considerable distance' from where she was held. Daisy would take the same route.

'To this day the warders and convicts in the Pretoria Central Prison will tell you how [Kraft] looked. She held her head well up, not proudly, not scornfully, but with the quiet dignity of a queen ... Once, in a film at the Bijou I saw the wife of a Zulu chief who walked like that. But there is no other queen alive in the world today who can walk amongst her subjects as [Kraft] walked between the warders on the gallows path.

'[Kraft] was hanged, and in being hanged she graced even the gallows. Many were pleased that day that they were not the hangman. And the warders who were present at the execution, and the prison governor, and even the doctor, were afraid to look at one another. It was as though each felt guilty at having been caught by the other in an act of shame.

'These stories of the gallows – these half-laughs with the hangman – will terrify Mrs de Melker long before they come to take her weight in order to calculate the height she has to drop, long before they measure the circumference of her neck in order to work out the size of the noose.'

On Christmas Eve 1932, Governor General George Villiers refused to grant a pardon or a reprieve or otherwise to exercise the Royal Prerogative of Mercy in respect of Daisy Louisa Hancorn Smith/Cowle/Sproat/De Melker. Harry Morris made a personal appeal to the minister of justice, but the decision of the Governor General could not be altered. 'No poisoner is ever reprieved,' Harry later wrote. Sidney and Eileen de Melker were summoned to the prison. The Bishop of Pretoria ministered to her, and gave her communion and a crucifix.

On 30 December, three days before the seventh anniversary of Daisy's marriage to Robert Sproat, preparations began early at Pretoria Central. The sun would have risen by five already, and prisoners were woken by a clanging bell at 5.30. After that, if Daisy should ask anyone the time, she was not to be told. An orderly offered her a tot of brandy, and the sheriff quoted the terms of her sentence.

The male convicts, who were normally marched through the hall at 7 am for breakfast, were kept locked in their cells until she had been led through. With a warder walking on either side of her, they walked the same route as Dorothea Kraft and finally reached double doors, behind which stood the scaffold. The bishop stood motionless in prayer, and Daisy clasped to her breast the crucifix he had given her.

'Tell my family your crucifix has been a great comfort to me during the last few days,' she said.

She entered the windowless whitewashed chamber, where from a beam hung six chains, each one tied to a ring. From one dangled a white plaited cord with a noose at the end. Daisy was placed on a pair of footmarks painted on the floor, and a cap was drawn over her head and eyes. The silence through the prison was uncanny, and the prisoners nearby could hear the fall of the trap door quite distinctly.

Within a few hours of her execution, a small group of relatives, including Sidney, Eileen and her sister Fanny McLachlan, stood by her grave in the English section of Brixton Cemetery, where her two husbands and her son lay buried. Her third husband put a bunch of white carnations on the simple coffin as it was lowered into the ground.

Afterword

The idea for Daisy and the killers came about by accident. She was a character in another book that I was researching, but suddenly I found myself taking an ever-lengthening detour to find out more about her. The more I dug into the Johannesburg of that time – a place rich in characters and stories, as it turned out – I started stumbling across other fascinating killers and charlatans, and the people who crossed their paths. Then, quite curiously, I started finding connections between many of them.

In my mind, I sometimes concocted a kind of genealogical chart – a criminal family tree, if you will – linking all the characters: Foster to Gibson to Morris to Schmulian back to Foster. Gibson to Hermanus Swarts to Dorothea Kraft to police chief Trigger to Irene Kanthack to Stephen Black to Bosman to Millin to Daisy and back to Morris again. The links and overlaps were just too incredible to pass up writing about.

That all of them lived during such a fecund time in Johannesburg's history made it all the more appealing. It is easy to forget that the city was trying to set itself up as one of the great metropolises of the world, and for a time it almost did. There was no place like it on the continent. And in the league of criminals and con artists, it was up there with the most notorious cities in the world, with a signature all its own.

Daisy herself remains largely an enigma, for whatever didn't come out at her trial was never made known. Certain books proved invaluable to me, mostly those by Benjamin Bennett, who was a crime reporter for the Argus newspapers at the time. Of all the crimes he covered, Daisy clearly fascinated him the most. And one can see why.

In today's age of social media, celebrities and movies, it is incredible to see how Daisy pre-empted it almost one hundred years ago. She was very aware of the newspapers, how she appeared in them, in word and picture, how people outside court reacted to her, and her celebrity. What happened to her film scenario, like so many things about her life, remains a secret.

As for the cast of characters, they each went their very different ways.

After her execution, Daisy's possessions were sold at auction. A man who bought a small radio couldn't get it to work and took it to a repair shop. Inside was found a small envelope with the words 'For dear old Sid' written on top. It contained a white powder, which the police analysed and found to be arsenic.

In the death notice of Sidney Clarence de Melker, who died at the age of 69 in 1953, Daisy's name was not mentioned.

If Harry Morris had actually succeeded in getting Daisy freed, another obstacle waited for her outside the court. A group of men dressed in khaki were waiting to arrest her. They were members of the British South Africa Police from Bulawayo, who were to take her to Rhodesia to be charged with the murders of three other people: her fiancé Bert Fuller, her uncle and one other person who wasn't identified.

If one included these three people and her children, it would have brought the number of Daisy's possible victims to ten.

Harry Morris had no doubt that Daisy killed Rhodes but wasn't sure if she'd done it with arsenic or some other poison. Nor did he believe she had done it for the endowment policy, but rather because he was the one person who could raise serious suspicions about her. There was a good chance he had seen things she had done to Cowle and Sproat, and when he didn't get what he expected when he turned 21, he might turn on her. In his memoir, Morris discussed the other four boys' deaths, and although he wouldn't comment on whether he thought Daisy had killed them, he wondered why Rhodes was spared, 'unless it was because he was the sturdiest of the lot'. Daisy, he said, 'was anxious to have a daughter'. In a cryptic remark, he added, 'Her next victim was to have gone about the time of her trial.' The likelihood was that it was Sidney de Melker.

In 1941, Morris travelled to Kenya to try what would become his most celebrated case, representing Sir Henry Delves Broughton, who was accused of murdering his wife's lover, the Earl of Erroll. The case brought to greater attention the infamous 'Happy Valley' set and was later made famous in the book, and then the film, *White Mischief*. Thanks to Harry, and his 'vital' knowledge of firearms, Broughton was acquitted. Asked afterwards if he thought that his client was guilty, Morris replied, in typical fashion, 'You know, dammit, I forgot to ask him.'

By the end of his career he had, in his estimation, taken part in at least 10 000 trials. His personal favourite, his 'royal flush', as he called it, remained his defence of the taxi-driver killer Dicky Mallalieu.

By 1947, with his eyesight failing him terribly, Morris's practice had declined so much that he did not receive a single brief. He died in October 1954. Justice WH Ramsbottom later said Morris had proved himself to be one of the great lawyers of his generation, and at his graveside it was said of him: 'He was a gallant defender of men.' He has often been referred to as 'the great defender', the name by which the English barrister Edward Marshall Hall had been known.

Sarah Gertrude Millin went on to see her thinly disguised novel based on Daisy's life published as *Three Men Die*. She also wrote a play about it. In her autobiography, she called Greenberg's speech at the end of Daisy's trial 'an expression of eternal justice – beautiful'. Morris also included the entire decision at the end of his autobiography.

Millin is barely remembered today, and if she is it is often with scorn for her views on race and miscegenation, set out most clearly in *God's Stepchildren*. Her biographer, Martin Rubin, questions why a woman so perceptive and intelligent was obsessed by the subject: 'One can in part blame her extremely limited education, which included no training in the social sciences and little in historical methods, yet Sarah Gertrude proved her ability to rise above her lack of education in other fields. One might attribute it also to life in a society impregnated with prejudice, but one must still wonder why Sarah Gertrude was unable to rise above the biases which were so common in the milieus where she lived.'

The Nobel Prize winner Nadine Gordimer, a fellow Jewish female

South African writer, described Millin as both 'remarkable' and 'a monster'. But Gordimer also said, in a speech in 1981, 'I think the day is coming when our emotional reaction to *God's Stepchildren* will be confined to its rightful place, and the novel will be examined again for what it is: an extraordinarily powerful and truthful unconscious depiction of the roots of apartheid's dishonesty, an establishment moral construct of prejudice, historically important to be set against the exposé of racialism that was thrust into an unwilling South African consciousness ...'

Millin's husband, Philip, became a Supreme Court judge but, quite shockingly, died of a heart attack in court, in the middle of a trial.

Herman Charles Bosman became one of the country's most famous authors of fiction. His prison experiences formed the basis for his semi-autobiographical book *Cold Stone Jug*. Bosman's books have never been out of print since 1951, when he died childless at the age of 46. Many of his works and watercolours were bought by the University of Texas in Austin.

Stephen Black remains one of the most overlooked (if not totally forgotten) artists South Africa has ever produced, partly because he defied categories: boxer, sports writer, journalist, screenwriter, novelist, playwright, iconoclast, bohemian, crusader and supporter of black writers such as Sol Plaatje and RRR Dhlomo. He is often called the first South African-born English playwright. Because he was always updating his plays, to keep them current with the latest news and vernacular, none of them were ever published. He died in August 1931 of liver cancer, and Bosman and Blignaut headlined the front page of their copycat magazine on 17 August with 'Stephen Black – The Man'. In a page-long paean to Black, they ended with the words, 'Sleep on, Stephen. You shall not be forgotten.'

The murder of Irene Kanthack remains unsolved.

After he was found not guilty of murdering Arthur Kimber, Dicky Mallalieu faced numerous other charges, mostly for forgery and fraud. But he and Gwen Tolputt were ordered to be deported, and after being escorted to Cape Town they were put on the *Llandaff Castle* in September 1932 and taken back to England.

The habitual criminal Andrew Gibson, when he last saw Harry Morris, swore to never commit a crime again. He returned to England, where, after he served his time in Bournemouth Prison, was sentenced in 1940 to ten years for manslaughter and forgery, in connection with the death of a woman after an abortion he'd performed, and for subsequently faking her death certificate. His medical shenanigans had finally caught up with him. He was 80 at the time, and had spent at least 46 of those years behind bars.

Notes

The following notes refer to the passage in which the reference occurs in the text. Full references to sources may be found in the References section.

CHAPTER 1

Page 6

Texas Jack John Baker 'Texas Jack' Omohundro had come across the five-year-old and his sisters after their parents were killed by Native Americans, and adopted them.

He took to selling liquor Most of the illicit liquor selling was done by 'poor whites (who bought a bottle and quickly sold it, usually for at least one hundred percent profit, usually to Africans) and Assyrians ... who dealt in car-loads of liquor ... and traded in the slum areas', according to Arthur N Wilson's 'The Underworld of Johannesburg', which appeared in Allister Macmillan's *The Golden City: Johannesburg*, published in 1933. Wilson was a crime reporter for *The Star*.

'This started him on a career of crime' See Wilson, 'The Underworld of Johannesburg'.

Page 9

Their routine was 'deadly monotony' Lago Clifford, article in *The Sjambok*, 1929.

Page 10

Charles Ernest Chadwick This was, according to some, Gibson's real name.

Page 11

falsity This was a word often used when the charge dealt with defamation.

'he must have been good company' Harry Morris, *The First Forty Years: Being the Memoirs of HH Morris, KC* (1948).

CHAPTER 2

Page 14

'the sentinel to the gates of hell' So hated were the magnates that in December 1913, Sir Lionel Phillips, one of the most important of them, was shot by an assassin while he walked from the Corner House to the Rand Club, just a few hundred yards away. The man, a mining trader named Misnun, described as a 'slightly built Russian Jew', was quickly apprehended. Asked why he did it, he replied, 'I did it because the mining people have twice ruined me.' Phillips, who was shot in the lung and liver, survived (*The Gold Fields*, 13 December 1913).

The Cowles could afford a maid Salaries for domestic workers were so low that even the most modest homes could afford one.

CHAPTER 3

Page 24

Even as he killed Mynott When the police arrived in Regents Park, they found the house in disarray, 'littered with stale bread and old newspapers'. Clothes lay scattered about, as did the gang's trademark disguises, false moustaches and cheeks, strands of fake hair, beards and tubes of face paint and dyes. On the washing line hung the dried meat they had prepared for their escape.

Page 25

He had seen the number 15 See Wilson, 'The Underworld of Johannesburg'.

Page 26

The rebellion, at least for the moment According to Hedley Chilvers, in *Out of the Crucible* (1929), 'Beyers was compelled to stay in Johannesburg. And the camp at Potchefstroom meanwhile broke up, so that his supreme opportunity to bring about rebellion passed. And it never recurred.' That wasn't exactly true, for he adds: 'Some days afterwards General Beyers went into open rebellion. General Botha took the field against him.' Beyers was assisted by General Maritz on the South West African border and General de Wet, who was organising in the Orange Free State. 'From the first, the fortune of war went against Beyers. He was harried about the country, and on November 8 was driven over the Vaal River. While crossing it he was shot and fell from his horse into the river.' After being dragged down the river, he eventually drowned.

When the news spread In 1933, Arthur Wilson called this 'the most remarkable crime story that has ever been written [and] more fantastic in its ramifications than any theme in fiction'. Which, given the city's notable crimes, was high praise.

Page 30

After climbing over Mezar's body The deaths attributed to the Foster Gang didn't end at the cave. By that stage, there were ten fatalities – one civilian, three policemen, a doctor, a Boer general, the three gang members and Peggy. Some reports claimed later that one of the policemen who had gone to fetch Peggy was so remorseful after her death that he took his own life. That brought the total to 11.

Three feet away from them The police found two letters on Foster, indicating that she wasn't meant to die in the cave. They said, 'My darling wife, Peggy, Goodbye for ever. May you forgive me for taking my life. I have no fear of death and, although I have been shot three times, I will never surrender. Max, and Boy [Mezar] will die with me, brave to the last. Kiss my baby ...' The other said: 'Goodbye from me and don't grieve for me. Judge Kotze has been the cause of all this. Goodbye my darling wife, Peggy. I love you still. Goodbye Mother, Aggie and the rest. Peggy you are the best little girl I know.'

CHAPTER 4

Page 31

'deserved every one' See Morris, *The First Forty Years*.

Mark Twain He made the comment in his book *Following the Equator: A Journey Round the World* (1897).

Page 32

city of gold and sin Bernard Sachs, *Multitude of Dreams* (1949).

1886 The real date of the city's founding, according to Chilvers in *Out of the Crucible*, was three years earlier, 1883, when the prospector Fred Struben found gold on a 'poorer' section of what would become the world's most profitable reef. It was only in 1886, however, that George Walker stumbled on the main leader.

University of Crime The term was apparently coined by the politician John X Merriman in a speech he made in Cape Town. One of the earliest condemnations of Johannesburg came from the 'eminent humorist, mimic, polyphonist, author, and composer' Charles DuVal, who lamented: 'Not a tree or shrub, not a patch of green, not a blade of grass, nought but an eruption of buildings scattered over an area fully a mile and a half long by an almost equal distance wide.' Granted, the mining camp was still only a few years old.

the mining camp exploded By 1890, the town had 26 000 people, and six years later, the number had quadrupled, to 102 000. By 1920, the total was 200 000.

Page 33

the incidents of crime The illicit sale of liquor, according to Arthur Wilson, was perhaps the biggest problem in early Johannesburg, stemming from an old Transvaal law banning the sale of alcohol to Africans. 'The drink scourge was a curse and the government did nothing to check it or keep order on weekends when indescribable orgies of drunkenness and tribal and faction fights occurred,' wrote Sir Lionel Phillips. His wife, Lady Florence, wrote: 'At times there were numbers of ghastly murders. The police are most inadequate and corrupt, and allow the illicit traffic in liquor to carry on under their eyes, it is said even to their profit.' Women began carrying weapons, she said, for 'the crime of rape assumed fearful proportions in Johannesburg, becoming at one point quite an epidemic, and all women went in terror for their own and their children's lives.' At that time, wrote Arthur Wilson, when the Africans 'lived like herded cattle in huts and dens, and the police were notoriously dishonest, and when no effective system of minimising the illicit trade in liquor had been established ... [Johannesburg saw the rise of] the Amalaita, the Ninevite and other native gangsters who have, at frequent intervals in the history of the Golden City and to this day, terrorised the law-abiding and inoffensive native and European community alike.'

'The Golden City's reputation' See Wilson, 'The Underworld of Johannesburg'.

'it was another type of prospecting' See Wilson, 'The Underworld of Johannesburg'.

Even though a killer was never found Deeming's name has often been mentioned in books and newspapers as a possible identity of Jack the Ripper.

Page 34

He 'explored the Never-Never-Land' See Chilvers, *Out of the Crucible*.

freebooter Another synonym for a lawless adventurer, for the world appeared to need many in those years. The Zulu word *skebenga* was more effective because it encompassed numerous types of con men.

Page 36

The scene following Von Veltheim's acquittal Von Veltheim was soon kicked out of the Transvaal and then the country. By 1908, ten years later, he was in court again, this time in London, for once again trying to extort money out of Woolf Joel's brother, Solly. A front-page story in *The New York Times* called him 'possibly the world's most widely known adventurer'.

'Londoners of all classes flocked in such numbers to the Guildhall' at the start of the trial. He caused a sensation in court by saying things like he was an agent for the French government, giving his address as no less than the Quai d'Orsay. After a lengthy trial, the 'baron' was sentenced to 20 years penal servitude on the Isle of Wight. In the 1920s, Von Veltheim turned up in Johannesburg again, and was stumbled across by the journalist Benjamin Bennett, who appears in these pages. He was deported and in 1924, wrote Chilvers, 'was sentenced to two years' imprisonment at Magdeburg, Germany, for inducing a merchant to finance an expedition to search for £100 000 worth of gold buried in the Transvaal'.

'This place showed distinct promise' See Morris, *The First Forty Years*.

CHAPTER 5

Page 38

'he had a couple of narrow shaves' See Morris, *The First Forty Years*.

'He also used his system' Harry Morris said that a doctor told him, 'I am quite convinced it was a piece of meat he had smuggled into the theatre.' He asked the doctor what happened to the patient: 'Oh well, she recovered.'

Dr Crippen Dr Hawley Harvey Crippen, an unassuming representative for Munyon's homeopathic remedies in London, was married to the overbearing Belle Elmore, a stage name for Kunigunde Mackanotzki, who had aspirations to be a vaudeville artist and singer. Things went badly between the two until the evening of 31 January 1910, when she was seen for the last time. Crippen told some people she had died, others that she had left him for someone else. By July, as the net was closing in on him, he and his assistant, who were lovers, caught a ship to Canada. A search of Crippen's house unearthed a headless body in a shallow grave, and it was found that Belle Elmore had died from the poison hyoscine, five grams of which Crippen had bought two weeks before she went missing. He was tried and found guilty of her murder, and hanged in November 1910.

Page 39

Plunkett saw the Gibsons off At the same time, it was reported that a young nurse who was meant to start working at the Belgravia Nursing Home had also vanished. She, like so many others, was 'an admirer of his skill and goodheartedness'. Both Gibson and the nurse, according to different people, said they were heading to Delagoa Bay for a short holiday. By the end of March, the *Rand Daily Mail* reported, '[t]he whereabouts of the young nurse also continue to be wrapt in mystery.' It was never clear who the nurse was, whether she was perhaps his wife, or what happened to her.

CHAPTER 6

Page 42

For anyone seeking relief   Clearly in demand, countless remedies were publicised across many columns of newspapers and magazines.

Page 43

Daisy told Alfie   Daisy claimed this at her trial.

Page 44

The new fever wing   The agglomeration of structures had been growing ever since the hospital began as a clump of tents on the hill in the earliest days of the mining camp, when 'at night patients could hear lions roaring on the vleis beyond Hospital Hill'.

He laced meat with strychnine   The poison law in Rhodesia was only changed and made more stringent in 1931.

Page 45

worth £95   It was attested at Daisy's trial that Fuller's estate was worth considerably more.

'spectacle of huge structures'   Sir Lionel Phillips, 1905.

CHAPTER 8

Page 50

'the public eye is very semitically filled in Johannesburg'   See Martin Rubin, *Sarah Gertrude Millin: A South African Life* (1977).

Page 51

The largest wave   One colourful description from the time was given by Bernard Sachs, of an area he used to go to as a teenager, which was between Ferreirastown and Chinatown. There one found sitting in 'queer little Russian cafes ... the long-bearded elders', men from Lithuania, Poland, Russia and Galicia, who 'talk in rapid Yiddish of the towns they left, Chuvl, Cracow, Dvinsk, Lemberg'. Nearby were Goldstone's café, Goldin's Kosher Restaurant, 'penny drinkshops' and the all-night Gaiety café, which was 'redolent of the nineteenth century music halls, and served as a reminder that Johannesburg had not yet shaken off its mining camp romancery', with characters who went by the names of Cucumber and Boots. Outside loitered pimps, prostitutes and criminals, while inside sat the *alte Afrikaner*, Jews who, like Benny's father, had arrived in the city a long time ago without their wives. They loitered for hours at the Gaiety playing dominoes, casino and the ten-card *klaberjass*. Soon enough, a small man named Joseph Gray would be extolling the virtues of communism, and Benny listened to stories about Lenin and Trotsky, who 'were leading downtrodden mankind out of bondage to undreamt of heights'.

Richard Curle   had, at about this time, started a friendship with the author Joseph Conrad, about whom he would later write several books.

Page 51

By 1916, the Jewish   One reference notes that the Jewish population almost doubled between 1904 and 1926, going from 38 000 to 72 000.
Louis Tumpowski   The common spelling for his name in the press at the
time was Tumpowski, although his grave in Lichtenburg identifies him as
Tumpowsky.

CHAPTER 9

Page 53

the 'Criminal Sessions'   The Supreme Court building also housed, quite
notably, the Diamond and Gold Detective Department.
For the past ten years   The one crime Harry never took on was treason,
and not because he didn't want to. 'This is a crime usually committed by
gentlemen,' he wrote, 'and gentlemen do not come my way.'

Page 54

'dear old lady'   See Morris, *The First Forty Years*.

Page 55

'the indeterminate sentence'   The indeterminate sentence had, since
the late 19th century, been used for 'habitual criminals convicted of committing serious crimes who had bad records'. See RG Nairn, 'The indeterminate sentence', *The Rhodesian Law Journal* 14(2) (1974): 105–143.

CHAPTER 11

Page 59

After other avenues failed   At the trial, a woman appeared who was meant
to be Bird's wife, Johanna. Bird was recalled at one point during the trial to
admit his 'immoral intercourse' with Kraft, he being coloured and she white.
He said he believed it was a bribe to get him to commit the murder.
doepa   Made of gum benzoin, obtained from cuts made in certain species
of trees. According to the *Dictionary of South African English*, *doepa* was
used in powder form or pieces, for flatulence or colic, or as 'a love potion or
magic potion, either taken by mouth or worn as an amulet, and believed to
give the user luck and power'. It was also used in the incense of some
churches, especially Russian and Orthodox.

Page 60

'having immoral relations'   From the transcript of Kraft's trial.

CHAPTER 12

Page 61

The drafts had been part Even though the robbery had never been solved, the key from the National Bank that was stolen during the heist was later found in the cave in Kensington on the body of one of the victims of the Foster Gang murder-suicide pact. The link to the robbery, as far as was possible, was made.

Page 62

nine men According to an act of 1917, jurors had to be white males between 25 and 60. White women, after they got the vote in 1930, were also allowed to serve on juries, but these had to be all-women juries in specially empanelled cases. Few were ever called.

'What he is telling you' To illustrate how a witness could send a perfectly innocent man to jail, Harry Morris liked to tell the story of Adolph Beck, an Englishman who in 1896 became one of the most famous victims ever of mistaken identity, all based on the false evidence of his accusers. Beck was convicted on two occasions of defrauding at least a dozen women, although it eventually turned out that he was in jail serving time for the first crime when the second crime took place. The guilty party in both cases turned out to be a man named Smith, who bore absolutely no resemblance to Beck.

'[W]ith a smattering of knowledge' In Harry Morris's experience, he had found that women lied more easily, readily and frequently than men, and showed no sign of uneasiness while doing so, while Scotsmen, the one nationality that stood out for him, were honest, both as witnesses and jurymen. Africans he struggled to read, because they usually testified in another language besides English, and he could never tell if they were blushing: 'There is no means of telling whether he is lying or not, except your client's word, and that is often less reliable. The native cannot blush. He neither stammers nor shuffles. For the most part he does not even look at you. He looks at the interpreter. If he did look at you his look would tell you nothing.'

Page 63

In 1907, Marshall Hall had defended Edward Marshall Hall was also meant to be Dr Crippen's lawyer, until his line of defence was rejected, and he bowed out before the trial began. Hall wanted to argue that Crippen had given his wife hyoscine as a depressant or anaphrodisiac, but had accidentally administered a fatal dose.

Page 64

The audible chuckling Benjamin Bennett, *Genius for the Defence* (1959).
Morris's movements Edward Marshall Hall, too, was a master of the the-

atrical in court. The author John Mortimer wrote in *The Guardian* (24 January 2001) that Hall 'was always preceded into court by three clerks, one carrying a pile of clean handkerchiefs, the next with a carafe of water and the third bearing an air cushion. If the prosecution evidence was impressive he would blow his nose, a loud and terrible trumpet, on the handkerchiefs; if it got more dangerous he would knock over the carafe of water; if it looked like becoming fatal he would slowly and deliberately blow up the air cushion, and so attract the jury's undivided attention.'

Page 65
perfect day   See Morris, *The First Forty Years*.

CHAPTER 13
Page 67
started sleeping with   From Swarts's testimony at his trial.

CHAPTER 14
Page 70
'bright and chatty'   See Morris, *The First Forty Years*.

CHAPTER 15
Page 71
Even though Johannesburg   Out of a countrywide population of six million, almost 140 000 died during the Spanish Influenza epidemic, most of them African and coloured, versus only 700 in Spain.
'[T]housands of people'   John R Shorten, *The Johannesburg Saga* (1970).

CHAPTER 16
Page 74
'how long afterwards'   A version of the conversation between Gibson and the killer Hermanus Swarts is repeated several times, at the trial and by Benjamin Bennett and Harry Morris, although the elements stay the same.
The patient said ... argument   From Gibson's trial testimony.

Page 75
'Suppose he was killed'   Gibson at his trial.

Page 80
A full decade   Interestingly, two black women who became the first to be executed after 1910, four years after Kraft, committed a crime that bore many similarities to that of the white widow. Ngqumbazi Tshange, who lived near Pietermaritzburg, conspired with her friend Maria Zondi to kill

her husband Mbanjwa. Putting *muti* in his food didn't work, so she contracted *skebenga*s to do it for her. One of them wanted three cattle, and then, when she couldn't provide that, money. In the end, the two women did it themselves and 'caved in [Mbanjwa's] head while they were all sleeping in the same hut'. Tshange's defence that he abused her – even though she had never laid charges against him – wasn't enough to sway the judges. She and Zondi were found guilty and hanged in 1925.

CHAPTER 17

Page 81

'The tears shed'   See Morris, *The First Forty Years*.

Page 83

A fight broke out   After only 20 minutes the jury found Leech not guilty. It was decided he had acted in self-defence.

At the centre   'People, it was inescapable, wanted sex and destruction. They craved for it.' Sarah Gertrude Millin, *The Night is Long* (1941).

duty and faithfulness   Millin's biographer, Martin Rubin, writes that she was 'obviously unnerved by any kind of sexuality (and) she deliberately sees it in its most malignant aspects ... It is odd that a woman who had experienced a marriage as happy and as close as her should hold so unfavourable a view of sex; and equally strange that a woman who had hardly led a sheltered life should write of sex like a neophyte.' See Rubin, *Sarah Gertrude Millin*.

'cling together through age'   Sarah Gertrude Millin, article in *The Outspan*.

sex and destruction   In her autobiography, *The Night is Long*, Millin recalls a passage from her novel *Three Men Die*, in which a doctor – who is seen as her voice in the book – is reflecting on the suspicious death of the main character's husband: '[It] suddenly struck him how often, indeed, sex and destruction were linked. (How easily murderers mated!) Was the reason, he pondered, that when the lid was removed everything boiled over together, all the terrible, fundamental instincts?

'"Terrible," thought Dr Stamp again, "but yes – fundamental, natural. Sex and destruction. Life and death. The beginning and the end."'

CHAPTER 18

Page 90

On 10 March   Marais did not die from four gunshot wounds and was found and taken to hospital. In a detailed declaration before he died, he described Long as the shooter.

Page 91

At a Special Criminal Court   A fourth man, Carl Stassen, was hanged for killing two Africans.

CHAPTER 20

Page 100

International acclaim had been   The novel *God's Stepchildren* became her most famous work, especially in the US, following its 1924 publication. It was also the one she became most criticised for, because it focused on a topic she wouldn't let go of – miscegenation. But in the 1920s, talking about race in this way was viewed very differently. Millin often spoke about how South Africans didn't appreciate her: 'While papers like the *New York World*, *Times*, *Post*, and critics like Mencken, Bromfield, Stallings were comparing me with the best they could think of, in South Africa I was referred to as "among South Africa's lesser-known writers" – though who the better known writers were I can't think.' Yet she was often referred to in the local press as 'celebrated', 'famous', 'great'. As one letter to the *Rand Daily Mail* noted in 1925, 'Two of the most considerable works of the past year have been produced by South Africans; we allude to "God's Step-children", by Mrs Sarah Gertrude Millin of Johannesburg, and "The Flaming Terrapin", by Mr Roy Campbell of Durban. Here we are, then, with a novelist of the first class and a poet of the very greatest distinction living and working in our midst, and there is scarcely a copy of the latest book by either of them to be purchased in the chief city of the Union.'

Page 101

Everything seemed to go wrong   Millin had invited a South African friend who she discovered, when he arrived, had grown a moustache since she had last seen him. In order for him to make a good impression on a young woman who was attending, she asked him to shave it off. He immediately did.

'She felt grateful to Lawrence'   Martin Rubin writes that another guest at the dinner, the painter Dorothy Brett, had a completely different recollection of the event, saying that Lawrence was captivated by Millin's descriptions of South Africa. She recalled him saying, 'Some day I will go to Africa with you [Frieda] and drive across the veldt.'

CHAPTER 21

Page 102

for the first time in her work   Benjamin Bennett said that it was perhaps because of this work that Daisy believed she knew how to handle doctors and also how to hoodwink them.

'a cheery and forceful personality'   See Bennett, *Genius for the Defence*.

CHAPTER 24

Page 109

'The emotional climate' Valerie Rosenberg, *Sunflower to the Sun: The Life of Herman Charles Bosman* (1976).

'cleaned, oiled and loaded, ready to use' See Rosenberg, *Sunflower to the Sun*.

Benny or Bernard Sachs had arrived in 1913, at the age of eight, with his mother and siblings from Kamajai in Lithuania.

Page 110

'mad genius' Bosman's friend Eddie Roux.

'a misfit' When Bosman returned for the short visit in 1926, he didn't even tell the young woman he had married several months earlier, Vera Sawyer. She only heard the news he was back in town after the murder. The marriage was seen by some as a prank, and didn't last long.

'an unhappy youth' See Sachs, *Multitude of Dreams*.

Page 111

and won third place Perhaps one of the most descriptive profiles of Bosman was written by his friend the artist Gordon Vorster: 'I think his father was Edgar Allen Percy Bysshe John François Oscar Fingal O'Flaherty Wills de Sade Rossetti Dante Shakespeare Oliver Onions. And he had a sister, Night, and a brother, Desert. And he was educated, in his own soul, by fine fires.'

Page 114

'Even the imagination was caged' Herman Charles Bosman, *Cold Stone Jug* (1949).

CHAPTER 26

Page 123

the owner of several properties The number of properties was identified at Daisy's trial – there were four in all – but not the locations. The other two, besides Tully Street and Terrace Road, were more than likely also in Turffontein.

CHAPTER 27

Page 131

He relied on the evidence The prejudices of the time were exacerbated, with white people seeing suspects everywhere. It was reported that in the hut of another African suspect, the police found photographs of nude white women, which caused an outpouring of letters to the newspapers. Some of them said this was what happened when bioscopes exhibited 'pictures of semi-nude white women in "artistic" [or abandoned] postures' and 'posters of a suggestive nature [that they] daily paraded through the streets, sometimes on lorries driven by natives'.

CHAPTER 28
Page 133
Daisy and Rhodes ... Meaker   It isn't always clear from court records where Daisy lived between her marriages, but she appears to have rented out her properties as much as possible, probably for the income she derived from them.

CHAPTER 29
Page 135
'I do not think he has an enemy'   Lago Clifford, article in *The Sjambok*. Clifford, known on radio as 'Uncle John', was a highly respected broadcaster who had been found guilty of indecent behaviour with several children. During his year-long imprisonment, he met Bosman: 'The young man undoubtedly has great literary gifts, some think genius.' On leaving jail, Clifford wrote a series of tragically moving and eye-opening articles on the conditions at Pretoria Central that were published in *The Sjambok*. Whether the accusations against him were true or not, Clifford realised that his life was ruined and he needed to move to another country after his release. It is unclear what happened to him.
'the last member of the Foster Gang'   Lago Clifford, article in *The Sjambok*.
Present at the execution   Clifford said that he got this information from a cleaner, the only person allowed in the execution chamber besides the officials.
'There was the tramping'   See Bosman, *Cold Stone Jug*.

Page 136
boxer turned journalist   Some of Black's early writing in Cape Town had been read and praised by Rudyard Kipling during one of his visits. The young journalist soon went to London, where he covered the Great War for the *Daily Mail*. Before starting *The Sjambok*, he had been living outside Nice with his French wife, attempting to farm.
'Years ago Johannesburg'   The actual quote by James Weston Leonard is, 'This place has more brains to the square inch than any other place in the world.'

CHAPTER 30
Page 139
writers abroad   Millin was especially friendly with the British authors

Winifred Holtby and Storm Jameson, both of them feminist, pacifist and anti-fascist. Millin and Holtby continued a friendship until the latter died, at the age of 37, of Bright's disease, an illness that would feature prominently in Daisy's trial. Jameson remained a friend for life.

CHAPTER 31

Page 140

'passionate sex affair'   *The Sjambok.*

Page 141

'Dear Hatty'   The spelling and grammatical mistakes have been left as they appeared in the letter.
Kroonstad murder   It is unclear what murder is being referred to, or if there even was one.

CHAPTER 32

Page 145

his lawyer would have to look at it   After a lawyer looked at the version Vermaak had written, the young man took it back to rewrite but never returned to Black's office again. In the end, Black never read it.

Page 146

exhaustive inquiry   Much of this information was disclosed in letters Black wrote to a retired police detective that were uncovered much later by the crime reporter Benjamin Bennett.

Page 147

original theory held by Colonel Trigger   Trigger himself was no longer in charge. He retired at the end of 1928, after nine years as the head of the criminal division.
Conan Doyle left the country   Doyle died the following year, 1930.
'murder in the plantation'   See Bennett, *Genius for the Defence.*

CHAPTER 37

Page 158

he would be dead   On 8 August 1931, barely a few weeks after *The New Sjambok* of Bosman and Blignaut had started, Black died of liver cancer. He was only 51. There was a large funeral at Brixton Cemetery, and one of his pallbearers was the former prisoner Lago Clifford, who had written all the prison exposés for his magazine. Rumours circulated that Black had been so depressed after all the libel suits against *The Sjambok*, and especially the 'damaging and relentless campaign' allegedly waged by the owners of Kinemas, that he had committed suicide. Kinemas was a fast-growing chain of theatres whose owners made huge, sometimes dubious claims about their successes, and Black had gone after them relentlessly. One of the issues he had raised was that Kinemas' ballyhooed 2 300-seat Plaza on Rissik Street, a theatre bigger than most in London or New York, had not dug foundations two years after it was announced. On the same day that the Plaza opened, shortly after Black's death, a malicious story started going around that his body had mysteriously been exhumed and dismembered, and that his limbs had been arranged to form the word 'PLAZA'.

Page 159

Roy Campbell   In spite of Bosman's criticism, Campbell and Plomer later went on to praise him.

last issues   *The New Sjambok*'s last issue was 14 November 1931.

'She is like a store-keeper'   'Their exchanges were venomous,' wrote Stephen Gray, 'and along with Millin Bosman tried to wipe out her associates (George Bernard Shaw and TS Eliot!). In the final analysis, their antagonism was classist: Millin, the (lawyer's) wife, stood for the establishment, including by extension the British press and the elitist PEN writers; Bosman stood for the working class (almost all of Bosman's characters are *platteland* types – the very people Millin held in abject contempt – and his major subject matter was labour).'

CHAPTER 39

Page 164

The Oxford Group   Originally known as the First Century Christian Fellowship, started in 1921 by an American named Frank Buchman, the group that came to South Africa in 1929 were mostly from Oxford, and a railway steward apparently put the sign 'Oxford Group' on their carriages. The name stuck.

CHAPTER 40

Page 167

Spilkin's Pharmacy   In Benjamin Bennett's book *Up for Murder*, he situates the place of purchase of poison at Spilkin's Extension Pharmacy, 65a Main Street, on the corner of Verona Street, more than a mile away from the main branch, at number 178. Spilkin had bought the second premises in 1931.

CHAPTER 43

Page 183

Hubrecht de Leeuw   In 1927, the town clerk of Dewetsdorp, a handsome young man who had been embezzling the town's money he was in charge of, was called to account by the mayor and two councillors. Given a deadline to return the money or face the consequences, De Leeuw chose instead to blow up the evidence in the town hall, and the three men with it. Scenes of carnage and burnt bodies still half-alive – though all three victims would soon be dead – were described after the event, and De Leeuw was quickly arrested. Given the sensational nature of the crime, which of course made headlines, and the good looks of the accused, women crowded the court. De Leeuw received his death sentence with unusual equanimity compared to many other criminals, who swore their innocence until the end, and was hanged.

CHAPTER 44

Page 187

His fight against capital punishment   Bosman, who was not beyond bearing a grudge – in their magazine, he and Blignaut had repeatedly attacked a female lawyer who had got a judgment against them on an insurance case – would also have learned that the man prosecuting Daisy, Cyril Jarvis, was the same man who had got him the death penalty.

CHAPTER 45

Page 188

'Daisy was a paradox'   See Morris, *The First Forty Years*.

Page 189

A quotation Maisels recalled   There are many renditions of this famous quotation. The full reference, from Blackstone's *Commentaries on the Laws of England* (Bk 4, Ch 14), is as follows: 'The killing may be by poisoning, striking, starving, drowning, and a thousand other forms of death, by which human nature may be overcome. Of these the most detestable of all is poison; because it can of all others be the least prevented either by manhood or forethought.'

Jean-Pierre Vaquier   Benjamin Bennett compares Daisy to the French poisoner, not only because he believed they both suffered from extreme vanity but also because both were caught out by a photograph in a newspaper. A London pharmacist recognised the inventor, who had been publicised in newspapers for his work, as a man who had signed his poison register with the improbable-sounding name of 'J. Wanker'.

CHAPTER 47

Page 196

Both Makins were found guilty   A third, and more recent case, from 1922, concerned Major Herbert Rowse Armstrong, a solicitor in Hay-on-Wye, on the Welsh border. After trying to poison a fellow lawyer with arsenic, he was arrested by Scotland Yard for attempted murder, whereupon more packets of arsenic were discovered at his home, raising suspicions about the death of his wife two years earlier. Her body was exhumed and found to contain large amounts of arsenic. Armstrong was found guilty of her murder and hanged, the only lawyer ever to be executed in Great Britain. The case was also referred to by Justice Greenberg in Daisy's trial.

CHAPTER 48
Page 198

Mallalieu was handsome   The slightly mismatched lovers-on-the-run story foreshadowed a similar one that would enthral the US within the next few years, that of Bonnie Parker and Clyde Barrow.

CHAPTER 61
Page 239

'On the one hand'   See Bennett, *Genius for the Defence*.

CHAPTER 62
Page 244

'he is oppressed'   See Bennett, *Genius for the Defence*.

CHAPTER 67
Page 274

the world's fastest plane   On 17 November, five days after Loew arrived, he boarded the Lockheed Orion at the Rand Airport, across Victoria Lake from Daisy's house in Simmer East. His captain, a man named James Dickson, was set on breaking the record for a commercial flight across Africa. They were headed for London. Five hours after take-off, *Spirit of Fun* made a quick and unscheduled landing at a small new aerodrome next to Victoria Falls before heading over the cataract for the short flight to the correct landing place in Livingstone, Northern Rhodesia. No one ever found out why Dickson landed at the small aerodrome, which had just opened. When *Spirit of Fun* took off, it spectacularly hit a tree and disintegrated. Dickson died instantly but the two passengers, Loew and his lawyer, miraculously survived. The story was in the news for days, with aviators dissecting what might have gone wrong, maps drawn to show the exact flight path, as Loew made his way slowly, by land, back to Johannesburg. The tragic story almost eclipsed Daisy's – but not quite.

CHAPTER 71
Page 293

'It seemed as if a blight lay over it   At least two more pamphlets appeared, written by the duo: 'Daisy De Melker's Ghost Haunts Central

Prison' and 'What Mrs. De Melker Thinks of Us'. Bosman and Blignaut even wrote a play on the subject and planned to stage it 'in a tin shanty at a fair'. In the end, they had to abandon the idea 'because their girlfriends (who were clearly going to play the main roles) were such poor actresses'.

Page 294

Daisy was placed Description of the execution procedure in Pretoria Central by Lago Clifford in *The Sjambok*.

Within a few hours of her execution Bosman made sure to be first to get in the last word. Knowing the interior of the prison, he prepared the news copy for Daisy's execution in advance, headlining his story 'How Mrs. De Melker Was Hanged'. On the morning of the execution, someone called the prison posing as the editor of *The Star* and got confirmation that she had indeed been executed by 8 am. Bosman's posters were on the street before anyone else's, and 'in time for late breakfast'.

References

BOOKS

Acutt, Renault Courtney. *Reminiscences of a Rand Pioneer: The Memoirs of Renault Courtney Acutt* (Ravan Press, 1977).

Aldaheff, Vic. *A Newspaper History of South Africa* (Don Nelson, 1976).

The Barnett Collection: A Pictorial Record of Early Johannesburg (The Star, 1965).

Beavon, Keith. *Johannesburg: The Making and Shaping of the City* (Unisa Press, 2004).

Benjamin, Arnold. *Lost Johannesburg* (Macmillan South Africa, 1979).

Bennett, Benjamin. *Murder is my Business* (Hodder & Stoughton, 1951).

Bennett, Benjamin. *Genius for the Defence* (Howard Timmins, 1959).

Bennett, Benjamin. *The Clues Condemn* (Hodder & Stoughton, 1969).

Bennett, Benjamin with Francois Pierre Rousseau. *Up for Murder: Accounts of Murder Trials in South Africa* (Hutchinson, 1934).

Berger, Nathan. *Jewish Trails Through Southern Africa* (Kayor Publishing House, 1976).

Berger, Nathan. *In Those Days, In These Times* (Kayor Publishing House, 1979).

Bolitho, Hector. *My Restless Years* (Max Parrish, 1962).

Bosman, Herman Charles. *Cold Stone Jug* (APB, 1949).

Bosman, Herman Charles. *My Life and Opinions*, edited by Stephen Gray (Human & Rousseau, 2003).

Busch, Noel. *My Unconsidered Judgment* (Houghton Mifflin, 1944).

Cartwright, AP. *The Corner House: The Early History of Johannesburg* (Purnell, 1965).

Chilvers, Hedley A. *Out of the Crucible* (Cassell & Co, 1929).

Chipkin, Clive. *Johannesburg Style: Architecture and Society 1880s–1960s* (David Philip, 1993).

Cohen, Louis. *Reminiscences of Johannesburg and London* (Robert Holden & Co, 1924).

Crisp, Ronald. *The Outlanders: The Men Who Made Johannesburg* (Peter Davies, 1964).

Collier, Joy. *The Purple and the Gold: The Story of Pretoria and Johannesburg* (Longmans, 1965).

Curle, Richard. *Wanderings: A Book of Travel and Reminiscence* (Kegan Paul, Trench and Trubner, 1920).

Devitt, Napier. *Memories of a Magistrate, Including Twenty-Five Years on the South African Bench* (HF & G Witherby, 1934).

Emden, Paul. *Randlords* (Hodder & Stoughton, 1935).

FitzPatrick, Sir Percy. *South African Memories* (Cassell, 1932).

Flather, Horace. *The Way of an Editor* (Purnell, 1977).

Fraser, Maryna (ed). *Johannesburg Pioneer Journals 1888–1909* (Van Riebeeck Society, 1985).

Gray, Stephen. *Free-lancers and Literary Biography in South Africa* (Editions Rodopi, 1999).

Gray, Stephen. *Life Sentence: A Biography of Herman Charles Bosman* (Human & Rousseau, 2005).

Gray, Stephen. *Remembering Bosman* (Penguin, 2008).

Gunther, John. *Inside Africa* (Harper & Brothers, 1955).

Hertz, Joseph. *The Jew in South Africa* (Central News Agency, 1905).

Jacobsson, Daniel. *Fifty Golden Years of the Rand* (Faber & Faber, 1936).

Jarvis, Cyril. *To Seek a Newer World: The Autobiography of a South African* (unpublished manuscript, Rhodes University).

Jeppe, Carl. *The Kaleidoscopic Transvaal* (C Juta & Co, 1908).

Johnson Barker, Brian and Mona de Beer. *A Vision of the Past: South Africa in Photographs 1843–1910* (Struik, 1992).

Kahn, Ellison. *Law, Life and Laughter Encore* (Juta & Co, 1999).

Knox, Patricia and Thelma Gutsche. *Do You Know Johannesburg?* (Unie-Volkspers, 1947).

Leyds, Gerald. *History of Johannesburg* (Nasionale Boekhandel, 1964).

Macmillan, Allister (ed). *The Golden City: Johannesburg* (WH & L Collingridge, 1933).

Macmillan, Allister and Eric Rosenthal. *Homes of the Golden City* (Hortors Ltd, 1948).

Macnab, Roy. *Gold Their Touchstone. Gold Fields of South Africa, 1887–1987: A Century Story* (Jonathan Ball, 1987).

Maisels, Issie. *A Life at Law* (Jonathan Ball, 1998).

May, Henry John (aka Herzl Joshua Schlosberg). *Red Wine of Youth* (Cassell & Co, 1946).

May, Henry John and Iain Hamilton. *The Foster Gang* (Heinemann, 1966).

Mendelsohn, Richard and Milton Shain. *The Jews in South Africa: An Illustrated History* (Jonathan Ball, 2008).

Millin, Sarah Gertrude. *The South Africans* (Constable & Co, 1926).

Millin, Sarah Gertrude. *Three Men Die* (Chatto & Windus, 1934).

Millin, Sarah Gertrude. *The Night is Long* (Faber & Faber, 1941).

Millin, Sarah Gertrude. *The Measure of My Days* (Abeland-Schuman, 1955).

Morris, Harry. *The First Forty Years: Being the Memoirs of HH Morris, KC* (Juta & Co, 1948).

Murry, Marischal. *Union-Castle Chronicle 1853–1953* (Longmans, Green & Co, 1953).

Musiker, Naomi and Reuben. *Historical Dictionary of Greater Johannesburg* (Scarecrow Press, 1999).

Neame, LE. *City Built on Gold* (Central News Agency, 1960).

Pegg, Henry Edward. *A History of Southern Africa* (Longmans, Green & Co, 1949).

Phillips, Lionel. *Some Reminiscences* (Ad Donker, 1986).

Rosenberg, Valerie. *Sunflower to the Sun: The Life of Herman Charles Bosman* (Human & Rousseau, 1976).

Rosenberg, Valerie. *Herman Charles Bosman: Between the Lines* (Struik, 2005).

Rosenthal, Eric. *Gold, Bricks and Mortar* (Printing House Ltd, 1946).

Rosenthal, Eric. *South African Saturday Book* (Hutchinson, 1949).

Rosenthal, Eric. *Other Men's Millions* (Howard Timmins, 1950).

Rosenthal, Eric. *The Rand Rush* (Ad Donker, 1974).

Rosenthal, Eric. *Memories and Sketches* (Ad Donker, 1979).

Rosenthal, Eric (compiler). *South African Dictionary of National Biography* (Warne, 1966).

Rubin, Martin. *Sarah Gertrude Millin: A South African Life* (Ad Donker, 1977).

Sachs, Bernard. *Multitude of Dreams* (Kayor Publishing House, 1949).

Saron, Gustav and Lewis Hotz. *The Jews in South Africa* (Oxford University Press, 1955).

Segrave, Kerry. *Women Serial and Mass Murderers: A Worldwide Reference, 1580 through 1990* (McFarland & Co, 1992).

Shorten, John R. *The Johannesburg Saga* (John R Shorten, 1970).

Slosberg, Bertha. *Pagan Tapestry* (Rich & Cowan, 1940).

Smith, Anna. *Pictorial History of Johannesburg* (Juta & Co, 1956).

Snyman, JPL. *The Works of Sarah Gertrude Millin* (Central News Agency, 1955).

Sowden, Louis. *The South African Union* (Robert Hall Ltd, 1945).

Swanson, MW (ed). *The Views of Mahlathi: The Writings of AWG Champion, a Black South African* (University of Natal Press, 1979).

Symonds, Francis Addington. *The Johannesburg Story* (Frederick Muller Ltd, 1953).

Taylor, James Benjamin. *A Pioneer Looks Back* (Hutchinson & Co, 1939).

Various authors. *Johannesburg: One Hundred Years* (Chris van Rensburg Publications, 1986).

Walker, Eric Anderson. *A History of South Africa* (Longmans & Co, 1928).

Weinthal, Leo. *Memories, Mines and Millions: Being the Life of Sir Joseph B Robinson* (Simpkins Marshall, 1929).

Wentzel, John. *A View from the Ridge: Johannesburg Retrospect* (David Philip, 1975).

BOOK CHAPTERS

Wilson, Arthur N. 'The Underworld of Johannesburg'. In *The Golden City: Johannesburg*, edited and compiled by Allister Macmillan (WH & L Collingridge, 1933).

ARTICLES AND PAPERS

Cartwright, MF. 'Stephen Black 1880–1931: A Chronology'. *English in Africa* 8(2) (September 1981): 91–94.

Dubb, Allie. 'Jewish South Africans: A Sociological View of the Johannesburg Community'. Occasional Paper 21, Rhodes University, Institute of Economic and Social Research, 1977.

Tomlins, Marilyn Z. 'Daisy de Melker: South Africa's First Serial Killer'. *Crime Magazine*, 2 December 2007. Available at https://www.crimemagazine.com/daisy-de-melker-south-africas-first-serial-killer-0.

Wade, Michael. 'Myth, Truth and the South African Reality in the Fiction of Sarah Gertrude Millin'. *Journal of Southern African Studies* 1(1) (October 1974): 91–108.

Zimmerman, Reinhard. 'The Contribution of Jewish Lawyers to the Administration of Justice in South Africa'. *Israel Law Review* 29(1–2) (Winter–Spring 1995): 250–290.

PAMPHLETS

Malan, Herman (Herman Bosman). 'The Life Story of Mrs. de Melker' (self-published, 1932).

Malan, Herman (Herman Bosman). 'Mrs. de Melker Under the Gallows' (self-published, 1932).

PERIODICALS AND NEWSPAPER ARCHIVES

The Daily News (London)
The Daily Telegraph (London), 1913–1932
The Gold Fields, 13 December 1913
Lantern, 1968–1969
The Natal Mercury, 1931–1932
The Natal Witness, 1931–1932
The New York Times, 1886–1932
The Outspan, 1927–1932
Rand Daily Mail, 1902–1932
The Sjambok, 1929–1931
South African Jewish Chronicle
South African Jewish Times
The Star, 1913–1932
Sunday Times, 1913–1932
The Times (London), 1913–1932
Vanity Fair, 1932–1933

Acknowledgements

This book was born out of another manuscript, so the thanks really go for both. First and foremost, I am most grateful to Helen Moffett, author and editor, who read both manuscripts many times, offered sage advice and always managed to stay excited about them. Thanks also to Marc Latilla, not only for your input on the maps but also for your labour-of-love blog johannesburg1912.com, which was a joy to stumble across and a very deep rabbit hole always worth falling into. I'm indebted to Stephen Gray, who sadly died in 2020 and who I met only briefly; he knew this era of Johannesburg better than almost anyone and covered the lives of two of its most colourful characters, Herman Bosman and Gray's own almost-namesake, Stephen Black. Thanks also to the library and archive stalwarts: Marike Beyers at the Amazwi South African Museum of Literature in Makhanda/Grahamstown (which was still called the National English Literary Museum when I began my research); Melanie Geustyn at the National Library of South Africa in Cape Town; Gabriele Mohale and Michele Pickover at Wits University's Historical Papers Research Archive; Diana Steele at the Johannesburg Heritage Foundation; and the Brenthurst Foundation. Bringing the city from a hundred years ago alive for me were the words of historian Kathy Munro, as well as other wonderful articles on the superb Heritage Portal website. Katie Mooney, who did some flawless research about Daisy for the women's prison exhibit on Constitution Hill, shared with me her insights. At the often overlooked and underfunded Johannesburg Library, which has the most jaw-dropping collection of records and newspapers – which drastically need digitisation before they are lost forever (I hope someone is listening) – I could always count on Sithembile Mkhize and Lungisani Silolo; and at Museum Africa, Kenneth Hlungwane. And last but not least, thank you to Gill Moodie at Jonathan Ball Publishers for her patient guiding of the project, which had several constantly moving parts. Of course, Johannesburg, a city that still seems to be as revered and reviled as it has always been, played no small role in the writing of this book – somehow, despite everything, it charms and inveigles its way into your core. Now as then, it remains utterly fascinating.

About the author

Ted Botha has worked for Reuters in New York and has been published in *The New York Times*, *Esquire*, *The Telegraph*, *Condé Nast Traveler* and *Outside*. He has written numerous books, including *Apartheid in my Rucksack*, the forensic thriller *The Girl with the Crooked Nose* and *Flat/White*, about living as an immigrant in a chaotic and battered tenement building in Harlem, New York. See more at www.tedbotha.com

Printed in the USA
CPSIA information can be obtained
at www.ICGtesting.com
LVHW012126250823
756160LV00009B/73